The comedies of
Corneille

For my mother and father

The comedies of
Corneille

Experiments in the comic

G. J. Mallinson

Fellow of Pembroke College, Cambridge

Manchester University Press

© G. Jonathan Mallinson 1984

Published by Manchester University Press
Oxford Road, Manchester M13 9PL
and 51 Washington Street, Dover
New Hampshire 03820, USA

British Library cataloguing in publication data

Mallinson, G. J.
  The comedies of Corneille
  1. Corneille, Pierre–Comedies
  I. Title
  842′.4   PQ1779

  ISBN 0–7190–0992–8

Library of Congress cataloguing in publication data
Mallinson, G. J.
  The comedies of Corneille.
  Bibliography: p.
  Includes index.
  1. Corneille, Pierre, 1606–1684--Comedies.   2. Comic,
The. I. Title.
PQ1779.M26   1984   842′.4   84–17582
ISBN 0–7190–0992–8

Phototypeset in Palatino by
Wilmaset, Birkenhead, Merseyside

Printed and bound in Great Britain by
Biddles Ltd, Guildford and King's Lynn

Contents

	Acknowledgements	vii
	Note on the presentation of texts	viii
	Introduction	1
I	*Comédie* in the 1630s: A decade of experiment	9
II	*Mélite*: A search for the comic	34
III	*La Veuve*: The actor and his role	55
IV	*La Galerie due Palais*: The actor and his feelings	77
V	*La Suivante*: 'Une voix demi-gaie et demi-sérieuse'	107
VI	*La Place Royale*: The comedy of fear	134
VII	*L'Illusion Comique*: The actor triumphant	163
VIII	*Le Menteur*: Reminiscence and development	188
IX	*La Suite du Menteur*: The play as entertainment	210
	Conclusion: Experiments in the comic	217
	Notes	222
	Bibliography	235
	Index	244

Acknowledgements

It is a pleasure to record here my gratitude to those who have given assistance in the course of my research: the Department of Education and Science and the Ministère des Affaires Etrangères for their substantial support; the Ecole Normale Supérieure for providing a friendly and stimulating environment in which to carry out the major part of my work in Paris; the Drapers' Company, whose funding of a Research Fellowship in Pembroke College enabled me to complete the final stages of this book; the British Academy for their generous grant towards the costs of publication; and Pembroke College itself for much and varied encouragement over a number of years. I should like to thank also Mrs Christine Bartram for typing so swiftly and efficiently two different drafts of this work, and the officers of the Manchester University Press for their help and cooperation.

In the course of my research, I have benefited greatly from conversations with teachers, colleagues and friends; to all these I offer my warm thanks. I express particular gratitude, however, to my two examiners, Professor H. T. Barnwell and Dr G. Jondorf for their helpful suggestions and comments on the doctoral thesis in which this book originated; to Professor J. Morel, who showed me much kindness during my time in Paris; to my supervisor, Professor O. de Mourgues, whose guidance, example and unfailing encouragement have been a constant source of inspiration; and finally, but not least, to my wife, Margaret, for her patient help with proofs and index, and for her boundless moral support from the beginning.

Note on the presentation of texts

In quotations from Corneille's comedies, I use the recent critical editions of the original texts, published by the Société des Textes Français Modernes or the Textes Littéraires Français. For the comedies where no such edition exists, namely *Le Menteur* and *La Suite du Menteur*, and for all other references to the works of Corneille, the text is that of the *Oeuvres*, edited by Charles Marty-Laveaux in the series Les Grands Ecrivains de la France. This edition is referred to in the footnotes as 'Marty-Laveaux', followed by the relevant volume number. All quotations from the works of Rotrou are taken from Viollet-le-Duc's edition of the plays; references to the relevant volume number are made by Roman numeral in the Notes.

A few other abbreviations are used in the course of the book to simplify the notes:

PMLA   Publications of the Modern Language Association of America
RHLF   Revue d'Histoire Littéraire de la France
STFM   Société des Textes Français Modernes
TLF   Textes Littéraires Français

Introduction

'Ses premières comédies sont sèches, languissantes et ne laissaient pas espérer qu'il dût ensuite aller si loin.'[1]

The *états présents* of Scherer,[2] May,[3] Couton[4] and Tancock[5] testify to critics' increasing interest in Corneille's work beyond a handful of tragedies written during a brief span of five years, and suggest a growing awareness of the depth and variety of his complete *oeuvre*. The comedies, in particular, have been subjected to close scrutiny, and much ground has been covered since that dismissive assessment of La Bruyère; what was once a neglected area of study is now one no longer and it has been seen to open on to some particularly interesting problems. Being among Corneille's earliest plays, these works promise to throw light on the maturing of his dramatic techniques and preoccupations; as comedies, they are a fascinating complement to later work in another register; and, on a more general level, they offer insight into the nature of a genre which was at a critical stage of its development. A single question, however, underlies these various lines of analysis, a question which all critics have considered, explicitly or implicitly, in their studies: how far and in what ways may the plays be seen as comic?

Corneille's comedies are clearly quite distinct from Classical traditions of the genre, and have roots in the pastorals and tragicomedies much in vogue at the time. Instead of avaricious old men and wily servants, parasites and pedants, he presents the adventures of young lovers, suffering and meeting setbacks in their amorous quests before being led finally to happiness. For many early commentators, the depiction in such plots of anger and jealousy, treachery and despair ultimately disqualifies the plays as comedies. Brasillach highlights in particular a *'style qui d'ailleurs a envie d'échapper à la comédie'*,[6] Dorchain speaks of destructive *'ruptures de tonalité'*,[7] Hatzfeld uncovers in them *'je ne sais quelle gravité qui n'est pas du genre comique'*,[8] and Brunetière criticises them for their constant explosions of lament: *'trop souvent, ou presque à tout coup, je ne sais quels accents tragiques ou, du moins, élégiaques s'y mêlent inopportunément aux futilités de la conversation mondaine et aux traits de la satire.'*[9] Even for as recent a critic as Brereton, such elements are seen to be quite incompatible with any form of comic vision: *'But even if taken only half seriously they seem inappropriate to comedy, as indeed is the violent distress or vindictiveness of some of the lovers as expressed in the course of the play.'*[10]

For other critics, however, the presentation of lovers' trials and ultimate joys is not seen to be inherently unsuitable to the genre. Already in the plots and characters of pastoral, Marsan sees the possibility of a refined form of comedy, neither grave nor farcical:

> *Ces intrigues qui reposent toutes sur les jeux de l'amour et de la fortune, ces angoisses des amants contrariés par des volontés étrangères, ou, mieux encore, par leurs propres scrupules, par leurs hésitations, leurs timidités, leurs accès de dépit, il y a là la matière d'une comédie nouvelle, non plus bouffonne et bruyante, toute de grâce et de délicatesse au contraire.*[11]

Gaiffe[12] and Nadal[13] stress the similarity of themes in the two genres, Voltz speaks of the *'réalisme des sentiments'* evident in both Racan and Corneille,[14] and Guichemerre is moved to categorise the plays *'parmi ces comédies qu'on pourrait appeler "sentimentales"'*.[15]

In this urbanised pastoral world, the dramatic impact of distress or passion is seen to be held in check. Characters' laments may be touching, but they never reach the heights of the tragic which earlier critics had imagined, and the troubles undergone are never anything but temporary; Rivaille argues thus in his thesis on the plays: *'L'émotion pathétique . . . effleure seulement l'âme des spectateurs sans y pénétrer.'*[16] The world of the comedies is held to be that of charming love imbroglios, sensitively and delicately observed in all their varied aspects of delight and despair. The *péripéties* are quite in keeping with the nature of the plots, and the plays imply the creation of a *comédie moyenne* which avoids the extremes of coarseness or violent dramatic outburst and which has its own particular tone; it is characterised thus by Voltz: '*Leur ton est très particulier: il allie, dans une atmosphère généralement détendue, l'enjouement d'un dialogue spirituel au pathétique discret d'une situation émouvante*' (p. 53).

Others go further, and see in these works the depiction of characters closely observed and drawn from life, living and loving in a particularised milieu. Lanson is absolute in his claims for the dramatist: '*Il avait du premier coup été droit au modèle éternel de l'art, la vie; il avait du premier coup la suprême grâce de l'art, la vérité,*'[17] and similar remarks are found in the analyses of Schlumberger[18] and Lemonnier.[19] These plays are conceived as *comédies de moeurs*, their settings consciously Parisian, their plots charming and not fantastical, their language neither crude nor stilted, their themes refined and suggestive. For Lancaster, Corneille helps to create '*a genuine comedy of manners, very largely free from the obscenity and brutality of the farce, the conventional characters of the pastoral and of Roman comedy, and the deeds of violence and changes of tone of the tragi-comedy*',[20] and more recent critics stress the same qualities which are seen to distinguish these plays from others of the period: their topicality and evocation of everyday life. Adam singles out this feature as the author's aim in his work,[21] Brereton speaks of his direct observation (p. 34) as does Küchler,[22] Yarrow sees in the plays '*many glimpses of seventeenth century life and society*',[23] and Maurens uncovers at their heart shrewd and ironical social insight: '*Décapons donc les comédies de leurs différents enduits, noblesse, lyrisme romantique ou baroque, pour retrouver le vrai Corneille, observateur malicieux de la jeunesse de sa province.*'[24] Indeed, so widespread is such an interpretation of the comedies that even when analysis of them leads to the conclusion that these elements of topicality do not lie at their heart, the plays are still judged as *comédies de moeurs*, albeit deficient ones: Dotoli summarises his position thus: '*Une lecture même superficielle suffirait pour nous faire comprendre que Corneille, malgré ses hautes qualités théâtrales et ses mérites quant à l'histoire de la comédie, n'avait pas encore montré tous les aspects d'une réalité quotidienne qu'il croyait présenter d'une façon complète.*'[25]

Such readings of the plays lead to the conclusion that Corneille's is a discreet, charming conception of comedy which is intended to arouse not laughter but a knowing, compassionate smile. Yarrow sees the dramatist's intention to observe man rather than to make him laugh (p. 98), Voltz stresses the refinement which takes the place of more obvious and unsophisticated effects (p. 54), and in his analysis of *La Veuve*, Harvey is led to this conclusion about Cornelian comedy in general: *'the impression remains that another sort of comic, a discreet, smile-provoking kind of humor permeates Corneille's early comedies.'*[26] For Maurens, these elements suffice to make the plays unequivocally comic, and they suggest a mixture of irony and sympathy in the presentation of the youthful adventures they depict: *'Ce comique d'humour fait l'originalité des cinq premières oeuvres de Corneille, lorsqu'il observait le coeur humain des adolescents avec un mélange de raillerie et de tendresse'* (*Préface*, p. 27). Other critics, however, having analysed what they see as charming and realistic in the plays, are often led to the opposite conclusion. For Adam, the dramatist's imputed desire to capture reality in his work takes him too far away from a purely comic vision of character and plot (I, 494); for Rivaille, comedy is only superficial and masks deeper preoccupations in his texts (p. 766), and Scherer crystallises what is a widespread understanding of the plays when he speaks of *'les premières comédies de Corneille, très nuancées et assez peu comiques'*.[27]

Similar conclusions are reached, often implicitly, by critics who stress in these plays what is seen to be a particular vision of contemporary society. Bürger compares Corneille's treatment of certain themes with that of his contemporaries, and concludes that his originality lies in the way he manipulates them to suggest the reality of his characters and their background: *'Corneille dagegen sucht die Künstlichkeit einzuschränken, indem er durch Umkehrung, Verknüpfung und Verwandlung von Motiven diesen eine neue Wirklichkeitshaltigkeit verleiht.'*[28] However, far from evoking a relaxed pastoral world where suffering is discreetly controlled, the plays are seen by these critics to portray deep conflicts of values and powerful tensions between characters. Love is not simply a charming emotion, freely expressed and happily concluded; it is inevitably subjected to the pressure of parental tyranny, tainted or thwarted by materialism, hypocrisy, inconstancy. Cruelty is uncovered in Corneille's comic universe by critics as early as Brasillach (p. 124), and such impressions are found more recently in the writings of Bürger, who devotes a chapter of his study to *'die Grausamkeit der Corneilleschen*

Komödienfiguren' (pp. 118–124), of Kerr[29] and of Moisan-Mor-teyrol, who speaks of *'ces jeunes loups que sont les héros des comédies'*.[30] For Doubrovsky, the world of the comedies bears no resemblance to the spontaneous world of youthful love so often evoked by other commentators, and he discovers in his readings: *'l'étonnante* cruauté *qui jaillit, à chaque scène, parmi ces êtres en porte à faux; cynisme, brutalités, mensonges, trahisons . . .'*[31] The grim fate of many heroines, seemingly thwarted in their search for happiness in love by the authority of parent or brother is often highlighted as Corneille's essential theme: Yarrow points out elements of social criticism (p. 87), Couton speaks of the *'réalisme et pathétique matrimonial'* felt in the plays[32] and Stegmann sees depicted here *'la laideur du monde bourgeois'*.[33]

The result is a picture of comedies which, far from being comic, are profoundly moving and disturbing. Couton is quite explicit about their impact: *'Ces situations apportent dans les comédies de Corneille les émotions qui attendrissent les coeurs'* (p. 43), and again, as in the remarks of earlier, less sophisticated critics, the plays are seen to prefigure in their themes, as well as in their language, the world of the tragedies. Thus Nadal states with regard to *Médée*: *'les comédies la préparent et l'annoncent par l'inquiétant problème amoureux qu'elles essaient d'esquiver'* (p. 79), and after an analysis of *Mélite*, Doubrovsky is already able to set the comedies in the wider context of Corneille's complete *oeuvre*: *'Dès cette première comédie, on trouve une présentation lucide des thèmes qui, en se compliquant et en s'approfondissant, vont susciter les grands mouve-ments de la dramaturgie cornélienne'* (p. 43).

The development to the tragic world which is implied in certain conclusions about the comedies is the evident starting point for other analyses. Critics often examine the protagonists of these plays in terms of the 'Cornelian hero' yet to be born. Nelson outlines a clearly defined hierarchy of moral values, dividing the characters into categories of true and false lovers, of heroes and lesser heroes;[34] Koch[35] and Fournier[36] conduct an investigation of the characters and the development of their reactions to problems and pressures imposed on them; Rivaille sees in the comedies the ever more obvious presence of heroes who use their will and intelligence to further a fundamental search for truth (p. 759), and Dort makes a conclusion in his study which is typical of many approaches to and interpretations of these plays: *'Toute la première partie de l'oeuvre de Pierre Corneille est recherche et découverte de ce héros cornélien'.*[37]

Other similarly thematic approaches do not examine the comedies as *comedies*, but situate the plays in a much wider philosophical context. Nadal evokes in them the mysterious and all-pervading influence of love (p. 80), and its unstable, capricious nature is analysed too by Lemonnier (p. 31), Cosnier,[38] and most particularly by Rousset, whose conclusion about these works is categorical: *'toutes les comédies de Corneille tournent autour d'un thème central: l'inconstance, "le change"'.*[39] Other critics emphasise fundamental problems of communication experienced by the characters,[40] and such notions are taken up by commentators who stress certain aspects of theatricality in the behaviour of the protagonists: Pedersen examines the whole question of deception in these terms,[41] and Rubin sees in the later comedies a search, through the playing of roles, of a more stable and ultimately more valuable state.[42]

Such analyses differ widely in their approaches, and yet, in their various ways they reach a single conclusion about the plays: that although they may be classed as comedies, they are not comic. In their remarks, critics clearly equate what is comic with what is amusing, and Corneille is seen as one for whom *comédie* did not necessarily, even partly imply the aim to arouse laughter. His work is held to be quite particular in its development of a discreet form of comedy, totally distinct from the more unsophisticated comic productions of the time. This interpretation is suggested in Emelina's judgement of the genre as it was to develop later in the century: *'la comédie, malgré les tentatives de P. Corneille, sera de plus en plus destinée – même très éloignée de la farce – à faire rire',*[43] and the same picture is implied in the following remark of Gill: *'Trente ans après la première représentation de Mélite, la gaieté, que Corneille avait pu rendre pendant quelque temps plus discrète, régnait de nouveau sur la scène comique française.'*[44]

Such an attitude, however, is unsatisfactory for two reasons. Firstly, it leads to an oversimplification of Corneille's *oeuvre*, implying that these early comedies constitute a homogeneous group. General statements about this body of plays as a whole are often inspired, one feels, by the more particular interpretation of a single play, and critics who single out the dramatic plight of Doris in *La Veuve*, the charm or topicality of *La Galerie du Palais*, the themes of hypocrisy or avarice in *La Suivante* or the nascent Cornelian hero in *La Place Royale*, are frequently led to trace similar elements in the rest of the corpus. The validity of this approach will be examined in subsequent chapters.

Secondly, and no less importantly, such interpretations of the plays inevitably distort the nature and range of other comedies written at this time. For dramatists in the 1630s, terms such as *comédie* and *comique* suggest not one, but several quite different forms of entertainment, a diversity which is clearly reflected in their work. Voltz makes the claim that Corneille's work was quite unique: '*Les premières comédies de Corneille sont trop personnelles pour avoir fait naître une école*' (p. 57), and yet, with the exception of Bürger, critics make little or no reference to the plays of his contemporaries. By so doing, they are ultimately led to simplify the extent of his originality. Very often, conclusions about his plays are reached largely with reference to the nature of the events they depict: young men and women falling in and out of love, daughters torn between passion and filial duty, villains who deceive and betray in the furtherance of their own ends. This approach, however, leaves two important questions unasked: how far are such themes commonplace in comedy of the time, and how far is this dramatist's treatment of them particular? It is only by studying this background that Corneille's conception of the genre may be properly analysed, and it is here that I shall begin.

I
Comédie in the 1630s
A decade of experiment

1

La Comédie à son entrée est suspendue, turbulente en son milieu, car c'est là que se font toutes les tromperies et les intrigues, et joyeuse à son issue.[1]

Le principal secret de pareils ouvrages, consiste à intriquer les accidens de sorte, que l'esprit du Spectateur demeurant suspendu entre la joye et la douleur, entre l'esperance et la crainte, ne puisse deviner où doit aboutir l'histoire, & se trouve agreablement surpris, par cet invisible noeud, qui desbrouille toute une pièce.[2]

For many writers of this time, the *comédie* is the play full of excitement and suspense, which depicts the thrilling adventures of lovers, ranging far in time and space and involving abductions, flights, imprisonment and duels. Ogier, writing in the preface to Schelandre's *Tyr et Sidon*,[3] argues that true theatrical entertainment depends on such involved incident: '*La poësie, et particulièrement celle qui est composée pour le théâtre, n'est faite que pour le plaisir et le divertissement, et ce plaisir ne peut proceder que de la variété des évenemens qui s'y representent*' (p. 153), and Rayssiguier, in the *Avis* to his adaptation of Tasso's *Aminta*,[4] remarks on the popularity of such plots with audiences who desire action in *comédie* above all else: '*la plus grande part de ceux qui portent le teston à l'Hôtel de Bourgogne veulent que l'on contente leurs yeux par la diversité et changement de la face du Theatre, & que le grand nombre des accidens & adventures extraordinaires leur ostent la cognoissance du sujet*'. In the plays themselves, dramatists constantly seek to evoke a world where anything seems possible, and exceptional events are, paradoxically, quite unexceptional. In du Ryer's *Clitophon*,[5] Act III Scene 10, the hero laments the cruel vagaries of fortune which underlie the aesthetic pleasure of such plots: '*Hé Dieux quelle fortune est égale à la nôtre, / Nous sortons d'un malheur pour entrer dans un autre'* (p. 104). In such plays as these, the depth of the protagonists' love is manifested in their resilience to misfortune and their courage in overcoming obstacles. For the hero in du Ryer's *Argenis et Poliarque*,[6] Act I Scene 2, adventure is the necessary prelude to happiness in love:

> *Un genereux amour mesprise les disgraces*
> *Et pour luy les dangers n'ont que de douces faces.*
> *Qu'on ne s'estonne point si je quitte nos bords,*
> *Il faut passer des mers pour avoir des tresors,* (p. 13)

and in Scudéry's *Le Fils supposé*,[7] Act I Scene 7, the heroine resolves to escape from the authority of a brother fiercely opposed to her choice of suitor; her flight is the first of many thrilling incidents in a complicated plot:

> *En vain mauvais Demon, tu souffles ta manie;*
> *Je me verrai bientost hors de ta tyrannie;*
> *Tes menaces en l'air ne m'espouventent point:*
> *Partons, puisqu'à l'amour, le courage s'est joint.* (p. 26)

The terms of this resolution are significant. Love may inspire the flight, and yet the focus is not so much on the emotion itself as on its manifestation in an act of courage and rebellion which contributes to the turbulent movement of the play.

The plots of some other plays are much less involved. Racan in *Les Bergeries*,[8] Mairet in *Sylvie*[9] or *Silvanire*, Baro in *Célinde*[10] or *Clorise*[11] and Rayssiguier in *Célidée*[12] depict events which are far less complex: the tricks of villains to win favours from the heroine, the struggles of lovers against the authority of parents. For such dramatists too, though, the entertainment of comedy ultimately derives from the tension and excitement involved in the protagonists' search for happiness. Characters may be led to lament the materialism of the times they live in: in Rayssiguier's *Tragi-comédie pastorale*,[13] Act IV Scene 3, for instance, Silvandre evokes thus the folly of the world: '*Puis qu'on n'estime point l'homme au siècle où nous sommes / Que par les biens tous seuls qui ne sont point aux hommes!*' (p. 99), and in the *Aspasie* of Desmarets de Saint-Sorlin,[14] Act I Scene 1, the hero bewails the vice to which his father has fallen prey:

> *Mon père qui surpasse en richesse le sien,*
> *Ne consentira pas à cet heureux lien.*

> *Dieux! quelle cruauté! que ma propre fortune*
> *Fatale à mes desseins me nuise & m'importune.* (pp. 2–3)[15]

Such incidents, however, do not so much suggest a penetrating indictment of contemporary manners as give expression to what is a simple and traditional source of dramatic conflict. In d'Alibray's translation of *Aminta*,[16] Act II Scene 1, the satyr's lament is voiced in exactly these terms: '*Et veritablement voicy l'âge doré, / Puis que l'or seul peut tout, & seul est adoré*' (p. 49), and in prefatory verses to *L'Inconstance punie* of La Croix,[17] the unidentified poet I.G.D. highlights what is clearly a popular theme in plays of the time, exploited to bring out heroic qualities in the protagonists:

> *D'un père ambitieux souffrir la tyrannie,*
> *Tenir ce qu'on promet, aimer parfaitement,*
> *Depeindre ces vertus, n'appartient proprement*
> *Qu'au loyal Caliris & à sa Melanie.*

In *Aspasie*, a girl is actually forced to marry the father of her lover, before the old man realises the cruelty of his desire, and in Baro's *Célinde*, the plot explodes into violence as the heroine attempts to kill both herself and the suitor she seems compelled to marry. Such is the aesthetic force of these plays that the spectators, like the characters, are kept uncertain of the outcome, and suspense is underlined by touching laments, like that of Diane in Rayssiguier's *Tragi-comédie pastorale*, Act IV Scene 1, as she imagines the bleak future:

> *Dieux qui m'avez donné ce que j'ay de beauté,*
> *En peut-on disposer contre ma volonté?*
> *Faut-il pour obéir aux raisons d'une mère*
> *Que j'attache à ma vie une longue misère?* (p. 84)

The importance of suspense in comedy was greatly discussed in these years, and a question much debated was the precise influence of an audience's prior knowledge of the plot on its reaction to the events depicted. For some dramatists, it seemed essential that the spectator should know no more than the most enlightened character; any intimation of the outline of the plot, given in the text itself or provided by a prefatory *Argument*, would undermine the impact of the drama. In the preface to his *Aminte*, d'Alibray openly argues in favour of leaving the audience doubtful as to the outcome of events: '*Outre que j'estime qu'il n'y a*

*rien de plus contraire au plaisir qu'on peut recevoir des ouvrages de
cette sorte, que d'en lire l'argument, parce que tout à coup il previent
nos attentes, & ne permet pas que nostre esprit demeure en suspens
dans l'incertitude des évenemens'*, and the same feelings are expressed in Baro's preface to *Clorise*, where he rejects the use of
an *Argument* at the head of his published work: *'Et jamais on n'a
veu qu'au recit d'un Poëme, on ait preoccupé les spectateurs par la
cognoissance du sujet; autrement, il seroit impossible qu'ils ressentis-
sent les passions qu'on leur veut inspirer . . .'*[18] If the thrills and
suspense which form the essence of such *comédie* are to be
sustained, if language is to have any direct and undistorted
force, then the facts of the plot must be carefully concealed; the
Prologue's analysis of such plays which heads this section is
taken from a brief debate at the beginning of Scudéry's play in
which the function of the *Argument* is called into question.

However, dramatic practice is very different from theory. It is
clear that an audience's knowledge of events did not necessarily
minimise their particular enjoyment of a play, and in his *Pratique
du théâtre*,[19] II 9, d'Aubignac suggests with great sensitivity that
spectators are quite happy to deceive themselves in such circumstances:

*Ils renferment toute leur intelligence dans les prétextes & les couleurs qui les
font mettre en avant, sans aller plus loing; ils s'appliquent à ce qui se dit de
temps en temps, & estant toujours satisfaits des motifs qui les font dire, ils ne
previennent point celles qui ne leur sont pas manifestées; si bien que leur
imagination se laissant tromper à l'art du Poëte, leur plaisir dure toujours.* (p.
178)

The frequency and popularity of plays adapted from known
tales in d'Urfé's *L'Astrée* is certain proof of this fundamental
aesthetic principle, and indeed, d'Alibray himself, in adapting
Aminta, was tacitly acknowledging and relying on his public's
ability to forget what it may already know.

Furthermore, where an audience may have superior knowledge in such plays, this is not exploited for essentially comic
effects. The comedy composed by Les Cinq Auteurs,[20] *La
Comédie des Tuilleries*, is a play constructed around a not very
probable misunderstanding known to the audience from the
exposition: the lovers believe that they are to be kept apart by
parental authority, whereas, in fact, they are betrothed to each
other. Yet, when the couple lament in Act III Scene 7, no irony

colours the impact of the lines. The pity of the lovers' imaginary ordeal is taken on its own terms; Corneille's lines have their own undistorted force, moving and beautifully balanced:

Aglante: *Aymons-nous, & souffrons; aymé de ce qu'on ayme,*
            On trouve des plaisirs dans la souffrance mesme.
Cleonice: *Aymons-nous, & souffrons; deux coeurs si bien d'accord,*
            Trouveroient des plaisirs dans les coups de la Mort. (pp. 86–7)

Significantly, the review of the play published in the *Gazette* of 10 March 1635 highlights above all '*la bonté de ses acteurs*' and '*la majesté de ses vers*'.[21]

This particular example clearly suggests the concern of certain writers to provide as much a poetic as a dramatic entertainment in their comedies, and the willingness of audiences to accept them as such. It is this desire which underlies and accounts for the glaring psychological incoherence in many characters, their uneven temper, their extreme gullibility. Treachery has only to be half-suspected, and the most passionate love may give way to violent hatred and anger. When the heroine thinks that her beloved is about to leave her for another in du Ryer's *Lisandre et Caliste*, Act III Scene 4,[22] her rage explodes at once:

> *Ces mains si laschement par les tiennes pressées*
> *Deschireront ce coeur qui reçeut tes pensées,*
> *Ce corps qui fut jadis l'idole de tes voeux*
> *Esteindra dans son sang les restes de ses feux:*
> *Et ma mort fera voir par ce sanglant spectacle*
> *Que tes nouveaux desseins ne trouvent plus d'obstacle.* (pp. 76–7)[23]

Furthermore, such laments are often expressed in terms which are singularly inappropriate. When, for instance, Arsidor comes to the rescue of a stranger in Scudéry's *Le Trompeur puny*,[24] Act IV Scene 6, and then realises that it is his bitter rival in love whom he had resolved to kill, his lament takes this form:

> *Sujet que je deteste, & qu'il faut que je serve,*
> *Je venois pour ravir ce que je luy conserve,*
> *Je combats contre moy, pour combattre pour luy,*
> *En un mot je me perds, le servant aujourd'huy.* (p. 89)

This particular stylisation is absurd in the context, suggesting an intellectualised reaction to deep disappointment which is quite out of place. Clearly, though, dramatic or psychological

verisimilitude is less important to the writer than this display of
his own linguistic agility.

This conception of the *comédie* as a poetic entertainment is
reflected particularly in those scenes where well-meaning
characters deliberately mislead others for the sake of hearing
them lament. In Rotrou's *Les Captifs*,[25] for instance, Philenie loves
and is loved by Tyndare, an imprisoned slave, but this love seems
doomed because the heroine has been betrothed since childhood
to the king's son who was abducted at birth. By Act V Scene 4, it is
clear that Tyndare is none other than Philenie's betrothed, but
the happy news is withheld from her for a moment. She is told
simply that the king's son has been found for her, and she is left
to struggle against this apparent threat to her happiness:

> Oui, vostre aveuglement souhaite à vostre fils
> Un mal dont vous plaindriez même vos ennemis.
> Ce n'est pas que ce sein enferme un coeur barbare;
> Il s'est laissé toucher aux charmes de Tyndare;
> Et ce joug que j'appelle un enfer aujourd'hui,
> M'eût été, je l'avoue, un ciel avecque lui . . . (IV, p. 177)

The heroine's mistake is apparent, but she is not conceived as the
butt of comedy in these lines. Deception leads to heroic dignity,
not ironical deflation, and Philocrate's exclamation of Act V Scene
5, '*Dieux! que ce passe-temps est merveilleux et raré*' (p. 178), does not
suggest any comic detachment deriving from his enlightened
knowledge of events, but rather his delight in the fluent
expression of noble sentiments. Like an actor who gives pleasure
to his audience by the accomplished performance of a role, the
character here entertains all those on stage.[26]

Indeed, that such interludes imply a focus on the individual
actor and his skill is more than simply a metaphor. In his *Examen*
to *Clitandre*, Corneille remarks on the popularity of long
monologues, both with the spectator and the player: '*c'étoit une
beauté en ce temps-là; les comédiens les souhaitoient, et croyoient y
paroître avec plus d'avantage*' (Marty-Laveaux, I, 273), and in the
'*Discours à Cliton*', published during the '*Querelle du Cid*', the
author remarks on the attitude of less discerning audiences to
such moments, and their interest not with dramatic context or
even the character depicted, but with the display of a popular
performer: '*ne venant au Théâtre que pour se divertir, ils sont aussi
contents d'ouyr de beaux vers, et de voir faire la Beaupré ou la Devilliers,*

que d'admirer telle ou telle Héroine qui leur estoit promise et à laquelle ils ne pensent plus.'[27]

In plays like these, the term *comédie* clearly does not necessarily connote the aim to make an audience laugh, and if amusing moments are included, they are conceived purely as interludes, often shamelessly farcical in nature. In Rotrou's *L'Heureuse Constance*,[28] the violent struggle of a king against his enemies is lightened by the ironical observations of a servant, Ogier, and the action of du Ryer's *Lisandre et Caliste* is interrupted in Act II Scene 1 by the amusing laments of a butcher, who suspects his wife of infidelity. Such comic elements neither affect the overall impact or presentation of the principal action, nor indeed are they considered to be a necessary adjunct of it. The arousal of laughter was often held to be an activity unworthy of such writers of *comédie*. Monléon's pride in his *Advertissement* to *Amphytrite*[29] is typical of these feelings: *'Je pardonne à la pauvreté de Padelle, lors qu'il fait rire mille crocheteurs à la place Dauphine, pour mieux vendre son bausme, mais je ne l'exempte pas d'infamie'*, and they are echoed again in Scudéry's preface to his *Apologie du théâtre*,[30] as he begins his defence of dramatists and the theatrical profession: *'Platon sans doute auroit eu raison, de bannir les Poëtes de sa Republique Ideale, s'ils n'avoyent point de meilleur employ, que celuy de faire rire.'* Their plots may not have the dignity of subject particular to tragedy, but nor do they imply in their presentation any form of ironical detachment from either action or character. Chapelain, when speaking of the genre of *tragicomédie*, makes a pertinent remark which underlines this point: *'Les modernes François l'ont fort mise en vogue, et par les personnes et par les mouvements l'ont plus fait tenir de la tragédie que de la comédie'* (*op. cit.*, p. 130). For such writers, the term suggests a pleasing mixture of incident and *beaux effets*, surprise and lyricism, a sequence of scenes intended to thrill and delight. Thus, when in Act V Scene 4 of Baro's *Célinde*, Amintor outlines the features of the tale which the audience has just enjoyed and which is to be put into dramatic form, he outlines the aims of many playwrights of this time: *'Allons en faveur de ces deux Mariages, opposer aux feux de la nuict ceux de vostre amour & de vostre joye, & faire graver sur l'Airain les merveilles de cette Histoire, afin qu'elle estonne esgallement, & qu'elle ravisse les yeux & les oreilles de la Postérité'* (pp. 216–17).

2

> *Les tourmens amoureus, quoy qu'ils fassent soufrir,*
> *Dans leurs puissans effaits ne font jamais mourir:*
> *Lon [sic] peut être amoureus, mais quoi qu'un Amant die*
> *L'on meurt fort rarement de cette maladie.*[31]

The kind of *comédie* just analysed concentrates on the excitement generated by the adventures of heroes in their quest for happiness; another form of comedy develops at this time however, where interest lies less in the protagonists' deeds than in their feelings. In this world setbacks to happiness are not mighty obstacles, but misunderstandings and uncertainties, lovers are not called upon to master powerful enemies, but simply themselves as they come to know their own heart and its various moods.

When characters are wrought with jealousy, for instance, their laments now are not simply the opportunity for expressions of violent anguish, but are seen in a discreetly comic light. In Beys' *Le Jaloux sans sujet,*[32] Act III Scene 2, for instance, Alindor's suspicions suggest a delicate blend of feelings, as love goes hand in hand with despair:

> *Que de mille regrets mon amour soit suivie,*
> *Et que j'erre aveuglé le reste de ma vie,*
> *Sans suite, sans dessein, bien loin de mon pays,*
> *Si tous deux à la fois il ne nous a trahis;*
> *S'il n'a secrettement quitté vostre service,*
> *S'il n'aime ma maistresse ou bien plustost Clarice,* (p. 50)

and in Rayssiguier's *Les Thuilleries,*[33] Act II Scene 1, Daphnide is quite aware that she cannot help loving the hero, even though she sees him forsake her; she may resolve to forget him, but realises that such a project would be quite vain:

> *Mais que tout ce discours esclatte follement,*
> *L'amour ne quitte pas un coeur facillement,*
> *Lors qu'il a mis le pied dessus nostre innocence,*
> *La raison veut en vain employer sa puissance.* (pp. 25–6)

In Rotrou's *Diane,*[34] Act II Scene 8, the heroine examines the nature of her attachment to a faithless lover; where affection is deep, it persists in all circumstances, and the mature lovers of these years are quite conscious of what such a paradox entails:

> *Helas! qu'un malheureux délibère aisément,*
> *Mais qu'il trouve de peine en l'accomplissement!*

> *Je ne puis l'oublier sans m'oublier moi-même,*
> *Je l'aime seulement; à cause que je l'aime*
> *L'auteur de mon repos me désobligeroit,*
> *Et je voudrois du mal à qui me guériroit.* (I, p. 292)

The sensitivity implied here is reflected also in dramatists' interest in the relationship of characters not in love with each other. In some pastoral plays, a scene depicting the rejection of a lover by an aloof lady had suggested the opposition of two wholly irreconcilable passions and often gave rise to that kind of poetic symmetry found, for instance, in Mairet's *Sylvie*, Act I Scene 3, as Sylvie turns away the sighing Philène:

Philène: *Justes Dieux! se peut-il qu'une bergère endure*
          Son pasteur à ses pieds d'amour se consumer?
Sylvie: *Mais plutôt se peut-il que ta fureur se dure,*
          Sachant que je ne puis ni ne te veux aimer? (161–4)[35]

In later plays, however, dramatists begin to suggest the possibility of feelings in such relationships which, although not those of love, have a certain warmth and human sympathy. In Baro's *Clorise*, Act I Scene 5, for instance, Alidor admits that he does not love Eliante, yet has pity for her hopeless longing: '*Mais je sens un regret qui m'afflige au mourir, / C'est dequoy je vous blesse & ne vous puis guerir . . .*' (p. 25) and the same feelings are suggested in Rotrou's *Florimonde*,[36] Act III Scene 5, as Theaste confesses to Cleonie that he has only feigned love for her:

> *Ce n'est pas ta beauté qui cause mon martyre,*
> *Et je te veux du bien assez pour te le dire;*
> *C'est encore beaucoup que je t'aime à ce point*
> *De te désabuser, et ne te jouer point.* (V, p. 452)

In plays of this kind, dramatists often seek to avoid arousing tension in the audience, a process clearly suggested in their presentation of a lover's despair. In many of the more lively comedies, such lament would be the prelude to a suicide attempt, and suspense generated by threats such as these of Rayssiguier's Aminta in Act I Scene 2, which were to be taken quite literally:

> *Tircis, pour le sçavoir j'ay fait tout mon effort,*
> *Et ne me reste plus que d'aller à la mort . . .* (p. 24)[37]

Where there were expressions of comfort, these would not reflect on the nature of the suffering, but simply reiterate the general principle that happiness invariably follows grief. In Scudéry's

Ligdamon et Lidias, Act II Scene 1, for instance, Aegide consoles Ligdamon in these terms:

> *La tempeste à la fin nous apporte le calme,*
> *Et l'homme courageux doit imiter la palme,*
> *Qui courbant quelquesfois dessous l'effort du faix,*
> *Se roidit, se redresse, & ne se rompt jamais,* (p. 28)

and in Mairet's *Chryséide et Arimand*,[38] Act I Scene 2, Bellaris uses the same argument to comfort Arimand: '*On n'a point jamais veu de si sanglant orage / Qui n'appaisast enfin sa fureur et sa rage*' (329–30).[39]

In several plays of the 1630s, however, the nature of this encouragement is quite different, as the *confident* puts the despair of love into perspective. In Rotrou's *Filandre*,[40] Act I Scene 4, for example, Cephise persuades Thimante that his violent anguish could never lead him to take his own life, however much he may believe it:

> *Thimante, il est aisé de parler du trépas:*
> *Je veux mourir souvent, et ne me hâte pas.*
> *La vie est à chacun une belle maîtresse;*
> *Tous l'aiment ardemment, quelque autre qui les blesse.*
> *La mort est en ce temps un rare effet d'amour;*
> *Et pour quoi qu'on en ait, on en a pour le jour . . .* (II, pp. 542–3)

and in the same dramatist's *Céliane*,[41] Act IV Scene 6, Julie expresses quiet confidence that her brother can recover from any disappointment in love which he may endure:

> *Ses maux ne sont pas tels que deux mois de tristesse*
> *Ne soient l'unique effet du tourment qui le blesse.*
> *De quelque désespoir qu'il paroisse agité,*
> *Croyez que de ce temps il sera limité . . .* (II, p. 310)[42]

In certain protagonists also, dramatists suggest a charming detachment from their feelings, an ability to view with irony those more violent reactions which belong properly to the world of literature. In Rotrou's *Célimène*,[43] Act I Scene 3, the heroine Florante, deceived by Filandre, views her plight with a calm humour. She may mouth the laments of many a heroine, but the dramatist makes quite plain that they are spoken '(*en*) *riant*':

Florante (riant):	*O sensible douleur! o perte irréparable!*
	Est-il à mes ennuys un tourment comparable?
	Qui m'ouvre les enfers? qui me perce le sein?
Filandre:	*Oh! vous n'en mourrez pas.*
Florante:	*Ce n'est pas mon dessein* (II, p. 90)

and in *Filandre*, Act V Scene 1, Cephise is quite resigned to defeat in her suit of love: she imagines the reaction of Filandre, also unhappy in his own quest, and refuses to imitate him in his despair:

> *Tu vas m'entretenir de la perte du jour;*
> *Et, si je connois bien ton débile courage,*
> *Tu ne vas témoigner que désespoir, que rage;*
> *Tu vas à ton secours implorer le trépas;*
> *Fais ce qui te plaira, mais je ne mourrai pas.* (II, pp. 593–4)[44]

The qualities outlined here characterise some of the more fascinating plays of this decade which conduct a sensitive examination of those pastoral ideals of conduct inherited from Tasso, Guarini and d'Urfé. In plays such as these, the dramatist implies a certain detachment from the characters and their feelings, a distance which derives from a sense of complicity between writer and audience, a mutual understanding of the problems of love which, although never minimising their importance, keeps them firmly in perspective. It is this understanding which lies behind the unexaggerated evocation of love and its effects which opens Coste's pastoral, *Lizimène*.

3

J'ay creu qu'en suitte de ces sujets si graves & si tristes, il te falloit donner quelque pièce Comique pour divertir ton esprit de leurs Histoires mellancoliques.[45]

In other plays of this period, however, dramatists seek quite different effects again, less obviously concerned either with creating suspense in the audience or in examining the feelings of the protagonists. In *Les Folies de Cardenio*, Pichou takes an episode from Cervantes, the struggle of Cardenio and Luscinde to find happiness in love, but devotes a great part of the play to the depiction of the hero's temporary madness and his comic meeting with Don Quixote, one no less mad than he; in Rotrou's *Bague de l'oubly*,[46] an essentially romanesque plot, dealing with the ambitions of two lovers to overthrow the king, is dominated by the confusion and misunderstanding which arise as the king successively puts on and takes off the magic ring of forgetfulness with which they hope to achieve their ends; and in *Les Galanteries du Duc d'Ossonne*,[47] Mairet produces a curious work where attention is fixed on the hero's adulterous adventures, simultaneously courting two women and priding himself on his own quick-wittedness in Act III Scene 5:

> *Comme une comédie a sauvé mon amour,*
> *Mon amour pourroit bien en causer une un jour,*
> *Car c'en est un sujet galant, comique et rare,*
> *Entre les plus parfaits dont la scène se pare.* (988–91)

Several plays published in these years follow quite explicitly in the traditions of classical comedy. In *Les Ménèchmes*[48] and *Les Sosies*[49] Rotrou exploits and adapts the comic potential in the comedy of confusion, and the preface to his later *Clarice*,[50] is a committed eulogy of Plautus: *'Il est impossible de s'esgarer dessus les pas de cet illustre Pere du Comique; ce qu'il a fait de beau l'est au dernier poinct, & ce qui ne l'est pas absolument pour luy, l'est parfaitement pour nous.'* Similarly, Mareschal's *Le Railleur*,[51] with its telling evocation of certain social types, is seen quite explicitly as an updating of Plautine techniques, and it is significant that in the preface to this play the dramatist refers to his *Véritable Capitan Matamore*[52] as his most accomplished and successful work: *'le Chef d'oeuvre de mes Comedies, sous le nom du Capitan ou du Fanfaron, que j'ay tiré de Plaute & accommodé à nostre Theatre aussi bien qu'à nostre Histoire & à nostre temps.'*

Other plays have roots in more farcical traditions with their presentation of such types as the aged lover and the deceived husband. Discret is an important figure here, and in the *Advertissement* to his *Alizon*, he distinguishes his play from the more exciting forms of drama, his own aim being simply to make an audience laugh; his *Dedicace* reiterates the point:

> *Estime qui voudra tous les sujets tragiques,*
> *Alizon qui fait rire a bien d'autres appas,*
> *Ceux-la font les humains si fort mellancoliques,*
> *Qu'il faut que celle-cy les tirent du trespas.* (p. 7)

Comic effects in this play are largely rudimentary in their grotesque distortion of pastoral elements, the elderly widow Alizon Fleurie recalling her past happiness with singularly inappropriate allusions:

> *J'estois son Alizon, son amour, son delice,*
> *J'estois sa Penelope, il estoit mon Ulysse;*
> *Chez nous tous les plaisirs estoient à l'abandon,*
> *Si j'estois son Astrée, il estoit Celadon,* (9–12)

and looking forward now to courtship from an eighty-year-old soldier, Maistre Hieremie.

In much the same style is Discret's later *Les Nopces de Vaugirard*,[53] whose preface, '*Epistre servant d'advertissement à ceux qui veulent rire*', gives an explicit indication of the dramatist's intentions. The plot depicts the farcical tale of a beautiful girl married to a wealthy but aged husband, where characters are seen to be completely, if rather unsubtly detached from all their suffering. In Act II Scene 1, for instance, the heroine Lidiane begins to outline the turbulent and distressing course of her life, only to pause with an ironical reflection not on the suffering itself, but on the time it would take her to finish her account:

> *Mais laissons ce parler, il est un peu trop triste.*
> *S'il falloit de mes maux reciter tout le cours,*
> *Trois jours ne suffiroient pour un si long discours.* (p. 26)

Le Docteur amoureux of Le Vert[54] is populated with characters who play parts for which they are clearly no longer suited. The dramatist draws robust comic effects from his heroine, the amorous and elderly Helene, who is quite aware of her deficiencies and yet blind to the consequences:

> *Malgré le temps usé de mes vieilles années,*
> *Que l'ordre du destin a presque terminées,*
> *Mon antique beauté pour se faire adorer*
> *Trouve encor des martyrs qu'elle fait souspirer,* (p. 7)

and in the doctor himself, Le Vert presents the traditional pedant, whose absurdly stylised and mock erudite language grotesquely distorts the tender feelings he would have it express in Act II Scene 2:

> *Mon coeur, mais coeur d'un homme accravaté de flame,*
> *Auquel vostre douceur peut servir de Dictame,*
> *Conduit par le respect & la timidité,*
> *Je viens solliciter vostre affabilité.* (p. 33)

This particular form of linguistic comedy has its most striking expression in those plays which present the traditional *péripéties* of an amorous plot in a single style. This is a form of the comic which rapidly loses its impact, but which suggests nevertheless a certain delight in sheer verbal virtuosity which is evident in these years. In the *Advertissement aux lecteurs* which prefaces the *Comédie de Chansons*,[55] the author proclaims with some pride the skill with which his play has been composed: '*Nous avons ici un ouvrage aussi ingénieux que l'on le sçauroit souhaiter. C'est une Comédie où il n'y a pas un mot qui ne soit un vers ou un couplet de quelque Chanson.*' This work, like Montluc's *Comédie de Proverbes*[56] or du Peschier's *Comédie des Comédies*[57] takes to the most extravagant lengths the detachment which can be created from the language of suffering. For Montluc's character, Thesaurus, distressed at the abduction of his daughter in Act I Scene 6, no sympathy is possible nor is it solicited in a lament which is the shameless accumulation of metaphors and popular expressions:

Helas mon voisin! j'ay perdu la plus belle roze de mon chappeau, la fortune m'a tourné le dos, moy qui avois feu & lieu, pignon sur ruë, & une fille belle comme le jour, que nous gardions à un homme qui ne se mouche pas du pied, qui m'eust servy de baston de vieillesse & d'appuy à ma maison . . . (p. 20)

Other comedies of this time work on less rarefied levels of verbal contortion and present in their different ways comic variations on the familiar characters of pastoral. Hylas, for instance, the dissident voice of *L'Astrée*, grows from the peripheral commentator of Mairet's *Silvanire*, Act I Scene 1: '*Aglante aime à l'antique, Hylas aime à la mode*' (67), to the central character of Mareschal's *L'Inconstance d'Hylas*,[58] who has no time for any doleful or lugubrious ideals. As he courts Stelle in Act IV Scene 3, he proposes a quite different attitude to love:

> *Ils pensent que l'amour n'est pas de bonne marque*
> *Si ce n'est sous des mots de souspirs, & de parque:*
> *Nostre effort n'en sera ni plus ni moins ardent;*
> *Laissons les tous mourir, & vivons cependant.* (pp. 94–5)

In this kind of play, lovers are destined to amuse, their setbacks in courtship suggesting less about the unpredictability either of fate or of the human heart, than about their essential ridiculousness. As Periandre courts Dorinde in *L'Inconstance d'Hylas*, Act I Scene 1, his supplications lack all heroic dignity:

> *C'est assez qu'une loy nous retiene caché*
> *Ce que sans vostre faute on eust vû sans peché;*
> *Il est vray que l'erreur en est plus grande à l'homme*
> *D'avoir ainsi quitté ce fruict pour une pomme.* (p. 3)

He bewails the consequences of the Fall here, but not only in general terms on account of the reticence which the heroine must needs show in her response to his pleas, but, more specifically, because of the very trappings of civilisation which frustrate his longing gaze. In such a context, the language of death which he then intones has a purely comic force; the hero is forced to try every possible argument in an attempt to prevail upon his beloved:

> Pour vous plaire est-ce assez de mourir sans le dire?
> Vous ne m'entendrez plus parler de mon martire,
> Ma perte seulement vous doit montrer un jour
> Ma foy dans vos rigueurs, vos traits dans mon amour. (p. 5)

In the traditional interview of the ardent lover and aloof lady, emphasis is placed no longer on the irreconcilability of diverse emotions, as had been the case in pastoral, but on the foolishness of the lover; his importuning suggests not love but the vain and awkward repetition of an outdated language. In du Ryer's *Amarillis*,[59] Act III Scene 1, the sighing Ergaste is firmly put in his place as he despairs of softening the heroine:

Ergaste: Hélas, je connois bien que tu veux que je meure!
           Mais je suis déjà mort aux plaisirs d'ici bas.
Amarillis: Quoy les morts parlent-ils? donc la voix nous demeure
           En dépit de l'assaut que livre le trépas? (p. 58),

and in Claveret's *L'Esprit fort*,[60] Act II Scene 1, the timid lover Cleronte is chastised by the onlooker Celirée: his laments are not seen as expressions of deep despair, but as verbal indulgence which serves no useful purpose:

> Vous l'aimez, & de grâce allez l'entretenir,
> Sans consumer vostre âme en des plaintes frivoles,
> Poursuivez les effets, quittez là les paroles . . . (p. 27)[61]

From here, certain dramatists are led to make more general statements about the spirit of the age, where pastoral ideals persist, but no longer in their original form. When Clarimand confronts Lyzante, the poet, in Mareschal's *Le Railleur*, Act III Scene 3, he remarks on the deep rift between literature and life, poetic expressions of despair being stylised and exaggerated. Lyzante had earlier rushed off the stage in a suicidal rage, but has now returned, safe and sound:

> On abuse du nom, le mal est bien divers
> De mourir en effet, ou de mourir en vers,
> Les Poëtes, les Amans, quand l'ardeur les convie,
> Meurent tous, & jamais ils ne perdent la vie. (p. 61)

In du Ryer's *Vendanges de Suresne*, Act I Scene 1, Philemon comments on the naivety and blindness of women besotted with romantic literature, and on the great success of fools whose only virtue is an acquaintance with pastoral novels:

> *Un homme de néant, bien poly, bien frisé,*
> *Par ces rares moyens se void favorisé,*
> *Pourveu qu'il sçache un mot des livres de l'Astrée*
> *C'est le plus grand esprit de toute une contrée;* (pp. 4–5)

and in *L'Advocat duppé*,[62] Act III Scene 2, Chevreau suggests the ridiculousness of the modern lover, not now a charming shepherd or a courageous warrior, but a timid lawyer whose clumsy attempt to beguile his beloved meets with symbolic failure:

> *Abordant son miroir je la voulois baiser,*
> *Croiant qu'ainsi mon mal se pourroit apaiser;*
> *Mais l'ingrate fuioit dans mon amour extrême,*
> *Et la pensant baiser je me baisois moy-mesme.* (p. 54)

These elements of *raillerie* which draw attention to the absurdity of behaviour inspired by literature rather than life lie at the heart of *Les Visionnaires* of Desmarets de Saint-Sorlin,[63] a play which exploits the comic potential of traditional literary language in a particularly sophisticated way. In pastoral, for instance, it is common for an aloof lady to regret that she is beautiful: in Gombauld's *Amaranthe*, Act I Scene 3, the heroine laments thus that she causes conflict and distress wherever she goes:

> *Qui sans faire du mal ne peut voir la clarté;*
> *Qui ne peut compatir avec la liberté;*
> *Qui ne fait qu'affliger ses amans, & soy-mesme;*
> *Qui rend leur ame triste, & leur visage blesme.* (p. 16)

In Hesperie, however, Desmarets transforms this attitude into a comic fixation, creating a heroine who is convinced that everybody is in love with her and who imagines their macabre attempts to win a place in her heart:

> *Je crains que quelqu'amant n'ait avant son trespas*
> *Ordonné que son coeur servît à mes repas.*
> *Souvent sur ce penser en mangeant je frissonne:*
> *Croyant qu'on le déguise, et qu'on me l'assaisonne!*
> *Pour mettre dans mon sein par ce trait décevant,*
> *Au moins après la mort ce qu'il ne put vivant.* (255–60)

Les Visionnaires offers a comic parade of such characters, each one with his or her own form of obsession, each one acting out a personal drama in the realm of the imagination. In his preface to this play, the dramatist openly dissociates himself from '*Poëtes, qui, pour contenter le vulgaire, font à dessein des pièces extravagantes, pleines d'accidens bizarres, de machines extraordinaires, et d'embrouillemens de Scenes, et qui affectent des vers enflez et obscurs, et des pointes ridicules au plus fort des passions . . .*' For Desmarets here, as for others at the time, the entertainment provided by the *comédie* is not that of excitement or poetic virtuosity. In plays such as this, the playwright is more concerned to amuse his public, to adapt the types and techniques of Classical comedy and farce or to exploit the comic potential of language and characters rooted in an outdated literary tradition.

4

Catastrophe est celle [ie. la partie] qui change toute chose en joie, et qui donne l'éclaircissement de tous les accidents qui sont arrivés sur la scène. Cette division est suivant l'ordre des comédies de Térence, que le Tasso et Guarini ont ponctuellement observé.[64]

For dramatists in the 1630s, clearly, the term *comédie* does not imply any single approach to the presentation of action and character; many possibilities are seen and exploited, and for many different effects. One constant feature is apparent, however, a feature evident on a purely formal, structural level: the *comédie* is the play with the happy ending, the play which sees the joyful resolution of all conflicts, establishes order and suggests a lasting sense of harmony, even justice.[65]

For the writer of the romanesque comedy, the final revelation of order comes as the dramatic climax, the ultimate and unexpected reversal which brings an end to all suffering. The dramatist convinces his public that all hope of happiness is lost for the protagonists and then produces a final surprise: order is achieved through the revelation of an identity hitherto unknown or misunderstood,[66] the granting of wealth and position,[67] or the resurrection of characters thought dead.[68] After the preceding tension and excitement, this emergence of harmony is all the more pleasurable as chaos is miraculously turned to order, despair to joy. At the end of *Silvanire*, Act V Scene 15, the chorus proclaims feelings common to many such plays:

> Ces amants que le Ciel a comblés de plaisirs,
> Après mille tourments soufferts en patience,
> Ont enfin toute chose au gré de leurs désirs;
> Ils bénissent leurs maux et font expérience
> Que le contentement est beaucoup mieux goûté
> Quand il a bien coûté . . . (2707–12)

and this attitude is reflected, too, in the observation of d'Aubignac in his *Pratique du théâtre*, II 10: '*car il est toujours d'autant plus agréable que de plusieurs apparences funestes, le retour & l'issue en est heureux & contre l'attente des Spectateurs*' (p. 190).

The final happy outcome certainly implies that no irremediable harm can be done in the world of comedy: hero and heroine are always seen to emerge unscathed from their painful quests. In *Aminte*, typically, d'Alibray's hero, like Tasso's is quite unharmed after the despair which had driven him to attempt suicide; the final order of comedy cures all ills and leaves no trace of the agonies undergone:

> Aminte est sain, sinon qu'il est un peu froissé,
> Et d'une égratigneure au visage blessé:
> Mais ce ne sera rien, il s'en mocque luy-mesme,
> Heureux d'avoir ainsi témoigné comme il ayme. (p. 148)

The world of order and stability to which hero and heroine then accede is expressed traditionally in the form of marriage. This creation of the happy couple conveniently expresses the end of suffering, chaos and confusion, and the advent of harmony and security; once the protagonists are married, then their trials are over, and no further harm or tribulations will befall them; the play will be complete. Thus, when Arthemise proposes to the hero in Beys' *Le Jaloux sans sujet*, Act V Scene 2, it is in these terms:

> Puisqu'ainsi de nous deux la fortune se jouë,
> Arrestons si tu veux son inconstante rouë;
> L'Hymen peut aujourd'huy contenter nos desirs,
> Achever nos travaux, commencer nos plaisirs,
> Bannir les ennemis de nostre douce vie,
> Et ravir le pouvoir de nous nuire à l'envie. (p. 89)

Significantly, indeed, such a proposal says little about the love which binds the couple and which, so often, has scant thematic importance. The emphasis is more obviously on the aesthetic principle involved in the termination of the play's events, and the dawn of order which marriage symbolises.

Such is the dramatic importance of this final triumph of harmony that nothing is allowed to tarnish its brilliance. The joy of the final scenes is shared by all, and characters who for the course of the play may have tried to thwart the happiness of the protagonists, either through tyranny or because of their own despised love, adopt new attitudes which authenticate the established order. In Scudéry's *Le Fils supposé*, Act V Scene 5, for instance, Cloridan who had earlier caused his sister to flee him with such courage, forgets his brutal opposition to her love, and admits the justice of his defeat:

> Vostre choix estoit juste, & mon jugement louche;
> Ne meslons rien d'amer avec cette douceur;
> Oublions l'un & l'autre, & nous aimons, ma soeur . . . (p. 117)

and in *Silvanire*, Act V Scene 13, Menandre is finally converted, recognising the value of his daughter's love for Aglante:

> Mes enfants, car pour tels je vous tiens sans contrainte,
> Bannissez de vos coeurs le soupçon et la crainte,
> Et que le souvenir de ce qui s'est passé
> Soit de notre mémoire à jamais effacé. (2543–6)

Alternatively, if no such changes of heart take place, the dissenting character simply disappears, taking with him none of the audience's sympathy, and in no sense dampening the intensity of the general joy. In Racan's *Bergeries*, Act V Scene 5, for example, Lucidas is excluded from the charmed circle, his moral turpitude, acknowledged by all concerned, disqualifying him from all claims to happiness. Damoclée's rejection of him has the consent of both the audience and the characters on stage:

> Laissez-nous en repos, esprit plein d'artifice,
> Vous offensez encor ces deux couples d'amants
> En retardant l'effet de leurs contentements. (2928–30)

Often, though, the primary order of the protagonists is complemented and intensified by the union of others. Marriage is what is expected at the end of comedy, and subsidiary characters are exhorted to join in the harmony: the remarks of Silvain and Palot in Gaillard's *La Carline*,[69] Act V, are classic in this respect:

Silvain: Viença Nicot, il faut qu'on te marie.
Palot: La saison veut que chacun s'apparie. (p. 79)

In the surging forward movement of the *dénouement*, indifference may change to love: Ydalie transfers her affections in the

Bergeries, as does Philène in Mairet's *Sylvie*, and Tirinte in *Silvanire*. And in Hardy's *Corine*,[70] Mélite happily forgets Caliste whom she had pursued in vain throughout the play, and accepts Arcas in Act V Scene 4, regretting only that time has been lost by her previous and misguided indifference to him:

> *Ne soyons plus qu'une ame, & qu'une envie,*
> *Et reparons de plaisirs amoureux*
> *Le temps perdu qui nous fit languoureux.* (1048–50)

Personal feelings are happily re-channelled; the past is forgotten for such characters, too, as they commit themselves totally to their new identities.

This emotional elasticity suggests certainly the absence of any internal coherence in the characters; such consistency is quite manifestly sacrificed for the sake of harmony. The order of *comédie* is far more geometrical than psychological; it is characterised by circles and smooth surfaces, unruffled by individualised characters or thoughts of suffering. This world is a wonderland, carefully created by the dramatist, full of marvels and surprises which lead finally to happiness. For the spectator, no other considerations matter; his delight at this order is as absolute as that of Daphnide in *L'Astrée*, Book 3, Chapter 12:[71] '*J'advoue avec vous, Alcidon, que voicy la contrée des merveilles, mais des merveilles pleines de bon-heur, puisqu'elle m'en faict voir aujourd'huy plus que je n'eusse jamais esperé*' (pp. 646–7). And indeed, this delight in order for its own sake is implied in the terms with which it is so often created. Behind the hand of Destiny which guides the protagonists through suffering to joy, is sensed the hand of the dramatist who similarly guides his audience. The *deus ex machina* is often used to make that final revelation which will turn chaos to order, and his omnipotence clearly reflects the dramatist's own with which he manipulates events for the greatest pleasure of his public. Clorimante is no prouder than du Ryer himself when, in *Cléomédon*,[72] Act V Scene 3, he announces himself thus: '*Je viens vous faire part d'un secret important / Qui vous doit estonner & vous rendre content*' (p. 90). The eulogy of *Amour* which comes in Racan's *Bergeries*, Act IV Scene 5, says nothing about the nature of love, and everything about Racan whose aim it is to thrill and delight his audience:

> *Grâces aux Immortels nos amants sont unis,*
> *Les pleurs sont apaisés, les tourments sont finis,*
> *D'une extrême douleur vient une extrême joie,*
> *L'on plaint à tort le mal que l'amour nous envoie,*
> *Qui vit dessous ses lois doit toujours espérer,*
> *Il fait rire à la fin ceux qu'il a fait pleurer.* (2173–8)

That this picture of love should veil only thinly the self-portrait of the dramatist himself is indeed significant. Here, as in all such *comédies*, the characters' feelings are of no interest to the playwright, and he attributes to love those features which characterise his own dramatic aims. Characters have no life of their own, and their love, be it reciprocated or not, is simply a pretext for action and adventure in the course of the drama; in the final scenes, it is inspired or fulfilled according to the exigencies of the aesthetic order. No resistance is offered, and the triumph of love, proclaimed so often at the end of *comédie*, implies no more and no less than the self-proclaimed triumph of the dramatist.

Other dramatists, however, were alive to the great improbability inherent in many such *dénouements*. Awareness of this is suggested, for instance, in d'Alibray's praise of *Aminta* in the preface to his own adaptation of the play: '*Quant à ce qui est de la conclusion de cette Pastorale, il n'y a rien de si naturel, ny qui vienne mieux au subject . . . aussi est-ce la partie la plus délicate, & qui endure moins de contrainte, & de gesne.*' The very *invraisemblance* which d'Alibray implicitly criticises here became for some dramatists the source of further comic effects. In Rotrou's *Diane*, for instance, the heroine decides to impersonate Lysandre, a hero once betrothed to the girl now loved by her treacherous suitor, Lysimant, and long believed to be dead; by doing this, Diane hopes to win back Lysimant, who would believe his new passion hopeless. Her performance parodies the theatrical artfulness of so many *dénouements*, as she proudly presents herself in Act III Scene 10, miraculously saved from a shipwreck:

> *Reconnaissez, Monsieur, ce gendre bienheureux*
> *Qu'enfin vous revoyez aussi sain qu'amoureux . . .*
> *. . . Oui, cet heureux amant*
> *Qui termine sa peine, et son éloignement,*
> *Que le Ciel a sauvé des efforts de Neptune*
> *Et qui revient chez vous établir sa fortune.* (I, p. 305)

However, the device becomes doubly ironical when fantasy turns into reality and the authentic Lysandre appears in Act V Scene 8 to perform just that function for which the heroine had resurrected him:

> *Quoy le temps vous a t'il mon portraict effacé?*
> *Ne vous souvient-il plus de cet heureux Lysandre*
> *Que vous avez jadis choisi pour vostre gendre?* (p. 333)

The speaker's lines echo those of the heroine herself who had played the part to perfection. Here, however, the surprise Lysandre sees around him is no longer that of an audience astonished by an unexpected return from the dead, but of one quite bewildered at this repetition of history.

The fortuity of fate raises other implications in du Ryer's *Vendanges de Suresne*, in which harmony is made possible by the propitious death of the hero's uncle, whose substantial bequest gives Polidor the qualities necessary for success in his suit. Irony is implied in the very unexpectedness of the event, but it is suggested further by the reaction of the heroine's father, Crisere. Throughout the play, he is presented as a typically avaricious parent, opposed to the impecunious hero and proudly asserting his authority in Act II Scene 5:

> *Et malgré les leçons que vous fait Palmedor,*
> *Un homme est assez noble alors qu'il a de l'or.*
> *On l'aime, on le respecte, on souffre ce qu'il ose;*
> *S'il sçait garder son or, il sçait beaucoup de chose.* (p. 49)

His change of attitude in Act V Scene 4, thus parodies the traditional conversion of a parent. Inspired as it is by this sudden bequest of money, it suggests now not so much the victory of enlightened thought, but an ironical persistance of blindness, a barely concealed delight that he has been satisfied in his own greedy desire:

> *Ses bonnes qualitez me font dire sans cesse*
> *Que le bien de son oncle est sa moindre richesse.*
> *Enfin il me ravit, & quand il n'auroit rien*
> *Son esprit ce me semble est un assez grand bien.* (p. 121)

In other plays, dramatists began to examine the possibility of suffering in *dénouements* traditionally so unruffled. A suggestive awareness of this possibility was apparent already in *L'Astrée*, IV 9. In his 'Histoire d'Alcandre, d'Amilcar, Circeine, Palinice et Florice', d'Urfé creates a plot in which six lovers court just three girls; Alcandre draws attention to the fact that some of them must inevitably be left disappointed: '*La comédie, à ce que j'ay ouy dire, finit tousjours en mariage; mais puisque nous sommes six, et que vous n'estes que trois, si faut-il de nécessité qu'il y en ait quelqu'un de nous mal content, car je sçay bien que je ne veux pas que celle que j'ayme soit partagée*' (p. 498). When the couples are finally paired in *L'Astrée*, V 4, the three lovers who are left alone quietly accept their fate; their disappointment is referred to, but not developed. The point, however, is taken up by Rayssiguier in his adaptation of the tale, *Palinice, Circeine et Florice*, in which the distress of one hero, Clorian, is made more explicit and tinged with a certain bitterness: '*Pour oublier du tout ces esprits inconstans, / Prenons pour medecins le depit & le temps*' (p. 108).

Suggestions of a different kind are implied in the ending of Rotrou's *Filandre*. In this play, Cephise and Filandre both suffer from the indifference of the ones they love. As early as Act I Scene 2, they discuss the traditional solution to their problem, Cephise speaking of the seemingly effortless transference of feelings which so often characterises and assures the atmosphere of unalloyed joy. The character's detachment from her emotions seems total here; she is willing and able to play any role:

> *Quoique pour Célidor, mon amour soit extrême,*
> *Je l'aime toutefois un peu moins que moi-même;*
> *Mon mal est violent, mais il n'est pas mortel:*
> *Suis mes sages conseils, et le tien sera tel.* (II, p. 534)

Nevertheless, the two villains attempt to sunder the relationship of the protagonists which frustrates their own passions. They fail, as is expected, and they are returned to the point of departure, where marriage to each other is the only possible outcome of the drama. This union takes place, indeed, but it is achieved with a curious suggestion of self-knowledge which adds a dimension to the traditionally automatic creation of order. Forgetfulness of an earlier attachment is not simply seen as a matter of course, and the past has its role to play in the harmony of the final scenes. Thus, in Act V Scene 1, Filandre points out, as he accepts Cephise:

> *Il est vrai, cet objet du tourment que j'endure,*
> *Avec fort peu d'efforts r'ouvriroit ma blessure;*
> *Mais tes yeux, secourus de la force du temps,*
> *L'ôteront de mon coeur, et nous serons contens.* (pp. 595–6)

The tenses are particularly suggestive here. The conditional suggests the potential survival of an unfulfilled and unfulfillable love which has been more than just the pretext for dramatic conflict, but, on top of this, is superimposed the future tense, as inevitable as the happy ending of comedy. The characters here play the roles allotted to them, but they suggest at the same time that they know what they are doing. The mechanics of the *dénouement* are ultimately left intact, and yet they are examined with a certain suggestive irony.

5

. . . c'est assez pour moi que vous n'ignorez pas la différence qu'il faut mettre nécessairement entre le cothurne relevé de Sénèque et l'escarpin bas de Plaute ou de Térence.[73]

Pour la piece, je l'ai acommodée à la nature du Poëme Comique, qui rebute en tout des vers & des sujets graves, pource que les uns ni les autres ne sont point de sa jurisdiction, & qu'elle se treuveroit defectueuse de ce qui embellit la Tragedie.[74]

The years which saw the creation of Corneille's earliest plays were years of constant experiment. Dramatists may make a broad distinction between the genres of tragedy and comedy, highlighting essential differences in the status of the characters, the language they use and the actions they perform, and yet, such distinctions made, it is clear that no consistency is apparent in their attitude to the effects which they seek to produce. For inspiration they look to traditions as diverse as those of Classical comedy, pastoral, farce and tragi-comedy, and range in their plays from exciting dramas to light-hearted amusement, from suggestive interest in the human heart to delight in linguistic ingenuity, from the glorification of heroes to incisive social comment.

This diversity is reflected on a linguistic level in the usage of the word *comique*. At times, it is applied to plays which are comedies in the broadest sense, but which are amusing in neither intention nor effect. Mairet describes his *Silvanire* as '*disposée à la comique*' and du Rocher his *Mélize*,[75] a traditional pastoral, as a *pastorale comique*. Conversely, Turlupin and Gros-Guillaume class themselves as '*maistres ès Arts comiques et récréatifs*' in their *Approbation* of the *Chansons* of Gaultier-Garguille;[76] Discret refers to his farcical *Alizon* as a '*pièce Comique*' in the *Advertissement*, and Montluc's *Comédie de Proverbes* is similarly designated.

Furthermore, on a more general level, only arbitrary distinctions are made between the terms *comédie* and *tragi-comédie*; not in such designations is there to be found an indication of the nature or impact of the plays themselves. Tragi-comedies such as Scudéry's *Ligdamon et Lidias* or Rotrou's *Cléagenor et Doristée*[77] may suggest a profusion of *péripéties* particular to this genre, and yet other plays so categorised are peopled by characters not of noble stock, whose deeds are less exciting and whose presentation is more deliberately comic: Mareschal's *L'Inconstance d'Hylas*, Pichou's *Folies de Cardenio*, Rayssiguier's *Palinice, Circeine et Florice* or Beys' *Le Jaloux sans sujet*. Conversely, comedies such as Rotrou's *Clorinde* or *Filandre* may imply more discreet preoccupations of this genre, uncluttered by romanesque thrills and excitement, and yet the same dramatist's *La Belle Alphrède* or Scudéry's *Le Fils Supposé*, similarly designated *comédies*, exploit just those elements.

Significantly, this particular range in the non-tragic drama of the time is often seen also within the work of individual dramatists. Pichou moves from the excitement of his *Filis de Scire*[78] to the farcical *Folies de Cardenio*, du Ryer from the poetic flights of *Argenis et Poliarque* to the comic topicality of the *Vendanges de Suresne*, Mareschal from the thrills of *La Généreuse Allemande*[79] to the incisive comedy *Le Railleur*, Rayssiguier from an adaptation of *Aminta* to the suggestive *Palinice, Circeine et Florice*, Beys from the suspense of *Céline*[80] to the discreetly ironical *Jaloux sans sujet*; and, most notable of all, of course, Rotrou extends in his *oeuvre* from adaptations of Plautus to thrilling tragi-comedies, from the creation of farcical comic types to the more subtly evoked lover. Corneille's own comedies, far from being produced in a literary wilderness, are deeply rooted in these years of fertile dramatic activity, and reflect many of the preoccupations here analysed. It is through a comparison with this work of his contemporaries that the nature and value of his own particular achievement may be properly seen.

II

Mélite
A search for
the comic

1

On n'avoit jamais veu jusques-là que la Comedie fist rire sans Personnages ridicules comme les valets boufons, les Parasites, les Capitans, les Docteurs etc. . . .[1]

Corneille's first comedy,[2] which depicts the attempt of Eraste to undermine the love of Tirsis and Mélite by persuading the hero that his mistress has forsaken him in favour of Philandre, has many features common to plays written in the last years of the 1620s and before: villainy motivated by despised love,[3] the use of forged letters,[4] madness,[5] false news of death.[6] These elements are frequently pointed out by critics, but in their analyses they are particularly apt to take at face value the presentation of both plot and character; the comedy is conceived as thrilling, moving or disturbing, but not as comic. Doubrovsky sees in the work the presentation of a precarious balance between beauty and fidelity in love (p. 41), as does Starobinski;[7] Yarrow (p. 63) and Rousset (pp. 205–6) stress the underlying theme of inconstancy and change; Adam sees in the portrayal of character no essentially comic perspective, (I, 482); Francq can find very little which would make an audience laugh;[8] Couton uncovers a *'réalisme discret'*,[9] Nadal sees it characterised by *'l'amertume, la violence, le deuil'* (p. 80), and Stegman goes so far as to speak of *'le ton émouvant'* of the play (II, 578). It is only in the more recent work of Maurens[10] and Poole[11] that critics have begun to move away from fundamentally thematic readings, and to look more closely at the dramatist's particular presentation of traditional scenes and characters.

If one considers certain scenes in *Mélite*, it is indeed impossible to distinguish between Corneille's work and many a tragi-comedy. When Tirsis believes himself betrayed in Act III Scene 3, for example, and laments in suicidal despair the treachery of his beloved, he is not presented as a comic hero, foolishly deceived by appearances:

> *Aussi le falloit-il que ceste ame infidelle*
> *Changeant d'affection, prist un traistre comme elle,*
> *Et la jeune rusée a bien sceu rechercher*
> *Un qui n'eust sur ce point rien à luy reprocher,*
> *Cependant que leurré d'une fausse apparence*
> *Je repaissois de vent ma frivole esperance.* (951–6)

The audience may be detached from the lament, knowing that such despair is unfounded, but, for all that, the hero is not viewed with irony. Tirsis is accorded here that same measure of sympathy due to many abused heroes and heroines of the time who have been deceived by villains.[12] And yet Corneille wishes to distinguish his play from others of the time. *Mélite* is designated *pièce comique*, a term found nowhere else before that date, and certain devices, traditional in tragi-comedy, are used here for originally comic effects.

The use of false news is such an instance. The announcement of a protagonist's death is frequently used to elicit pity from the audience: in Tasso's *Aminta*, for example, reports of Silvia's and then Aminta's death suggest the tragic end to all hope of happiness; and in La Croix, *L'Inconstance punie*, Act V Scene 4, the thought of her lover's fate inspires a long lament in the heroine. When the suicide of Tirsis is announced in Act IV Scene 3, the audience is as deceived as the characters on stage, but Corneille's subsequent dramatic emphasis is quite particular. The news is not dwelt on for its own sake, expressed through the reactions of loved ones, but it is used rather to highlight the foolishness of the schemers who have brought it about. In Act IV Scene 5, the dramatist stresses not the despair of the heroine but the short-lived joy of Eraste, whose plot significantly backfires. He may delight at the apparent success of his ruse:

> *Allons donc sans scrupule, allons voir ceste belle,*
> *Faisons tous nos efforts, à nous r'approcher d'elle,*
> *Et taschons de r'entrer en son affection,*
> *Avant qu'elle ait rien sceu de nostre invention,* (1367–70)

but is confounded in the very next scene, when he learns that
Mélite is quite out of reach and has died herself at the news of
Tirsis' death; in his guilt and frustration, the villain loses his
wits. And in Act IV Scene 7, stress is placed on the fatuity of the
cowardly Philandre, who has been convinced by Eraste, that
Mélite does in fact love him. Unaware that Tirsis is thought
dead, he now summons up the courage to challenge this rival to
a duel:

> *Rival injurieux dont l'absence importune*
> *Retarde le succez de ma bonne fortune,*
> *Et qui sçachant combien m'importe ton retour*
> *De peur de m'obliger n'oserois voir le jour.* (1499–502)

Attention is fixed not on the pathetic plight of the hero, but on
the folly of the schemer, totally out of touch with events. His
attribution of cowardice to Tirsis shows how little he under-
stands heroic despair, and it is fitting indeed that this character's
most eloquent expression of valour should come at a time when
there is no danger to him at all.

The meeting of Philandre and Tirsis in Act III Scene 2 reveals
another transformation of a scene traditional in tragi-comedy. In
several plays prior to *Mélite*, the confrontation of rivals in love
leads to outbursts of violence and death. In Auvray's *Madonte*,[13]
Act II Scene 6, *Dorinde*,[14] Act V Scene 6, Mareschal's *La Généreuse
Allemande*, Act V Scene 3 duels actually take place on stage, and
in Scudéry's *Ligdamon et Lidias*, Act I Scene 3, Lidias' brief
challenge to his enemy underlines the audience's expectations
from such meetings: '*Il suffit, le discours sied mal dans les combats, /
C'est pourquoy pour mourir mettez le pourpoint bas*' (p. 22).

In *Mélite*, however, the presentation and intention of the
scene is quite different. In Tirsis, Corneille stresses the comic
irony of one who inadvertently reveals his love to an apparent
rival, thinking thereby to increase his joy. He sees himself as:
'*Tirsis dont le bon-heur au plus haut point monté, / Ne peut estre
parfaict sans te l'avoir conté*' (805–6), and then adds some lines
later: '*Mon bon heur est plus grand qu'on ne peut soupçonner, / C'est
quand tu l'auras sceu qu'il faudra t'estonner*' (817–18). As his
confidence increases, so too does the ironic force of his remarks.
Corneille creates a fine climax as Tirsis protests faith in the
heroine's love, quite unaware that in a previous scene Philandre
has resolved to abandon Cloris, his mistress and Tirsis' sister, in

favour of Mélite. The comparison Tirsis draws here is comically ambiguous: '*De sa possession je me tiens aussi seur / Que tu te peux tenir de celle de ma soeur*' (841-2).

Philandre, too, is deliberately presented in a comic light. In his claims to the affections of the heroine, he does not so much threaten the happiness of the protagonist as appear ridiculous in his own right. When he reads out the *fausses lettres*, sent apparently by Mélite but in fact by Eraste, he may partly fuel Tirsis' despair, but, more importantly, he is seen to reveal his own vanity and gullibility in the face of such ironical missives: '*Je commence à m'estimer quelque chose puis que je vous plais, et mon miroir m'offence tous les jours ne me representant pas assez belle comme je m'imagine qu'il faut estre pour meriter vostre affection*' (p. 66).

Such gullibility is complemented by the exposure of the character's cowardice. Again Corneille shows a fine sense of comic balance as Philandre moves from self-assurance in his victory over Tirsis with this tangible evidence: '*Te voylà tout resveur, cher amy, par ta foy / Crois-tu que celle-là s'adresse encor à toy?*' (893-4) to a frantic struggle to avoid a duel. When Thersandre meets his rival in *Madonte*, Act II Scene 6, he is eager to defend what he believes to be a token of the heroine's love:

> Cet anneau que je porte à ton désavantage
> Ne peut pas aysément souffrir qu'on le partage,
> Il faut que ma valeur le merite à son tour,
> Qu'il couronne ma force ainsi que mon Amour, (p. 54)

but not so Corneille's deceived character. Philandre finds himself in a heroic scene in which noble demands are made of him, and he is not equal to the task:

Philandre: Quant à moy, ton trespas me cousteroit trop cher,
Il me faudroit aprés par une prompte fuite
Esloigner trop long temps les beaux yeux de Melite.
Tirsis: Ce discours de bouffon ne me satisfaict pas,
Nous sommes seuls icy, despeschons, pourpoint bas.
Philandre: Vivons plustost amys, et parlons d'autre chose. (906-11)

Behind the casuistry of the character's excuse, Corneille reveals the presence of the coward. The retort of Tirsis does not simply suggest the speaker's own despair but underlines the ridiculousness of Philandre, and the threat which he makes finally forces his interlocutor to drop all pretence, and to speak in his true voice.

Comedy of a similar kind is found in the meeting of Cloris and Mélite in Act IV Scene 2. The encounter may be announced in terms of bitterness and scorn in Act III Scene 5, when the angry Cloris threatens to present the heroine with the letters she has seemingly written to Philandre, not realising that Mélite is quite ignorant of this deception:

> *Je la feray rougir, cette jeune esventée,*
> *Lors que son escriture à ses yeux presentée*
> *Mettant au jour un crime estimé si secret,*
> *Elle recognoistra qu'elle ayme un indiscret,* (1099–102)

but in the confrontation itself, Corneille exploits the potential for comic misunderstanding and confusion. Instead of angry remonstration and protest, the scene begins with carefully worded irony from Cloris, announcing her good intent with a malicious smile:

> *Je cheris tellement celles de vostre sorte,*
> *Et prends tant d'interest en ce qui leur importe,*
> *Qu'aux fourbes qu'on leur faict je ne puis consentir,*
> *Ny mesme en rien sçavoir sans les en advertir.* (1267–70)

Corneille skilfully and deliberately prolongs the misunderstanding, as each character is seen to talk at cross-purposes. A comic movement is traced from confident assertions on both sides, as each puts forward her case:

> Mélite: *Je renonce à choisir une seconde fois,*
> *Et mon affection ne s'est point arrestée,*
> *Que chez un cavalier qui l'a trop meritée.*
> Cloris: *Vous me pardonnerez, j'en ay de bons tesmoins,*
> *C'est l'homme qui de tous la merite le moins,* (1278–82)

to ever-increasing frustration and bewilderment. For Mélite, Cloris' criticism of her lover suggests a curious lack of respect for Tirsis, while for Cloris, Mélite's continued defence of her choice implies a quite shameless unconcern about her theft of Philandre's affections. Mélite's disbelief is beautifully suggested, as she thinks herself mistaken firstly about the identity of Cloris and then about the seriousness of her accusations: '. . . *Doncques pour me railler, / La soeur de mon amant contrefait ma rivale?*' (1306–7), and this is complemented by Cloris' own incredulity, convinced that Mélite's is simply a performance of polished deception: '*Doncques pour m'esbloüir, une ame desloyale / Contrefait la fidelle?*' (1308–9). This

counterpointing of accusation and suspicion is then so stylised as
to reach another comic crescendo as each heroine is led to accuse
the other of treachery and ill-intent which is known to be absurd:

Cloris: *Vous voulez m'affiner, mais c'est peine perduë,*
          Melite, que vous sert de faire l'entenduë?
          La chose estant si claire, à quoy bon la nier?
Mélite: *Ne vous obstinez point à me calomnier,*
          Je veux que si jamais j'ay dit mot à Philandre . . .(1327–31)

Suffering or anger have no dramatic force here; emphasis is placed
wholly on the characters' incredulity and ignorance of the truth.

Most significant of the themes taken over by Corneille in *Mélite*,
however, is that of madness. The madman is a familiar, but
complex figure in plays of this time, and is used by dramatists for
several different effects. On one level, he may be presented as
pitiful, folly being seen as a striking reflection of mental suffering.
In Racan's *Bergeries*, Act III Scene 4, for example, Arthenice is
moved to sympathy at the sight of the crazed Alcidor: '*Quelque mal
que je veuille à sa déloyauté, / J'ai pitié de le voir en cette extrémité*' (1577–
8), and in the same way Corneille's Eraste invites such a response
as he evokes in his madness the torment endured by the thought of
his misdeeds:

          Tout ce qu'il a de fers, de feux, de fouets, de chaisnes
          Ne sont auprés de toy que de legeres peines,
          On reçoit d'Alecton un plus doux traitement,
          De grace, un peu de trefve, un moment, un moment. (1663–6)

However, a madman's ragings may also be developed not in
order to suggest the pitiful plight of the speaker, but rather as
imaginative passages enjoyable for their own sake. Apocalyptic
visions are characteristic of the mad heroes in both Pichou's *Folies
de Cardenio* and Rotrou's *L'Hypocondriaque*, and again Corneille
takes this traditional opportunity to entertain his audience as
Eraste evokes a descent into the Underworld, searching for the
shades of the ones he has offended:

          Vous donc esprits legers, qui faute de tombeaux
          Tournoyez vagabonds à l'entour de ces eaux,
          A qui Caron cent ans refuse sa nacelle,
          Ne m'en pourriez-vous point donner quelque nouvelle? (1477–80)

Scenes such as Act IV Scene 9, following the madman's encounter
with Philandre, or Act V Scene 2, prior to the arrival of the nurse,

are conceived as shameless interludes of linguistic colour. In his *Examen* of the play, Corneille may be embarrassed by the incidents, but he stresses their popularity at the time: '*La folie d'Eraste n'est pas de meilleure trempe. Je la condamnois deslors en mon ame; mais comme c'estoit un ornement de Theatre qui ne manquoit jamais de plaire, et se faisoit souvent admirer, j'affectay volontiers ces grands égaremens . . .*' (p. 137). Implied here is an exhibition of the poet's skill and the actor's virtuosity; language is taken on its own terms, with little regard for the speaker or the context. Isnard's remarks on Pichou's *Folies de Cardenio*, which he published in a preface to the same writer's adaptation of *Filis de Scire* emphasise this particular dramatic function: '*Certes, j'advouë franchement d'avoir esté ravy plusieurs fois de ces admirables façons de parler, qu'on y rencontre presque par tout, & de m'estre laissé tout à fait transporter à ces divines conceptions qu'il fait naistre par l'esprit d'un insensé, & qui font paraistre ses folies mille fois plus belles que toutes les moderations de la sagesse.*'

But the madman in general and Eraste in particular has another important purpose. Critical opinion is divided between those who insist on the 'tragic' effect and intention of these scenes,[15] and those who interpret them as purely comic.[16] Such a division of reactions is not surprising, the less so as it reflects the curiously ambiguous reaction of contemporary audiences which mingled compassion with amusement. Silandre's remark on the madness of Liridas in *Climène* of La Croix,[17] Act II Scene 1, occasioned by the speaker's successful wooing of a girl loved by them both, stands for many such in literature of this time:

> *Mais grace à mon bon heur, une melancholie*
> *A tellement changé son amour en folie,*
> *Que ses sens esgarez, son foible esprit démis*
> *Fait rire en mesme temps & pleurer ses amis.* (p. 19)[18]

Furthermore, Corneille's immediate predecessors are quite alive to the potential for comedy, not to say farce, in the depiction of a character largely out of control of his faculties. In La Croix, *Climène*, Act V Scene 1, and Pichou, *Les Folies de Cardenio*, Act IV Scene 2, the dramatists write interludes of farcical brutality as their crazed heroes mistake innocent bystanders for their enemies and attack them. Corneille follows also in this tradition. In Eraste's folly, he may create *beaux effets*, but he intends equally to make his audience laugh. In Act IV Scene 6, the hero mistakes his servant Cliton for Charon, and urges him to ferry him across the Styx, resorting finally to a leap on to his shoulders: '*Il se jette sur les espaules de Cliton, qui l'emporte du Theatre*'; these elements are taken up later in Act V Scene I as the servant complains to the *nourrice* of the beatings he has endured:

> Eust-il peu, sans en perdre entierement l'usage,
> Se figurer Caron des traits de mon visage,
> Et de plus me prenant pour ce vieux Nautonnier
> Me payer à bons coups des droits de son denier? (1599–602)

More significant, though, is Eraste's meeting with the *nourrice* in Act V Scene 2, and his mistaking her for the heroine he seeks. Again such confusions are not uncommon in scenes of madness before *Mélite*, and are often exploited for their largely grotesque humour, as the madman sees beauty in the most unlikely subjects. In the anonymous *Folie de Silène*,[19] Act III Scene 4, the mad Silène is seen to force his attentions on a *vieillard amoureux*, his master, and in Pichou's *Folies de Cardenio*, Act IV Scene 2, Cardenio, mistaking the *barbier* for Luscinde his beloved, gives expression to his passion, much to the discomfiture of his interlocutor:

> Agreables transports, amoureuses delices,
> Que vous avez bien tost allegé mes supplices,
> Vous me ravissez l'ame au moindre souvenir
> Du supreme bonheur qui me doit avenir. (p. 80)

It is significant, though, that Corneille avoids the potential for crude innuendo in such an encounter, and creates comic effects in a more sophisticated way. Irony is apparent at the start of Eraste's address to the nurse, as the deranged character speaks the traditional lines of a repentant hero in a context which is singularly inappropriate:

> Je voy desja Melite, ah! belle ombre voicy
> L'ennemy de vostre heur qui vous cherchoit icy,
> C'est Eraste, c'est luy, qui n'a plus d'autre envie
> Que d'espandre à vos pieds son sang avec sa vie. (1673–6)

The contrast is traditional, but Corneille goes further in his treatment of it, concentrating on the hero's gradual return to his senses. The juxtaposition of sublime and banal is beautifully suggested through the evocation of the lady's eyes, in poetic terms so radiant, in reality so dull. As Eraste apostrophises his beloved, he is led to recognise that his effusions are quite out of place:

Eraste: *Ce n'est que de vos yeux que part ceste lumiere.*
Nourrice: *Ce n'est que de mes yeux! désillez la paupiere,*
            Et d'un sens plus rassis jugez de leur esclat.
Eraste: *Ils ont de verité je ne sçay quoy de plat.* (1683–6)

The formula '*je ne sçay quoy*', traditionally associated with the indefinable beauty of the lady is now used to describe the nurse's own particular ugliness; this last vestige of the poetic vision in the hero's newly found sanity suggests, in the language itself, the transition from illusion to truth on which the comedy is based.

The hallucinations of the deranged hero are now held side by side with banal reality. The imagined victory over the inhabitants of Hell is reduced to the flight of servants from an unpredictable lunatic:

Eraste: *Je ne m'abuse point, j'ay veu sans fiction*
            Ces monstres terrassez se sauver à la fuite,
            Et Pluton de frayeur en quitter la conduite.
Nourrice: *Peut-estre que chacun s'enfuyoit devant vous*
            Craignant vostre fureur et le poids de vos coups. (1706–10)

The mask of the madman is slowly peeled off. As reality asserts itself once more, the mythological quest conducted by Eraste is revealed for what it is: an illusion, a role.

That Corneille derives both excitement and comedy from his madman is not in itself original; this diversity of function is found already in plays before *Mélite*. Striking, however, is his careful juxtaposition of the two effects in this scene with the *nourrice*. It suggests, on one level, a more subtle interest in the comic potential of the type, going beyond mere farcical violence or crudity. But it is significant, too, in the wider context of the play itself. The performance of an inappropriate role which is highlighted here in Eraste's folly is not simply a comic interlude in *Mélite*, but lies at the very heart of it.

2

Mais prens garde sur tout a bien joüer ton roolle.[20]

Corneille's sensitivity to the comic potential of his plot is immediately apparent in his presentation of Philandre, easily

persuaded by Eraste that Mélite has fallen in love with him. It is
not unknown in plays before *Mélite* for a character to be falsely
persuaded of a lady's love, and it is a theme which does not
necessarily give rise to comedy. In Auvray's *Madonte*, Thersandre
is similarly deceived by a villain that Madonte loves him, and for
him this news represents the success of a long and faithful
devotion. His reaction of Act II Scene 4 is one of noble delight:

> *Enfin l'Amour fléchi par ma perseverance*
> *Me permet de le suivre avec de l'esperance;*
> *J'ayme & je suis aymé d'un soleil que les Dieux,*
> *S'ils afectoient le change auroient mis dans les Cieux.* (p. 40)

Corneille's use of such a character is, however, quite different.
Whereas Auvray stresses his hero's dignity, Corneille places the
emphasis on his gullibility. In Act II Scene 7, Eraste is seen to
delight in the manipulation of his victim at his weakest point, his
vanity:

> *C'est donc la verité que la belle Melite*
> *Fait du brave Philandre une loüable elite,*
> *Et qu'il obtient ainsi de sa seule vertu*
> *Ce qu'Eraste, et Tirsis ont en vain debatu?*
> *Vrayment dans un tel choix mon regret diminue,* (643–7)

and, as the scene develops, attention is fixed on the gradual
success of the ruse and the reduction of Philandre's heroic
stature. He is betrothed to Cloris, Tirsis' sister, but as his vanity
gets the better of him, his rejection of Mélite's 'suit' in the name of
this love progressively loses all conviction. He moves from
protests of Cloris' superior virtue: *'Un peu plus de respect pour ce que
je cheris'* (662), to concern about the promise he has given her: *'J'ay
promis d'aymer l'une, et c'est où je m'arreste'* (667), and finally to fear
for his loss of reputation: *'J'en serois mal voulu des hommes et des
Dieux'* (669).

Philandre is certainly not the first treacherous lover in plays of
this period. In Pichou's *Folies de Cardenio*, Fernant abandons his
betrothed Dorotée in order to pursue Luscinde, and in the same
dramatist's *L'Infidèle Confidente*,[21] Act II Scene 3, Lisanor is quite
open about the perfidy he proposes:

> *Que je trouve de peine à résoudre mon âme*
> *Aux foibles sentimens de ma première flame,*
> *Que le changement plaist, & que la nouveauté,*
> *Est puissante à l'esclat d'une aimable beauté.* (pp. 34–5)

Corneille, however, makes of Philandre a more obviously comic creation who, like a gullible *fanfaron*, happily and ridiculously plays the part of heroic lover, only too willing to believe that women are apt to fall at his feet. His speech of joy in Act III Scene 1 is laden with irony, as Corneille underlines the frailty of the evidence which elicits such vain protestations from the fool:

> *Tu l'as gaigné Melite, il ne m'est plus possible*
> *D'estre à tant de faveurs desormais insensible,*
> *Tes lettres où sans fard tu dépeins ton esprit,*
> *Tes lettres où ton coeur est si bien par escrit*
> *Ont charmé tous mes sens de leurs douces promesses,*
> *Leur attente vaut mieux, Cloris, que tes caresses.* (775–80)

In his *Examen*, Corneille points out the *invraisemblance* of Philandre's general reaction to Eraste's deception, seeing this as a fault in the play: '*Avec tout cela, j'advoüe que l'Auditeur fut bien facile à donner son approbation à une Piece, dont le noeud n'avoit aucune justesse. . . . Ce Philandre est bien credule de se persuader d'estre aimé d'une personne qu'il n'a jamais entretenuë*' (p. 136), yet it is this very improbability which, in the original text, Corneille exploits. Philandre's gullibility is not a dramatic weakness, it is a comic strength.[22]

It is this focus on the performance of an inappropriate role which also characterises Corneille's comic transformation of a scene frequently found in pastoral, the argument of two characters about the nature and value of love.[23] Such scenes traditionally serve the purpose of highlighting the ideal quality of a hero, prepared to suffer in the name of a love whose properties are unknown to or rejected by a more cynical interlocutor. In Act I Scene 1, Eraste clearly models himself on such perfect lovers as he defends his noble intentions in wanting to marry Mélite against the worldly objections of Tirsis, who at this early stage of the play, professes himself uninterested in such ideals. For Eraste, Mélite's lowly position is of no importance:

> *. . . Trêve de ces raisons,*
> *Mon amour s'en offence, et tiendroit pour supplice*
> *D'avoir à prendre advis d'une sale avarice,*
> *Je ne sçache point d'or capable de mes voeux*
> *Que celuy dont Nature a paré ses cheveux.* (52–6)

Just as Thélame, the prince, is prepared to defend his love of a shepherdess in Mairet's *Sylvie*, so this suitor casts aside all other values in favour of his passion.

In scenes such as this, comedy is traditionally provided by the *esprit fort*, happily unheroic in his outlook. In *L'Astrée*, Book I Chapter 8, the first debate of Silvandre and Hylas culminates in the categorical victory of the ideal; the perfect lover easily outargues his ridiculous opponent, whose function is simply to amuse: '"... *on peut bien aimer comme moy, et mal aimer comme vous; et ainsi on me pourra nommer maistre, et vous brouillon d'amour."* A ces derniers mots, il n'y eut celuy qui peust s'empescher de rire' (p. 291). Tirsis is one of many such cynics of the time, for whom the language of love is just a game:

> *Tous ces discours de livre alors sont de saison,*
> *Il faut feindre du mal, demander guerison,*
> *Donner sur le Phoebus, promettre des miracles,*
> *Jurer qu'on brisera toutes sortes d'obstacles,*
> *Mais du vent et cela doivent estre tout un.* (63–7)

The parody of traditional formulae in such lines echoes the language of Auvray's lover in '*Les Rodomonts sous les Courtines*':

> *Dissimuler nos feux, forger mille artifices,*
> *Cacher aux plus rusez les desirs de nos coeurs,*
> *Adorer deux beaux yeux, leur offrir nos services,*
> *Les nommer nos Soleils, nos Roys & nos Vainqueurs ...* [24]

To this, Corneille adds a comic attachment to money which leads his anti-heroic lover to the most farcical of statements, as he looks forward with pleasure to what is the very antithesis of all pastoral endeavour: marriage with an ugly wife:

> *La beauté, les attraits, le port, la bonne mine,*
> *Eschauffent bien les draps, mais non pas la cuisine,*
> *Et l'Hymen qui succede à ces folles amours*
> *Pour quelques bonnes nuits, a bien de mauvais jours. ...*
> *C'est assez qu'une femme ayt un peu d'entregent,*
> *La laideur est trop belle estant teinte en argent.* (117–20; 123–4)

However, Corneille gives to Tirsis a further and more significant function in this scene. His remarks are not only comic in their own right, but also manifestly inconvenience Eraste, who unlike d'Urfé's Silvandre, constantly struggles to defend himself. The *esprit fort* does not simply debate the value of love like Hylas, but also, and more importantly, he casts doubt on Eraste's commitment to what he says, suggesting, indeed, that the hero is just playing a part:

> *Que je te trouve, amy, d'une humeur admirable,*
> *Pour paroistre eloquent tu te feins miserable,*
> *Est-ce à dessein de voir avec quelles couleurs*
> *Je sçaurois adoucir les traits de tes malheurs?* (21–4)

From the opening lines of the play there are hints that Eraste is slightly distant from his role of heroic lover, surprised himself at the form it takes: *'Parmy tant de rigueurs n'est-ce pas chose estrange /* *Que rien n'est assez fort pour me resoudre au change?'* (1–2), and this soon shades into foolishness and incompetence. In Mareschal's *La Généreuse Allemande*, Act I Scene 2, Aristandre had proposed to introduce Adraste to the beauty he loves, seeing this as an appropriate punishment for his profane interlocutor:

> *Lors que tu la verras, cette Ame de ma vie,*
> *Qui tient dessous sa loy ma raison asservie . . .*
> *Ses regards te feront hayr la liberté,*
> *Adorer mon supplice & ma captivité.* (pp. 14–15)

Eraste makes the same proposal, but far from suggesting confidence, it reveals this character's desperate attempt to win the argument, resorting to a ploy whose potential folly his own words unwittingly imply:

> *Allons, et tu verras dans ses aymables traits*
> *Tant de charmans appas, tant de divins attraits,*
> *Que tu seras contraint d'advoüer à ta honte,*
> *Que si je suis un fou je le suis à bon conte.* (131–4)

When Mélite finally appears in the next scene, he has lost all self-assurance, forced now to admit his failure as the noble spokesman of ideal love:

> *Je me suis donc picqué contre sa mesdisance*
> *Avec tant de malheur, ou tant d'insuffisance,*
> *Que les droits de l'amour bien que pleins d'equité*
> *N'ont peu se garantir de sa subtilité.* (145–8)

Significantly, however, Corneille suggests in these opening scenes not only the comic discountenancing of an apparently ideal lover, but also of the *esprit fort*. Such a movement had already been traced by Mareschal in his *Généreuse Allemande*, but a comparison here reveals again Corneille's more obviously comic intentions. When introduced to the fair Camille in Act II Scene 3, the cynical Adraste immediately falls in love. His reaction is one of noble renunciation:

> *Je sçay que mes efforts yroient contre le vent,*
> *Si j'osois indiscret vous aymer d'autre sorte*
> *Que sous cette amitié qu'Aristandre me porte;*
> *Je sçay bien que luy seul possede vostre coeur,*
> *Qu'il merite luy seul d'en estre le vainqueur. . . .* (p. 33)

Corneille, though, does not suggest the dignity of his character, but rather his attempts to disguise a sudden and evident lack of self-control. From early protestations of confidence in the opening scene: '*Allons, et tu verras que toute sa beauté / Ne me sçaura tourner contre la verité*' (135–6), Tirsis is led to make remarks of ever increasing ambiguity when in the presence of the heroine. His early admission of her beauty: '*Sur peine d'estre ingrate il faut de vostre part / Recognoistre les dons que le Ciel vous depart*' (187–8), leads finally to a covert declaration of love: '*Et prenant desormais des sentimens plus doux / Ne soyez plus de glace à qui brusle pour vous*' (195–6). For the audience, and for Mélite, this sudden reversal is both obvious and comic: Tirsis' claims to self-control have been found to be quite vain: '*Pour voir si peu de chose aussi tost vous desdire / Me donne à vos despens de beaux sujets de rire*' (205–6).

This particular presentation of both characters is sustained in Act I Scene 3, in which Eraste's jealousy becomes apparent. Again, this is a meeting of rivals which could give rise to tense and exciting drama. In a similar situation in Hardy's *Gésippe*,[25] the hero's distress is the centre of dramatic attention. In Act I Scene 5, Gésippe is seen to curtail his friend's praise of the heroine, open about the suffering it causes him: '*Abrégeons des discours si pleins de courtoisie, / Qu'ils ont desja chez moy logé la jalousie*' (261–2). Corneille, however, suggests a more obviously comic angle of vision. Eraste's ridiculousness is evident from the beginning of the scene, as his expression of self-satisfaction underlines simultaneously his own stupidity: '*Maintenant suis-je un foû? meritay-je du blasme? / Que dis-tu de l'object, que dis-tu de ma flame?*' (213–14), and the character's feelings of insecurity are comically suggested through language which, superficially, expresses confidence in his rival. There are no hints of suffering here: the audience is detached from the action, its attention fixed on Eraste's struggle to remain calm:

> *Confesse franchement qu'elle a sceu te ravir,*
> *Mais que tu ne veux pas prendre pour ceste belle*
> *Avec le nom d'amant le tiltre d'infidelle.*
> *Rien que nostre amitié ne t'en peut destourner.* (220–3)

And, what is true of Eraste is true also of Tirsis, beneath whose
protestations of detachment Corneille makes quite clear the
expression of love. Eraste's attempt to keep in control of his
language is complemented by that of Tirsis, who is more and
more uncomfortable as the *esprit fort*:

> *Que veux-tu que j'en die? elle a je ne sçay quoy*
> *Qui ne peut consentir que l'on demeure à soy:*
> *Mon coeur jusqu'à present à l'amour invincible*
> *Ne se maintient qu' à force aux termes d'insensible,*
> *Tout autre que Tircis mourroit pour la servir.* (215–19)

As Tirsis proposes to write a sonnet in her honour, he is seen to
struggle vainly to conceal the fact that language which he has
formerly used with such happy unconcern has now taken on a
new meaning for him:

> *J'ayme bien ces discours de plaintes, et d'allarmes,*
> *De souspirs, de sanglots, de tourmens et de larmes,*
> *C'est de quoy fort souvent je basty ma chanson,*
> *Mais j'en cognoy, sans plus, la cadence et le son.* (233–6)

Throughout this play, Corneille transforms traditional scenes,
deriving comic effects from the presentation of characters known
and seen to be playing roles. In Act II Scene 5, Cloris questions
her brother about his love. Such meetings of brother and sister
are frequent in pastoral, presenting the hero with an opportunity
to confide the secret of his heart. In Mairet's *Sylvie*, Act I Scene 4,
Thélame answers the enquiries of Méliphile with a spontaneous
openness: 'Comme on permet le mal qu'on ne peut empêcher, / Il faut
bien découvrir ce qu'on ne peut cacher' (275–6).[26] Corneille, however,
presents his hero in a more obviously comic light. Instead of
being frank, Tirsis tries to persuade his sister that he still spurns
love, and that the passionate sonnet he has written is on behalf of
another. The awkwardness of his argument is at the centre of
attention, as he mentions this third party four times in the space
of a short speech, convincing neither himself nor Cloris:

> *En faveur d'un amy je flatte sa maistresse,*
> *Voy si tu le cognois, et si parlant pour luy*
> *J'ay sceu m'accommoder aux passions d'autruy.* (510–12)

And as he reads out the verses, he vainly tries to persuade his
sister that he is only playing a part, and that his heart has no place
in what he expresses:

> *Tu sçais mieux qui je suis, et que ma libre humeur*
> *N'a de part en mes vers que celle de rimeur.* (533–4)

Such a presentation of the hero is quite particular to Corneille at this time. In Claveret's *L'Esprit fort*, a comedy which appeared shortly after *Mélite*, Criton, the cynic, is quite open about his defeat in Act IV Scene 5, as he falls in love with the heroine:

> *Qu'oubliant à regret la loy des forts esprits*
> *Ce retour soit tesmoin qu'une fille m'a pris,*
> *Qu'un petit Dieu vainqueur pour la seconde grace*
> *Anime un feu secret dans mon ame de glace.* (p. 92)

Corneille, however, shows himself sensitive to the comic potential in a character who continues to play a part, even when he has lost all conviction in it.

It is this particular perspective which the dramatist seeks even at moments potentially rich in suspense. In Act II Scene 3, for instance, Eraste threatens the happiness of Tirsis, contemplating a duel with his rival:

> *Il suffit, les destins bandez à me desplaire*
> *Ne l'arracheroient pas à ma juste cholere.*
> *Tu demordras parjure, et ta desloyauté*
> *Maudira mille fois sa fatale beauté.* (477–80)

On a first level, the language is quite traditional, and in its formulation it echoes the anger of Poliarque in du Ryer's *Argenis et Poliarque*, Act II Scene 2, a hero equally resolved to free his mistress from the attentions of a rival suitor:

> *À quoy tient maintenant que ma force assouvie*
> *N'arrache à Licogène, & l'amour, & la vie,*
> *Et qu'un coup genereux n'immole à mes fureurs*
> *Cet infame subjet de toutes mes erreurs?* (p. 24)

However, whereas Poliarque's language of bravery corresponds to the courageous nature of the speaker, Eraste's does not; whereas Poliarque is a hero, Eraste only plays the part. Beneath the familiar dramatic stance, Corneille makes clear to the audience the presence of a *fanfaron*, for whom such mighty protestations are simply a mask. At the end of the speech, this pose is abandoned as the character uses familiar logic to justify his own lack of courage; it is not the dramatic role itself which the audience is invited to enjoy, but the character's comic performance of it:

> *Quel transport déreglé! quelle estrange eschappée!*
> *Avec un affronteur mesurer mon espée!*
> *C'est bien contre un brigand qu'il me faut hasarder,*
> *Contre un traistre qu'à peine on devroit regarder,*
> *Luy faisant trop d'honneur moy-mesme je m'abuse,*
> *C'est contre luy qu'il faut n'employer que la ruse.* (485–90)

This process is significant. Corneille may not avoid the use of traditional heroic language in this play, and yet he constantly seeks to make his audience aware of the speaker as well as the role he plays. In this way he tries to reduce the conventional tension and excitement of much comedy, and to suggest a particular comic perspective.

3

Mais deslors je ne m'assujettissois pas tout à fait à cette mode, et me contentay de faire voir l'assiette de son esprit, sans prendre soin de le pourvoir d'une autre femme.[27]

In some respects, the *dénouement* of *Mélite* is quite traditional. The lovers are miraculously resurrected from the dead, and rejoice now in their hard-earned happiness. Tirsis' speech of joy in Act V Scene 4 is undistorted and immediate in its impact:

> *Maintenant que le sort attendry par nos plaintes*
> *Comble nostre esperance, et dissipe nos craintes,*
> *Que nos contentemens ne sont plus traversez*
> *Que par le souvenir de nos travaux passez,*
> *Chassons le, ma chere ame, à force de carresses . . .* (1787–91)

and echoes the equally spontaneous joy of Aglante in *Silvanire*, Act V Scene 8, after a more obviously thrilling adventure.

> *Maintenant que le Ciel de nos larmes touché*
> *Nous a rendu le bien qu'il nous avait caché,*
> *Vous plaît-il pas, Ménandre, et vous sage Lérice,*
> *Que sans plus différer nostre hymen s'accomplisse?* (2279–82)

At the same time, however, Corneille changes the impact of other conventional features. Like *Silvanire*,[28] for instance, *Mélite* may forgive the villain whose ill-conceived ruse has brought happiness for the protagonists:

> *Vostre fourbe inventée à dessein de nous nuire*
> *Avance nos amours au lieu de les destruire,*
> *De son fascheux succez dont nous devions perir*

> *Le sort tire un remede afin de nous guerir.*
> *Donc pour nous revancher de la faveur receüe,*
> *Nous en aymons l'autheur à cause de l'issue . . .* (1927–32)

but this formulation is seen in a cynical light by the *nourrice*; behind a traditional stance is suggested indifference and selfishness:

> *Ils ont tous deux leur conte, et sur ceste asseurance*
> *Ils tiennent le passé dedans l'indifference,*
> *N'osant se hazarder à des ressentimens*
> *Qui donneroient du trouble à leurs contentemens.* (1947–50)

This detachment is quite striking in Corneille's treatment of Philandre, Cloris and Eraste. In Act V Scene 3, Philandre returns to Cloris, full of repentance after his ridiculous infidelity, asking for the forgiveness which he might reasonably expect:

> *Ah, ne remettez plus dedans vostre memoire*
> *L'indigne souvenir d'une action si noire,*
> *Et pour rendre à jamais nos premiers voeux contens*
> *Estouffés l'ennemy du pardon que j'attends.* (1743–6)

Such a situation is indeed not uncommon in plays of the time. In Pichou's *Folies de Cardenio*, Act V Scene 4, the wronged Doristée takes back the faithless Fernant: '*Laissons le souvenir des outrages passez, / Je trouve que mes maux sont bien recompensez . . .*' (p. 117), and in Rotrou's *L'Hypocondriaque*, Act V Scene 5, conversely, the deserted Aliaste is happy to recover Cleonice who had pursued another hero throughout the drama. This is a convention of *comédie* expressed by Cloris herself, whose opening lines in the play offer pardon to a lover who fears that he has offended her: '*Ne m'espouvente-point, à ta mine je pense / Que le pardon suivra de fort prés ceste offence*' (253–4). Tradition suggests the inevitability of this re-alliance, and yet, having built up the expectations of the audience, Corneille deliberately disappoints them: Cloris is quite intractable in her refusal:

> *Tes protestations ne font que m'offencer,*
> *Sçavante à mes despens de leur peu de durée*
> *Je ne veux point en gage une foy parjurée,*
> *Je ne veux point d'un coeur, qu'un billet aposté*
> *Peut resoudre aussi tost à la desloyauté.* (1738–42)

The particular nature of this reaction is seen in Act V Scene 5, when she joins Mélite and Tirsis, and tells them of Philandre's repentance. The heroine tries to bring Cloris round to harmony, urging her to forgive, but this traditional role is rejected categorically:

Mélite: *Ma soeur, ce fut pour moy qu'il oza s'en desdire.*
Cloris: *Et pour l'amour de vous je n'en feray que rire.*
Mélite: *Et pour l'amour de moy vous luy pardonnerez.*
Cloris: *Et pour l'amour de moy vous m'en dispenserez.* (1883–6)

The dismissal of Philandre may suggest the dramatist's glee at the downfall of the gullible,[29] but it reflects also a more sensitive interest in Cloris herself and her inability to forget deception so easily. By the end of the play, this heroine is proposed as a partner for Eraste, a pairing which Corneille was later to regard as quite *invraisemblable*,[30] but which, in the comedy itself, has its own suggestive force. Tirsis may express here the conventional attitude, having no doubt that this match is a happy one and willingly giving his consent:

> *Bien que dedans tes yeux tes sentimens se lisent*
> *Tu veux qu'auparavant les miens les autorisent,*
> *Excusable pudeur, soit donc, je le consens*
> *Trop seur que mon advis s'accommode à ton sens . . .* (1971–4)

but in Cloris' own response, Corneille leaves room to imply a more ambiguous uncertainty, as she hesitates to love again simply on demand: '*Aymez moy seulement, et pour la récompense / On me donnera bien le loisir que j'y pense*' (1983–4).

The dramatist's reluctance to fulfil conventional patterns is ultimately expressed in the heavy irony which concludes the play. It is suggested that the nurse offer herself to the abandoned Philandre: '*Entrons-donc et tandis que nous irons le prendre / Nourrice, va t'offrir pour maistresse à Philandre*' (2007–8). Such a matching of comically incongruous characters was not without precedent in comedy; in Gaillard's *La Carline*, for instance, Turquin, an amorous satyr is paired off with Francine, an old servant. The *nourrice*, however, refuses, and images of prosperity and fertility, traditional at the end of comedy,[31] are replaced here with an evocation of frustration and barrenness: '*Allez, je vay vous faire à ce soir telle niche / Qu'au lieu de labourer, vous lairrez tout en friche*' (2019–20). The tone of the *nourrice* is certainly original, as she suggests that the happiness of the protagonists may only be illusory. For some critics, these lines suggest a serious threat to the lovers, a perplexing shadow across the light-heartedness of comedy;[32] another critic, however, sees here the authentication of Love's victory, thrown into relief by the nurse's bitter acknowledgement of defeat.[33] This character, though, should not be seen in isolation. Set in the wider context of the *dénouement*, she is seen to reflect that distance from tradition which Corneille achieves in these final scenes. What she implies about the hero and heroine with her crude and cynical wit, the dramatist himself has implied about the secondary characters, suggesting, without going any further, the arbitrary and unconvincing way in which order is conventionally created. The conclusion of the action is seen from a distance, the joy of hero and heroine muted, and the formal patterns of comedy, through Corneille's refusal to fulfil them totally, thrown into relief.

4

En tout cas, elle est mon coup d'essay . . .[34]

As a *coup d'essai*, *Mélite* is fascinating. It is clear that parts of the play fall very much into the broad tradition of tragi-comedy written at the time. Moments in Eraste's madness or Tirsis' laments, particularly, suggest that delight in language for its own sake which is such an integral part of the poetic entertainment provided by some *comédie*. Equally clear, however, are the attempts to create comic effects largely free of farce or verbal crudity. *Mélite* is not the first play to seek comedy outside the stereotyped characters of a classical tradition: Schelandre in *Tyr et Sidon*, Pichou in *Les Folies de Cardenio*, Auvray in *Dorinde*, Rotrou in both *L'Hypocondriaque* and *La Bague de l'oubly* do this already in their use of the madman and the *inconstant*. However, whereas in these plays, such comedy remains an interlude, albeit extended over several scenes in certain cases, in an essentially thrilling plot, Corneille seeks more obviously to avoid dramatic suspense and to sustain a comic focus throughout, often transforming traditional scenes in a strikingly original way. The meeting of rivals is no longer exciting, but amusing, and characters in their various forms of madness are seen trying to convince in parts which are not theirs to play: the coward sees himself as the hero, the lover pretends to be the *esprit fort*, and the rejected suitor longs to be the *pastor fido*. Notable, too, though, is the *dénouement* of the play. In the detachment which Corneille suggests here from tradition, he is the first dramatist to give expression to a theme which will become more and more frequent in the 1630s: the illogicality of a convention which so effortlessly creates harmony between characters at the end of comedy. In *Mélite*, Corneille's unease is first articulated; its implications will be more rigorously examined by him in the comedies which follow.

III

La Veuve
The actor
and his role

1

Si tu n'es homme à te contenter de la naïfveté du stile, et de la subtilité de l'intrique, je ne t'invite point à la lecture de cette piece, son ornement n'est pas dans l'esclat des vers.[1]

The warning issued by Corneille in his *Avis* to the reader of *La Veuve* is a significant one. What he had implied in his designation of *Mélite* as a *pièce comique*, is now explicitly stated as he distinguishes his new comedy from the form of romanesque tragi-comedy, full of involved *péripéties* and colourful language, such as he had himself written in *Clitandre*, the previous year. The originality of this stance, though, should be carefully examined. In his claims to simplify both plot and language, he was not being essentially innovatory. In the preface to *Silvanire*, Mairet criticises as *'invraisemblables'* those plays which offer a profusion of events, and defends on these grounds a limited duration for the play's action: *'il me semble que les Anciens ont eu juste raison de restreindre leurs sujets dans la rigueur de cette règle, comme la plus propre à la vraisemblance des choses, et qui s'accommode le mieux à nostre imagination'* (p. 485). Similarly, several writers in these first years of the 1630s stress in their prefaces the importance of *'naïveté'* in dramatic language, seeing this also as a prerequisite for that verisimilitude sought at the time. In his *Dédicace* to *Lizimène*, Coste refers to the *'naïveté de son langage'*, hoping that this will be *'capable de . . . donner quelque satisfaction'*; in d'Alibray's important *Advertissement* to his adaptation of *Aminta*, he rejects the use of inappropriately intellectualised language in general, and the *pointe* in particular: *'aussi ne faut-il guere d'artifice pour exprimer la naïveté d'une passion; il ne faut point tirer de l'esprit ce qui doit venir du coeur, ny songer à une belle conception lors que l'âme ne demande qu'à enfanter'*, and in his preface to *Silvanire*, Mairet also remarks that he has removed all *pointes* from his play: *'évitant comme ils [i.e. les modernes Italiens] ont fait cette importune et vicieuse affectation des pointes et d'artifices, qu'on appelle* cacozélie' (p. 48). It is against this background that Corneille's often quoted remarks should be seen, suggesting not so much unprecedented assertions about the nature and function of comedy, but a further statement in the developing reaction against the burdensome rhetoric of tragi-comedy and a move towards an aesthetic of *vraisemblance*: 'La *Comedie n'est qu'un portraict de nos actions, et de nos discours, et la perfection des portraicts consiste en la ressemblance'* (p. 5).

Where Corneille distinguishes himself from these other dramatists, however, is in his general conception of his play. Whereas Mairet and d'Alibray, as has been seen earlier, see the pleasure of the *comédie* deriving from their creation and resolution of suspense, Corneille clearly seeks other effects. *La Veuve*, like *Mélite*, contains many elements of plot which, in other writers, may give rise to exciting and tense conflict: Alcidon kidnaps Clarice in an attempt to win her away from Philiste, and Doris, Philiste's sister, struggles to find happiness as two equally unsuitable partners in marriage are proposed to her. Corneille's presentation of such events, however, is quite particular.

The abduction of the heroine is an example of this. Such incidents are certainly popular in more romanesque tragi-comedies. In du Ryer's *Argenis et Poliarque*, the villainous act of Act IV Scene 2 leads to brutal conflict on stage, and in Rotrou's *L'Hypocondriaque*, Act II Scenes 3 and 4, Lisidor's attempts to abduct Cleonice meet with failure and death at the hands of the hero, a fate which equally befalls the scheming Clorante in Auvray's *Dorinde*, Act IV Scene 3. When Alcidon abducts Clarice in *La Veuve*, however, it is not the violence of the deed which is stressed so much as the enthusiasm which his accomplice, the heroine's *nourrice* brings to her part, changing roles with flair and accomplishment: *'Sortons de pasmoison, reprenons la parole, / Il nous faut à grands cris joüer un autre roolle'* (1167–8). And it is this, rather than the horror of the act, which is underlined immediately afterwards, in Act IV Scene 1, as Lycas tells the news to his master, Philiste. Interest lies not with the touching plight of an abducted heroine but with the theatrical display of the nurse, miming the mad rage of so many heroines, and setting innocent onlookers to flight:

> Seule en ce grand logis elle court haut et bas,
> Elle renverse tout ce qui s'offre à ses pas,
> Et sur ceux qu'elle voit frappe sans recognoistre:
> A peine devant elle oseroit-on paroistre
> De furie elle escume, et fait tousjours un bruit
> Que le desespoir forme, et que la rage suit . . . (1197–202)

Corneille's deliberate avoidance of tension is evident also in his presentation of the potentially bitter and tense conflict between Philiste and his mother Crysante in their choice of a husband for Doris; it is a conflict often singled out by critics as characteristic of what is held to be the play's bleak atmosphere.[2] It has been seen already, however, how tyranny exerted by parents is something of a commonplace in pastoral. It is a dominant theme, for instance, in *Silvanire*, where the dramatic focus centres on the heroine's struggle against the authority and avarice of her father, as she tries to defend her love for Aglante against such pronouncements of insensitivity as this of Act I Scene 2:

> Je sais bien le pouvoir que m'a donné sur elle
> L'inviolable droit de la loi naturelle;
> Elle s'y résoudra de force ou de douceur . . . (151–3)

Doris finds herself caught up between Philiste who insists that she should marry Alcidon, unaware that he only feigns love for her, and Crysante who urges her towards the wealthy but ridiculous Florange. Their tyranny over her, however, is a source of comedy, as these characters are seen to exercise their unfeeling authority not with the threatening openness of Mairet's Menandre, but in the name of reason and humanity. Crysante, for instance, constantly speaks language which is inappropriate to the circumstances. Alcidon admits in Act I Scene 2 that his courtship of Doris merely serves to conceal his passion for Clarice, but in the following scene, Crysante comically reveals her ignorance as she encourages her daughter towards what seems to her the perfect match:

> Ne crain pas que je veuille user de ma puissance,
> Je croirois en produire un trop cruel effet
> Si je te separois d'un amant si parfait. (174–6)

Finally enlightened as to Alcidon's true motives, she promptly
reveals further misconceptions in Act I Scene 4. Turning her
attention to the suit of Florange, she happily believes that Doris,
like she, readily considers wealth to be a more than adequate
substitute for affection. As she speaks with confidence about her
daughter's willingness to accept this proposal, there is no sense
of cruel coercion, but of absurdly misguided benevolence:

> *Non qu'elle en face estat plus que de bonne sorte,*
> *Il suffit qu'elle voit ce que le bien apporte,*
> *Et qu'elle s'accommode aux solides raisons*
> *Qui forment à present les meilleures maisons.* (289–92)

In Act III Scene 3, Philiste is presented as equally out of touch; he
can criticise the blind avarice of his mother, and yet, in his ardent
defence of Alcidon's suit, his own ignorance is clear:

> *Moy dont ce faux esclat n'esbloüit jamais l'ame*
> *Qui cognois ton merite autant comme ta flame,*
> *Je luy fis bien sçavoir que mon consentement*
> *Ne dépendroit jamais de son aveuglement,*
> *Et que jusqu'au tombeau quand à cét hymenée*
> *Je maintiendrois sa foy que je t'avois donnée.* (939–44)

From this opposition of characters Corneille creates in Act III
Scene 7 a scene of carefully orchestrated comic confusion.
Crysante rightly sees the folly of Philiste's continued support of
Alcidon, and Philiste justifiably scorns his mother's favouring the
wealthy Florange. They accuse each other of blindness, but are
unable to see it in themselves:

> Crysante: *Estant riche on est tout: adjoustez qu'elle mesme*
> *N'aime point Alcidon, et ne croit pas qu'il l'ayme.*
> *Quoy? voulez-vous forcer son inclination?*
> Philiste: *Vous la forcez vous mesme à cette eslection,*
> *Je suis de ses amours le tesmoin oculaire.* (1087–91)

Such discrepancies between characters' protestations of enlightenment and the actual intent or effect of their words have
literary precedents. In Baro's *Célinde*, for instance, the hero's
mother is typically avaricious, forcing Floridan to abandon the
impecunious Parthénice for the wealthy Célinde. Yet, having
exerted such authority over her son, she can speak words of
tolerance to Célinde's father, in Act I Scene 2, deploring, as it now
suits her purpose, the exercise of parental authority in matters of
love: '*mais le souvenir de ce que j'ay esté, & une expérience particulière*

m'enseignent qu'il ne faut jamais user de violence sur les inclinations d'une fille bien née' (p. 31). Corneille's interest though, is not in the hypocrisy of his characters but precisely in their quite inadvertent ignorance. Comedy and not tension is what he seeks as he presents the mother and son quite out of control of the language they use. At the end of the scene, Crysante laments that her daughter seems doomed to marry one she does not love. The defence of a vulnerable daughter by an enlightened parent is certainly a traditional feature of pastoral and tragi-comedy. In Scudéry's *Le Trompeur puny*, Act IV Scene 1, the queen defends Nerée against an authoritative king: *'Voulez-vous qu'un himen, où vostre main la force, / Se commence en tristesse, & finisse en divorce? . . .'* (p. 74), and in *Silvanire*, Act V Scene 9, Lérice bewails the avarice of Menandre at the height of a tense conflict: *'O! père sans pitié, ton avare faim d'or / Fera tant qu'à la fin nous la perdrons encor . . .'* (2327–8). Corneille, however, gives to the role a particular ironic twist. The mother is seen to defend her daughter against an absurd marriage, and yet with the same words, and quite unwittingly, she pushes her into one even more ridiculous:

> *Desplorable! le Ciel te veut favoriser,*
> *D'une bonne fortune, et tu n'en peux user.*
> *Rejoignons toutes deux ce naturel sauvage,*
> *Et taschons par nos pleurs d'amollir son courage.* (1113–16)

Attention is fixed not on the dramatic conflict but on the comic discrepancy between character and words, on traditional language of enlightened thought which reveals the speaker's blindness beneath.

At certain points, though, it seems that drama breaks out, and that Corneille's comic vision is blurred. Such a moment would seem to be Doris' monologue of Act IV Scene 9, a speech which evokes the cruel fate of daughters, victims of others' authority and tyranny:

> *Qu'aux filles comme moy le sort est inhumain.*
> *Que leur condition me semble deplorable!*
> *Une mere aveuglée, un frere inexorable,*
> *Chacun de leur costé prennent sur mon devoir*
> *Et sur mes volontez un absolu pouvoir . . .* (1570–74)

It is a speech which is often taken seriously by critics,[3] and yet it would be quite inappropriate to see the outburst as unique at the time and indicative of a penetrating social awareness particular to

Corneille. The language is quite traditional, and Doris is no more bitter in her indictment of misplaced parental values than countless other heroines of tragi-comedy. Her words echo, for instance, those of Melanie in La Croix, *L'Inconstance punie*,[4] Act I Scene 2, who is similarly subjected to tyranny:

> *Que la condition de fille est importune,*
> *De n'estre seulement libre en sa volonté*
> *Puis qu'il faut que la bonne & mauvaise fortune*
> *L'empesche de sortir de sa captivité.* (p. 15)[5]

Furthermore, set in its context it has a specific and clear comic function. Had it followed the argument of Philiste and Crysante in Act III Scene 7 which was analysed above, a scene where Doris' fate is effectively in the balance, the impact might have been largely pathetic. Corneille, however, waits until the end of Act IV, and inserts this speech immediately after a scene in which happiness for Doris is finally prefigured. Alcidon seeking to rid himself of the heroine in order to facilitate his courtship of Clarice feigns magnanimity and urges her to transfer her affections to Celidan, a hero whose virtue and love of Doris is already known to the audience. In her reaction to what she rightly recognises as a hypocritical gesture, the heroine is now temporarily blinded to this promise of joy; the ironical inappropriateness of her lament is made clear.

Similar comic irony is implied in the presentation of another vulnerable girl at a seemingly tense moment: Clarice, just prior to her abduction, when, in Act III Scene 8, she expresses delight in her reciprocated love of the hero:

> *Mes voeux sont exaucez,*
> *L'aise à mes maux succede,*
> *Mon sort en ma faveur change sa dure loy,*
> *Et pour dire en un mot le bien que je possede,*
> *Mon Philiste est à moy.* (1122–6)

That this speech of joy should occur as early as Act III does not in itself suggest an ironical presentation of the heroine, of course. In other plays of the period, conflict is seemingly resolved before the final Act: in Baro's *Clorise*, Act III Scene 6, Eliante, formerly aloof, accepts and rejoices in the suit of the hero; in du Ryer's *Clitophon*, Act III Scene 5, Charmide announces the end of suffering for the care-torn protagonists; in Mairet's *Chryséide et Arimand*, Act IV Scene 2, the protagonists are reunited, only to be separated again later; and in Racan's *Bergeries*, Act III Scene 4, the lovers are reconciled with a parent previously opposed to their passion, and the company looks forward to imminent happiness: '*Guérissez-vous tous deux pour jouïr des plaisirs / Qu'un heureux hyménée apprête à vos désirs*' (1653–4). In such cases, the joy is shared by the audience, as unaware as the characters of the trials to come; its untimely expression indicates defective construction rather than comic intentions on the dramatist's part. Corneille, however, is careful to underline the ignorance of his heroine. The audience has knowledge of the planned abduction, and, set in this context, Clarice's joy seems particularly out of place:

> *Qu'il fait bon avoir enduré.*
> *Que le plaisir se gouste au sortir des supplices!*
> *Et qu'après avoir tant duré*
> *La peine qui n'est plus augmente nos delices!* (1147–50)

As the attack draws closer, Corneille has his heroine stress again and again the feeling traditional at the end of comedy that joy is all the sweeter after suffering. The expectations of the audience are exploited to undermine and give an ironical force to a familiar theme, and Corneille creates not so much dramatic tension or sympathy for the defenceless heroine, as a more obviously comic suspense.

2

Le plus beau de leurs entretiens est en equivoques, et en propositions dont ils te laissent les consequences à tirer; si tu en penetres bien le sens, l'artifice ne t'en desplaira point.[6]

Corneille certainly seeks to avoid the tension and excitement of tragi-comedy in this play, but such an intention is again not without precedent. Mareschal in his *L'Inconstance d'Hylas* and Rotrou in his *Les Ménèchmes* had turned to d'Urfé and Plautus for amusing plots of amorous intrigue and confusion, and in *L'Esprit fort*, Claveret gave much attention to the comic portrayal of various kinds of lover, from the *esprit fort* to the *esprit foible*, from the timid Cleronte to the jealous Orilame.

In many ways, Corneille takes over and develops comic themes sketched out already by his predecessors—the ironical presentation of the awkward lover is such an instance. In Mareschal's *L'Inconstance d'Hylas*, Claveret's *L'Esprit fort*, or Scudéry's *Le*

Trompeur puny, there are brief interludes in which a lover is seen in a ridiculous light, his language wooden and archaic, his courtship lacking all spontaneity and warmth. Similarly, in Baro's *Clorise*, Act IV Scene 3, Eraste is seen to court the heroine in the following terms, launching into talk of eternal devotion within seconds of meeting her:

> *Donc beauté que j'adore, & pour qui je souspire,*
> *Augmentez d'un subject l'estat de vostre Empire,*
> *Et croyez que la mort seule me peut ravir*
> *La gloire que mon ame attend de vous servir* . . . (p. 97)

language which elicits this dry remark from his father: *'Je voy qu'à ce discours elle n'est guere esmeuë'* (p. 97). Doris' treatment of Florange, although reported by her rather than directly presented, exploits all the comic potential in amorous rhetoric whose force is blunted:

> *Il m'aborde en tremblant avec ce compliment,*
> *Vous m'attirez à vous ainsi que fait l'Aymant,*
> *(Il pensoit m'avoir dit le meilleur mot du monde)*
> *Entendant ce haut stile aussi tost je seconde*
> *Et respons brusquement sans beaucoup m'esmouvoir,*
> *Vous estes donc de fer à ce que je puis voir.* (207–212)

Corneille is more explicit than Baro, however, in his investigation of this awkwardness, setting it in a context which suggests a world apart from the idealistic realms of *L'Astrée*; a rift is apparent between fiction and life, the language of literature and the language of love. In Act I Scene 4, Geron explains to Crysante that the foolish Florange merely reproduces the rhetoric he has acquired from books. Such language now, though, can no longer faithfully express the reality, nor indeed the complexity of feelings:

> *Madame, je vous jure, il peche innocemment,*
> *Et s'il sçavoit mieux dire, il diroit autrement,*
> *C'est un homme tout neuf, que voulez vous qu'il fasse?*
> *Il dit ce qu'il a leu* . . . (271–4)

Florange is also significant, however, as a foil to the avarice of Crysante. In Act I Scene 3, the mother is quite clear about his suitability as a partner for Doris, however ridiculous he may be. For such as she, love does not motivate courtships, but the desire to make a good match:

> *Au demeurant fort riche, et que la mort d'un pere,*
> *Sans deux successions encores qu'il espere,*
> *Comble de tant de biens, qu'il n'est fille aujourd'huy*
> *Qui ne luy rie au nez, et n'ait dessein sur luy.* (229–32)

The importance of money in the choice of a partner is not in itself a theme new to pastoral or comedy as has been seen, but whereas other dramatists make of it a serious threat to the happiness of perfect lovers, Corneille is the first to transform it for comic purposes, suggesting an ironical distance from the idealism of fiction and a shrewd insight into the character who speaks.

A different form of detachment is developed by Corneille in the presentation of his hero, Philiste. In certain respects, this character follows broadly in the tradition of many pastoral lovers, shy and hesitant in the declaration of their passion. In d'Alibray's *Aminte*, Act II Scene 3, the hero insists on keeping silent about his longing, and in Rayssiguier's *Tragi-comédie pastorale*, Act II Scene 4, Silvandre is made to speak in this way about his love for Diane:

> *Mais je veux cependant attendre en patience,*
> *Et contre cet obstacle employer ma science,*
> *Taschant de l'obliger par ma discretion*
> *A recognoistre un jour ma juste affliction.* (p. 50)

And indeed, in *L'Astrée*, I 6, Daphnis thus advises the amorous Filandre, suggesting that such reticence in courtship is ultimately the surest way to a lady's heart, advice vindicated by the success of Aminta and Silvandre: '*De sorte que j'estime ceux-là bien advisez qui se font aimer à leurs bergères, avant que de leur parler d'amour; d'autant qu'amour est un animal qui n'a rien de rude que le nom, estant d'ailleurs tant agréable, qu'il n'y a personne à qui il desplaise* (pp. 217–18). Philiste certainly heeds the advice of his pastoral models, echoing it closely as he explains to Alcidon the course and intention of his courtship in the opening scene of the comedy:

> *Ajustons nos desseins à ses intentions,*
> *Tant que par la douceur d'une longue hantise*
> *Comme insensiblement elle se trouve prise.*
> *C'est par là que l'on seme aux Dames des appas*
> *Qu'elles n'evitent point ne les prevoyant pas.*
> *Leur haine envers l'amour pouroit estre un prodige*
> *Que le seul nom les choque et l'effet les oblige.* (36–42)

As Corneille points out in his *Avis*, this figure provides the opportunity to develop a charming ambiguity in language, as love is expressed through words of civility and respectful distance. This is suggested as early as the opening scene, when Philiste tells Alcidon of the kisses he exchanges with Clarice in the daily social round:

> Mais ils tiennent bien peu de la ceremonie;
> Parmy la bien-seance il m'est aisé de voir
> Que l'amour me les donne autant que le devoir, (74–6)

and it is developed in Act I Scene 5, when the hero and heroine are first seen together. Philiste makes a seemingly general statement about the humour of lovers, unable to disguise the passion they feel:

> L'esprit d'un amoureux absent de ce qu'il ayme
> Par sa mauvaise humeur fait trop voir ce qu'il est,
> Tousjours morne, resveur, triste, tout luy desplaist,
> A tout autre propos qu'à celuy de sa flame
> Le silence à la bouche, et le chagrin en l'ame, (354–8)

but this he then echoes pointedly as he gladly accepts Clarice's suggestion that they spend the following day together:

> Jamais commandemens ne me furent si doux,
> Puisque loin de vos yeux, je n'ay rien qui me plaise,
> Tout me devient fascheux, tout s'oppose à mon aise,
> Un chagrin eternel triomphe de mes sens. (372–5)

Clarice rejects this particular formulation, but in so doing she draws attention not only to the point being made by the hero, but also hints at her own hesitant acknowledgement of the compliment being paid her:

> Si (comme tu disois) dans le coeur des absents
> C'est l'amour qui fait naistre une telle tristesse,
> Ce compliment n'est bon que vers une maistresse. (376–8)

No open declaration of love is made, but beneath the protagonists' words, Corneille suggests the charming interaction of modesty and longing.

But while the charm of love may be implied in such reticence, a more obvious ridiculousness may also be suggested in the bashful lover. In Claveret's *L'Esprit fort*, the titular hero, brash in his rejection of love, is complemented by Nicandre, the *esprit foible*, equally extreme in his silent pining, as he explains in Act I Scene 6: 'Tant de respect à mon amour est joint, / Que je n'osay jamais *luy declarer ce point'* (p. 21), and in Cleronte, the same dramatist presents a character who, through the mockery of Celirée in Act II Scene 1, is made alive to his foolishness in fearing to court on his own behalf: *'Ton agreable humeur m'aprend en peu de mots, / Que la crainte en amour est la vertu de sots'* (p. 28).

Corneille is also certainly aware of this comic potential in his hero, and in the second meeting of his protagonists in Act II Scene 4, he exploits it fully. The confrontation of hesitant lover and lady of superior birth is not unknown in plays before *La Veuve*. In Boisrobert's *Pyrandre et Lisimène*, Act I Scene 3, Lisimène is seen to encourage the hero to declare himself, in spite of the apparent difference in their station. The heroine is quite direct in her own protestation of love: *'Nous sommes tous heureux, par l'effort de ton bras, / J'offencerois le Ciel, si je ne t'aimois pas . . .'* (p. 11), and this elicits from the subservient Pyrandre a correspondingly spontaneous declaration:

> *O bonté sans exemple en l'object le plus beau*
> *Que jamais éclaira le celeste flambeau!*
> *Princesse, honneur du monde, adorable merveille,*
> *Que je suis glorieux, s'il est vray que je veille . . .* (p. 11)

Corneille's presentation of a similar encounter is, however, quite different. Like Lisimène, Clarice is open about her love: *'Ne desguisons plus rien, mon Philiste, il est temps / Qu'un adveu mutuel rende nos feux contents . . .'* (617–18), but instead of encouraging the expected passionate avowal from her lover, the heroine is met with incredulity, ranging from accusations of a cruel deception: *'Vous me jouës, Madame, et cette accorte feinte / Ne donne à mes amours qu'une mocqueuse atteinte'* (623–4), to a lingering reluctance to believe what he hears: *'N'ayant jamais esté digne d'un tel honneur / J'ay de la peine encore à croire mon bon-heur* (641–2). Such hesitation suggests not only the charm of love, but also the comic blindness of one who refuses to see the truth, of one who, so fully committed to his role of hesitant lover, is unable to abandon it when it is no longer appropriate. As the hero shows his ever-present difficulty in declaring himself openly, the frustration of the heroine is seen to increase, from her early surprise and disbelief: *'Quelle façon estrange! en me voyant, brusler / Tu t'obstines encor à le dissimuler'* (625–6), to complete desperation: *'Cesse de me tuer par cette deffiance, / Qui pourroit des mortels troubler nostre alliance?'* (635–6). The potential for comedy in the presentation of the reticent hero is exploited here in a scene of careful stylisation and balance.

The greater part of Corneille's comic imagination is concentrated, however, on the figure of Alcidon, whose role as a deceiving villain is again quite particular. It is not uncommon in plays before *La Veuve* to have humorous interludes based on the hypocritical play-acting of a schemer. In Auvray's *Dorinde*, Ardilan's treacherous attempts to persuade Darinée of his love provide entertainment for all, not least for the intended victim:

> *Voicy tout à propos cet amoureux de Cour*
> *Qui sçait bien contrefaire un veritable Amour;*
> *Dieux! qu'il donne de mal à sa teste baissé,*
> *Pour feindre que je suis presente à sa pensée.* (p. 42)

And, in a similar way, when Scudéry's villain, Cleonte, tries to persuade the hero, Arsidor, that he has won the favours of the heroine in *Le Trompeur puny* Act II Scene 5, emphasis is not on the hero's suffering but on the delight with which the deceiver protests an experience of love which the audience knows to be nothing more than a product of his fertile imagination:

> *Brisons là ce discours, apprenant de ma bouche,*
> *Que le tombeau d'Amour se trouve dans la couche,*
> *Lors qu'on possede tout on n'espere plus rien,*
> *Et luy qui vit d'espoir meurt privé de ce bien.* (p. 37)

However, what Auvray and Scudéry make an interlude in essentially thrilling tragi-comedies, Corneille develops to a much more sophisticated degree.

Alcidon is presented as the role-player *par excellence*, the one who revels in performance. As early as the opening scene, he expresses disapproval of Philiste's timidity in love: reticence would ill-suit one such as he:

> *Ce n'est pas là mon jeu; le joly passetemps*
> *D'estre aupres d'une Dame, et causer du beau-temps . . .*
> *Touche, pauvre abusé, touche la grosse corde,*
> *Conte ce qui te meine, et ne t'amuse pas*
> *A perdre sottement tes discours et tes pas.* (47–8; 54–6)

And when, in Act III Scene 1, he discovers that Celidan loves Doris, but has overcome the passion for the sake of his friend, Alcidon laments that he has missed the opportunity to play a heroic role, the performance of this noble gesture clearly being as pleasurable to him as the thought of winning Clarice:

> *Je souffre maintenant la honte de sa perte,*
> *Et j'aurois eu l'honneur de te l'avoir offerte,*
> *De te l'avoir cedée, et reduit mes desirs*
> *Au glorieux dessein d'avancer tes plaisirs.* (847–50)

Through this character, Corneille parodies certain heroic scenes to an extent quite without parallel before his play. The sacrifice of personal love out of friendship for another is a familiar event in pastoral and tragi-comedy. It occurs on several occasions in *L'Astrée* (I 5, I 10, II 1), in Hardy's *Gésippe*, Act II Scene 2, Pichou's *Filis de Scire*, Act II Scene 3, and in Baro's *Clorise*, Act V Scene 6, when Eraste nobly gives up his love of the heroine:

> *Pour moy, j'aymerois mieux estre privé du jour*
> *Que de t'avoir ravy l'object de ton amour.*
> *Ton Adieu m'a touché tantost de telle sorte*
> *Qu'on m'eust pris pour un Tronc dont la racine est morte.* (p. 134)

In Act IV Scene 4, Alcidon casts himself in such a role, but the impact of his performance is not uplifting, like that of Baro's hero, but comic. It is known that this love is only feigned, and attention is fixed not on the language itself, but on the character who speaks it:

> *Long temps à mon sujet tes passions contraintes*
> *Ont souffert et caché leurs plus vives atteintes,*
> *Il me faut à mon tour en faire autant pour toy:*
> *Hier devant tous les Dieux je t'en donnay ma foy,*
> *Et pour la maintenir j'esteindray bien ma braise.* (1355–9)

As the scene continues, Corneille underlines the distortions implied in this performance by revealing, beneath the heroic façade, the true identity of the speaker. Alcidon slowly loses control of his language and is able to disguise only thinly his unheroic desire to rid himself of the unwanted Doris so that he may be free to force his attention on Clarice:

> *C'est faire mon devoir te quittant ma Doris,*
> *Et me vanger d'un traistre espousant sa Clarice?*
> *Mes discours, ny mon coeur n'ont aucun artifice,*
> *Je vay pour confirmer tout ce que je t'ay dit*
> *Employer vers Doris mon reste de credit.* (1374–8)

It is a display which is no more convincing to the audience than it is to Celidan, who, from this moment, seeks to counter the villainy of his friend:

> *Il me cede à mon gré Doris de bon courage,*
> *Et ce nouveau dessein d'un autre mariage*
> *Pour estre fait sur l'heure et tout nonchalamment*
> *Ne me semble conduit que trop accortement.* (1391–4)

Corneille's comic exploitation of this role-playing leads to some particularly subtle and original effects, apparent, for instance, in the presentation of Alcidon's courtship of Doris in Act II Scene 5. In certain plays of the period, comedy derives from the spectacle of a character feigning love for a lady. In Auvray's *Dorinde*, Act II Scene 1, a scene alluded to already, the villainous Ardilan protests love, only to be disbelieved by the astute Darinée:

Ardilan: *Vous pouvez-vous connestre, & ne me croire pas,*
          Quand je dis que vos yeux me livrent au trépas . . .
Darinée: *Ha véritablement je croy que votre erreur,*
          Troublant votre raison veut passer en fureur, (pp. 33–4)

a fate which also awaits Hylas in his feigned declaration to Dorinde in Mareschal's *L'Inconstance d'Hylas*, Act I Scene 2. And in Claveret's *L'Esprit fort*, much of the play's comic force derives from the hero's struggles to conceal his love for Angelie by paying court to the heroine's two sisters, Orante and Celirée. In Act I Scene 3, Claveret suggests the irony of such an encounter by having the hero forget momentarily the identity of the one he addresses:

> *. . . Ange. Orante est l'image*
> *A qui je dois sans feinte adresser tous mes voeux,*
> *C'est mon unique espoir, le sujet de mes feux,*
> *Et la seule beauté dont le pouvoir me lie.* (p. 18)

That Orilame can simply substitute one name for another is significant. It underlines the fact that, as also in Auvray's scene, the protestation of love is itself undistorted, and that its comic impact is achieved by the audience's knowledge of context alone, which the dramatist is careful to exploit.

In comparison with these examples, the originality and virtuosity of Corneille's scene can be properly evaluated. When Alcidon boasts of his role-playing to the nurse in Act I Scene 2, he likens himself to d'Urfé's ideal lover, suggesting that his language is also indistinguishable from that of the heroes he impersonates:

> *A m'en ouyr conter, l'amour de Celadon*
> *N'eut jamais rien d'esgal à celuy d'Alcidon,*
> *Tu rirois trop de voir comme je la cajolle,* (135–7)

but in the actual presentation of the scene, this is not the case. Here, Alcidon so manipulates his language that, while seeming to protest his love for Doris, he effectively states the opposite; sincerity of expression lies behind an elaborate theatrical mask. He presents himself as the traditionally timid lover, but in such a way as to suit his own purpose:

> Doris si tu pouvois lire dans ma pensée
> Et voir tous les ressorts de mon ame blessée,
> Que tu verrois un feu bien autre et bien plus grand
> Qu'en ces foibles devoirs que ma bouche te rend. (679–82)

The performance is impressive in its own right, but Corneille develops the comedy even further in his presentation of the heroine. Whereas both Darinée and Orante disbelieve their scheming suitors quite openly, Doris plays the villain's game herself, and with greater accomplishment. Alcidon's joy is countered and rendered comic by Doris' own:

> Quitte, mon cher soucy, quitte ce faux soupçon,
> Tu douterois à tort d'une chose si claire,
> L'espreuve fera foy comme j'ayme à te plaire,
> Je meurs d'impatience attendant l'heureux jour
> Qui te monstre quel est envers toy mon amour. (694–8)

Here, irony is not simply imposed from without on a scene which, in other circumstances, may be taken at face value. It is built into the language itself, and the audience is constantly aware of both role and reality, mask and face, as traditional formulations of passion are seen to express absolute indifference. Comedy no longer simply derives from an apparent discrepancy between the speaker and the role he plays, but, more subtly, from the juxtaposition within the role itself of truth and falsehood, spontaneous expression and calculated deception. It is a scene of which Corneille was particularly proud, alluding to it explicitly in his *Avis*, and having Doris refer back to it in Act III Scene 4, underlining the comic enjoyment it provided: 'Croyez moy qu'Alcidon n'en sçait guere en amour / Vous n'eussiez peu m'entendre et vous tenir de rire . . .' (1014–15). Here, the dramatist refines a comic language of ambiguity to suggest the character who both *plays* and *is*; it is quite without precedent in plays of this time, and is not the least significant part of the comedy's originality.

Similar ambiguity is found in Alcidon's opening speech of Act III Scene 3. In this scene, the villain seeks some excuse to abduct

Clarice, and he plans here to accuse Philiste of conniving in
Florange's suit of Doris. He plays the role of outraged lover, who
sees deception rife in the world:

> *Je resvois que le monde en l'ame ne vaut rien,*
> *Au moins pour la pluspart, que le siecle où nous sommes*
> *A bien dissimuler met la vertu des hommes,*
> *Qu'à grand peine deux mots se peuvent eschapper*
> *Sans quelque double sens afin de nous tromper,*
> *Et que souvent de bouche un dessein se propose*
> *Ce pendant que l'esprit songe à toute autre chose.* (910–16)

Comedy derives on a first level from Alcidon's visible delight in
his performance, prefacing his deception of the hero with this
sweeping observation on man. There is more than just accomplished play-acting in these lines, however. The words Alcidon
speaks also have a layer of truth, and are seen to refer just as
appropriately to his own proposed deception of Philiste, as they
are intended to refer to Philiste's fictitious deception of him. The
villain here plays a part for the hero's benefit, fixed in his stance of
disabused lover, but at the same time, with the same words, he
openly comments on this very part he plays. The actor is both
committed to and detached from his role; it is from this particular
perspective that the full comic force of the speech derives.

Corneille adapts this same angle of vision in Act II Scene 3.
Here the *nourrice* is seen to defend her seemingly treacherous
attitude to Philiste, as the hero confronts her after she has tried
vainly to turn the heroine's mind towards Alcidon. The sudden
surprise of a villain caught in the middle of a treacherous act is a
scene familiar in comedy. In Rotrou's *Les Ménèchmes*, Act III Scene
5, Orazie overhears her husband lament his fruitless courtship of
Erotie, and he is then forced to explain himself:

> *L'ai-je dit sans dessein, ne te voyois-je pas*
> *Écouter mes discours, et marcher sur mes pas?*
> *Conserve si tu veux cette créance vaine:*
> *Je ne parlois ainsi que pour te mettre en peine.* (I, p. 551)

In *La Veuve*, Corneille carefully builds up to the nurse's
explanation, suggesting her astonishment and dismay at being
thus caught out, as she moves from instinctive questions: '*Et bien,*
quoy? qu'ay-je fait?' (525), and inarticulate exclamations: '*Ah,*
ah . . .' (528), to the start of her defence: '*De grace quatre mots, et tu*
seras content' (530). The encounter is certainly comic, as the

villainess displays remarkable quick-wittedness, talking herself
out of an impossible situation:

> Moy qui de ce mestier ay la haute science,
> Et qui pour te servir brusle d'impatience,
> Par un chemin plus court qu'un propos complaisant
> J'ay sceu croistre sa flame en la contredisant,
> J'ay sceu faire esclatter avecques violence,
> Un amour estouffé soubs un honteux silence,
> Et n'ay pas tant choqué que picqué ses desirs
> Dont la soif irritée avance tes plaisirs. (547–54)

At the same time, however, Corneille adds a further dimension to
a traditional comic scene as he suggests through these same
words the nurse's own feelings of self-reproach. Victory for
Philiste means defeat for her own treacherous plan, and the
smiling mask of confidence and pride which she is forced to
adopt here hides a face grimacing at her effective incompetence.
The lines have one meaning for Philiste, one for the nurse, and
both for the audience. At the end of the scene, Philiste expresses
his uncertainty about the truth of what he has been told:

> Soit une verité, soit une illusion,
> Que ton subtil esprit employe à ta defence,
> Le mien de tes discours plus outre ne s'offence, (570–2)

but his words, rather than suggesting a grave metaphysical
doubt as to the nature of reality, underline more obviously the
comic principle behind this scene. The nourrice's words are
both true and false; role and reality are carefully brought
together.   –

The same comic focus is apparent, finally, in Alcidon's
downfall of Act V Scene 9. Persuaded by Celidan that Philiste is
dead and that Clarice is ready to reciprocate his affection, the
villain enters in this last scene, confident of victory, only to see
the lovers happily reunited. Told by Clarice of Celidan's desire to
marry Doris, Alcidon resorts again to his role of heroic fury at this
apparent threat to his love and honour:

> O honte! ô creve-coeur! ô desespoir! ô rage!
> Qui venez à l'envy deschirer mon courage . . .
> Je mourray bien sans vous, dans cette trahison
> Mon coeur n'a par les yeux que trop pris de poison,
> Perfide, à mes despens tu saoules donc ta braise,
> Et mon honneur perdu contribuë à ton aise? (1935–6; 1941–4)

There is great drama here as Alcidon plays a familiar part, echoing the words of many a villain defeated in love. In du Ryer's *Argenis et Poliarque*, Act V Scene 5, the defeated Licogene only wants to die:

> *Injurieux subjets de mes peynes diverses,*
> *Astres sanglans, auteurs de toutes mes traverses,*
> *Qu'ay-je encore à souffrir devant que vostre effort,*
> *M'arrache du pouvoir d'un miserable sort?* (p. 99)

But Corneille is not simply reproducing a heroic speech to be enjoyed out of its dramatic context, nor is he just delighting in comic overstatement. These lines are not merely a piece of studied play-acting, but they also contain the suggestion of a spontaneous outburst which merges comically with the histrionic display. Alcidon realises indeed that he has been deceived by Celidan, not in his wooing of Doris but in his skilful arousal of the villain's hopes to win Clarice. As he comes on stage, he sees that he has been fooled, and cannot retain his despair. The mask does not hide his face, but is superimposed suggestively on it.

In plays of the time, comedy may derive from the presentation of characters acting certain parts, but in scenes such as these, Corneille clearly refines the juxtaposition of role and reality, detachment and commitment to a degree which has no parallel in the works of his contemporaries. He goes beyond the simple exploitation of the audience's knowledge of context, and he suggests instead through the language itself, the comedy of the theatrical performance, of the actor who is constantly visible beneath the persona he embodies.

3

Voila mon homme pris, et ma vieille attrapée.[7]

The *dénouement* of *La Veuve* is in many ways more conventional than that of *Mélite*. The theme of the *traistre trahy* is certainly not uncommon in plays before this. In *Silvanire*, the plans of the deceiving Tirinte are seen to work against him, and he is led to repentance and marriage with Fossinde; and in Scudéry's *Le Trompeur puny*, the villainous Cleonte fails to separate the hero and heroine, and is finally killed in a duel. In *La Veuve*, however, Corneille is more concerned to develop the comic potential in such a theme, having the deceiver reveal himself to be more

gullible than those he would deceive. His early triumph of Act III
Scene 2, as he successfully convinces Celidan of the innocence of
his schemes: '*Bons Dieux! que d'innocence et de simplicité; / Ou pour la
mieux nommer que de stupidité . . .*' (885–6) is only shortlived, and
he is defeated by an actor more convincing than himself. In Act V
Scene 3, he is outplayed by Celidan, and is persuaded that his
treachery has brought him happiness. Celidan brings to his
performance that same enthusiasm which Alcidon constantly
displayed, as he distorts the outcome of events, recounting the
words of a heroine apparently ready to turn her affections to the
villain:

> . . . *J'ay perdu ce que j'ayme,*
> *(Dit elle) mais du moins si cét autre luy mesme,*
> *Son fidelle Alcidon m'en consoloit icy,*
> *Qu'en le voyant mon mal deviendroit adoucy!* (1663–6)

Alcidon's expression of self-satisfaction at the end of the scene
echoes that of Act III Scene 2, but now it is the villain's gullibility
and lack of control which Corneille makes comically manifest:

> *O l'excellent amy! qu'il a l'esprit docile!*
> *Pouvois-je faire un choix plus commode pour moy?*
> *Je trompe tout le monde avec sa bonne foy.* (1688–90)

And yet, in his creation of order, Corneille hints once more at
the arbitrary way in which it is brought about. Suggestions of this
are found in the presentation of Philiste, who is denied his
traditional role as saviour of the heroine and the creator of order.
In Gombauld's *Amaranthe*, Act III Scene 2, Alexis boasts of his
successful rescue of his beloved: '*Quand l'effort que j'ay fait me
cousteroit la vie, / C'est un grand heur pour moy que de l'avoir servie*' (p.
76), but Philiste has no such triumph. Although having several
attributes of the traditional pastoral lover, Corneille's hero differs
from the model in this important respect, and his final happiness
is tainted by the thought that it has been achieved without his
contribution:

> *Mon ame en est ensemble et ravie, et confuse,*
> *D'un peu de lascheté vostre retour m'accuse,*
> *Et vostre liberté me reproche aujourd'hui,*
> *Que mon amour la doit à la pitié d'autruy.* (1807–10)

In Act V Scene 7, Clarice reflects not on the heroism of her lover,
but on the inevitable mechanics of the plot which have brought
them back together:

> *Que t'importe à present qu'un autre m'en delivre,*
> *Puisque c'est pour toy seul que Clarice veut vivre,*
> *Et que d'un tel orage en bonace reduit*
> *Celidan a la peine, et Philiste le fruit?* (1819–22)

The hero is here impotent, at the mercy of events which, in this case, have turned out in his favour.

Similar detachment is suggested in the ultimate salvation of Doris. It is characteristic of the play's essential irony that the true partner for this heroine should be proposed to her not by Philiste or Crysante, whose motives are ostensibly honest, but by the villainous Alcidon in Act IV Scene 8:

> *Ce Cavalier au reste a tous les avantages*
> *Que l'on peut remarquer aux plus braves courages,*
> *Beau de corps et d'esprit, riche, adroit, valeureux,*
> *Et sur tout de Doris à l'extreme amoureux,* (1551–4)

and when his suit is favoured by Crysante, it is in terms which are again heavily ironical. Continuing to speak the language of an enlightened parent, Crysante recalls her love for Celidan's father which had met with parental opposition:

> *S'il m'aymoit je l'aymois, et les seules rigueurs*
> *De ses cruels parens diviserent nos coeurs,*
> *On l'esloigna de moy veu le peu d'avantage*
> *Qui se trouva pour luy dedans mon mariage . . .* (1781–84)

She laments here that material preoccupations should have undermined the happiness of two lovers, and yet it is precisely Celidan's wealth rather than his affection for Doris which she welcomes:

> *Non Monsieur, croyez-moy, vostre offre nous honore,*
> *Aussi dans le refus j'aurois peu de raison,*
> *Je cognoy vostre bien, je sçay vostre maison . . .* (1772–4)

This hero, then, appears as the miraculously ideal solution to the conflict, the perfect lover, the wealthy suitor and the sincere friend, the embodiment of those values which Crysante and Philiste have so ardently, but comically defended. Harmony is achieved as if by magic, and yet it is in a significant way. Succeeding where Philiste is shown to be deficient, Celidan throws into relief the shortcomings of the traditional hero. The attributes of valour and fidelity, conventional in tragi-comedy, are replaced by those of the actor whose skill and inventiveness restore a lost order. Such a character will feature more and more prominently in Corneille's later comedies.

4

Sur cette maxime je tasche de ne mettre en la bouche de mes Acteurs, que ce que diroient vray semblablement en leur place ceux qu'ils representent, et de les faire discourir en honnestes gens, et non pas en Autheurs . . .[8]

In the *Avis* to the reader of his play, Corneille clearly dissociates himself from that form of tragi-comedy which sacrifices all verisimilitude for the sake of exciting *péripéties* or displays of rhetoric. For him, the *comédie* is more than simply a sequence of largely unconnected poetic set pieces, whose motivation is arbitrary and whose expression is ill suited to the circumstances. Language should be appropriate to the character concerned.

Such a stress on the *vraisemblance* of comedy has important consequences in *La Veuve*. On one level, it lies behind Corneille's visible attempt to suggest a topical and recognisable setting for his play. Allusions here to dances, social visits and to Paris itself develop from and take further several such references found in plays before this: the brief evocation of the capital in Racan's *Bergeries*, Act II Scene 4, the setting of Claveret's *L'Esprit fort* on the *'route d'un Parc, près de Versaille'*, or the allusions to the *Feste de Paris* throughout the anonymous *Mercier inventif*.[9] And indeed, in the character of Florange, whose wealth is seen by Crysante to be more than adequate compensation for his ridiculous lack of spontaneity, Corneille suggests a comic detachment from the ideal world of fiction where heroes are heroic and marriages made of love.

Also, however, and more importantly, these remarks have a significance which suggests unity in the play not simply as a *comédie de moeurs*. The importance accorded to the relationship of language and speaker is reflected in the varied comic force of *La Veuve*, from the transformation of potentially tense scenes of tyranny to the parody of the eloquent lover, from the charm of hero and heroine whose words of modesty betray tender longing to the elaborate theatrical displays of the villains who superimpose sincerity on falsehood. Language here is never seen on its own terms, but always in relation to the one who speaks it. The potential for comedy here is seized on and exploited by Corneille to its full extent, and he produces a play of comic sophistication which was without equal at the time of its creation.

IV

La Galerie du Palais
The actor
and his feelings

1

> *Que tu sçais, cher amy, lire dans les esprits!*
> *Et que pour bien juger d'une secrette flame,*
> *Tu penetres avant dans les ressorts d'une ame!*[1]

It is *La Galerie du Palais*, above all, which leads critics to speak of charm and realism in Corneille's comic *oeuvre*. In his *Examen*, the dramatist points out with pride how the *nourrice*, that remnant of classical comedy and farce, has been replaced by a *suivante*,[2] and this move towards a more realistic depiction of action is reflected, too, in the title of the play itself and the scenes of bustle and commerce which recreate the atmosphere in the *galerie du Palais de Justice*.

For some critics, the chief interest and originality of the play lies in these very scenes.[3] There is indeed a certain shrewd observation of the keen business instinct in these stall-holders, as, for instance, in the lament of the *lingère* in Act I Scene 4:

> *Je perds bien à gaigner de ce que ma boutique*
> *Pour estre trop estroitte, empesche ma pratique,*
> *A peine y puis-je avoir deux chalands à la fois,*
> *Je veux changer de place avant qu'il soit un mois . . .* (85–8)

and yet Corneille was certainly not the first dramatist to introduce merchants on stage. In *Le Mercier inventif*, Act I, a pedlar arrives to sell his wares at the *Feste de Paris*, in Coste's *Lizimène*, Act IV, a similar character appears, and in du Ryer's *Lisandre et Caliste*, Act II Scene 1, the action is interrupted, as was noted in the first chapter, by the amusing conversation of a butcher and his wife. The presence of such scenes suggests, then, not so much

Corneille's inventiveness as his ability to seize on elements clearly popular in the works of his contemporaries and to adapt them for his own purposes.

To a certain extent the genre scenes to which the title of the comedy refers are purely episodic. In his *Examen* of the play, Corneille was to be slightly concerned about the justification of his title for this very reason: *'Ce tiltre seroit tout à fait irregulier, puisqu'il n'est fondé que sur le Spectacle du premier Acte, où commence l'amour de Dorimant pour Hyppolite, s'il n'estoit authorisé par l'exemple des Anciens'* (p. 149). Nevertheless, and more obviously than in the other plays alluded to, they complement what is seen to be the dramatist's replacement of exciting adventure with a more sensitive portrayal of the human heart: the plotting of Hippolyte who loves Lysandre, but is loved by Dorimant, the hesitations of Célidée uncertain about her feelings for either, and the jealousies of both heroes, each easily convinced that he has been deceived.

By the time of *La Galerie du Palais*, this kind of play was becoming quite familiar. In Claveret's *L'Esprit fort*, attention is fixed on the comic relationship of lovers, ridiculous and at times quite charming in their suspicions and misunderstandings; in *Amarillis*, du Ryer retains a pastoral background and depicts a sequence of jealousies and rival love affairs; in *La Bourgeoise*,[4] Rayssiguier concentrates on the persistent attempt of the heroine to come between two lovers and to win the hero for herself, and in two plays of Rotrou, *Céliane* and *Diane*, the dramatist replaces the suspense of tragi-comedy with the more discreet entertainment provided by his heroines' search to win back the heart of faithless lovers.

The first Act of Corneille's play sets a tone of discreet charm and harmony. In Act I Scene 2, Pleirante approves of his daughter Célidée's manifest love of Lysandre, and his words of encouragement have none of the ironical undertones which characterised Crysante's quite misplaced enlightenment in *La Veuve*:

> *Ne pense plus, ma fille, à me cacher ta flame,*
> *N'en conçoy point de honte, et n'en crains point de blâme:*
> *Le sujet qui l'allume a des perfections*
> *Dignes de posseder tes inclinations.* (25–8)

The scene is quite straightforward and undistorted, presenting the simple, but touching avowal of love from a daughter to the father she can trust:

> *Monsieur, il est tout vray, son ardeur legitime*
> *A tant gaigné sur moy que j'en fay de l'estime:*
> *J'honore son merite, et n'ay pû m'empescher*
> *De prendre du plaisir à m'en voir rechercher.* (33–6)

Similarly, in the scenes which follow, Corneille takes pleasure in the examination of Dorimant's sudden love for Hippolyte, whom he glimpses in the *galerie*. Love is not accepted simply as a given fact of the drama, but there is interest clearly in its inception and growth. Lysandre notices his friend's curiosity as to Hippolyte's identity, and is given lines which reflect his sensitive understanding of the heart: '*Ta curiosité deviendra bien tost flame: / C'est par là que l'Amour se glisse dans une ame*' (209–10). When Dorimant begins to rage at the beating which his servant has endured in a vain attempt to follow Hippolyte home, Lysandre is quick to analyse the true motives of the outburst:

> *Ce desir, à vray dire, est un amour naissant*
> *Qui ne sçait où se prendre, et demeure impuissant;*
> *Il s'esgare et se perd dans cette incertitude,*
> *Et renaissant tousjours de ton inquietude,*
> *Il te monstre un objet d'autant plus souhaité,*
> *Que plus sa cognoissance a de difficulté.* (267–72)

Dorimant's remark to Lysandre quoted at the head of this section clearly indicates Corneille's principal interest here, and what is seen in particular terms in the dialogue of these two characters is suggested, too, on a more general level, in their earlier conversations about love and its presentation in poetry. Such preoccupations were becoming more and more evident in plays of this time. In *La Pèlerine amoureuse*,[5] Act V Scene 5, Rotrou inserts a discussion on art between Lucidor and Filidan, the latter stressing that only the lover is qualified to write about the heart and its complexities:

> *Dois-je rien ignorer? et puis-je, si je n'aime,*
> *Savoir ce qu'en un coeur peut une ardeur extrême,*
> *Exprimer ce qu'Amour a d'amer et de doux,*
> *Ce que dit un amant, ce que pense un jaloux. . . ?* (II, pp. 512–13)

Rotrou's scene is a curious interlude in a plot of disguised lovers and feigned madness. Corneille's discussion, however, is entirely consonant with the atmosphere of the preceding scenes, as he carefully prepares the way for the investigation of feelings which is to follow. In Act I Scene 7, Lysandre moves from that traditional mockery of bookish rhetoric seen already in the mouth of Tirsis to a more suggestive interest in the evocation and analysis of love, for which such stereotyped language is manifestly unsuited:

> O pauvre Comedie, objet de tant de veines,
> Si tu n'és qu'un portrait des actions humaines,
> On te tire souvent sur un original
> A qui, pour dire vray, tu ressembles fort mal! (173–6)

Significantly, the opening scenes of the play are concerned just as much with such reflections as they are with the exposition of the plot. More obviously than anywhere else in his comedies so far, Corneille shows interest not so much in villainous attempts to separate lovers, but in the nature of love itself, its charms and its precariousness. Florice's remark in the first scene is indeed less the threat of a schemer as she plans to aid Hippolyte in her pursuit of Lysandre, than it is a shrewd observation on the human heart:

> Je veux que Celidée ait charmé son courage,
> L'amour le plus parfait n'est pas un mariage;
> Fort souvent moins que rien cause un grand changement,
> Et les occasions naissent en un moment. (13–16)

2

Le Stile en est plus fort, et plus dégagé des pointes dont j'ay parlé, qui s'y trouveront assez rares.[6]

Corneille may move explicitly away from the heavy rhetorical language of tragi-comedy, but still in this play there are moments of colourful outburst, particularly in the mouth of Lysandre. In many ways this character falls into the mould of the traditional pastoral hero who lives only for his love and is subjected to violent despair when it is threatened. When Célidée seems to betray him, his laments recall those of Céladon (*L'Astrée* I 4), Alcidor (Racan, *Les Bergeries*, II 5), Arsidor (Scudéry, *Le Trompeur puny*, I 7) or Philidor (du Ryer, *Amarillis*, III 3), but Corneille, like some other dramatists of this time, suggests detachment from such passion. In Claveret's *L'Esprit fort*, Act IV Scene 7, for instance, Orilame has an outburst of jealous rage, and yet it is carefully set in a comic context. The audience knows that his supposed rival is the ridiculous *esprit fort*, whom the heroine moreover only pretends to love, and the violence proposed is seen not so much as the thrilling prelude to bloodshed, but as a more discreetly comic suggestion of naivety:

> *Amour, rage, transports, quels rets leur doi-je tendre?*
> *Souffriray-je un affront sans épancher leur sang?*
> *Leur iray-je plonger un poignard dans le flanc?*
> *Les iray-je esgorger aupres de ma maistresse?* (p. 99)

Similarly, in Act IV Scene 4, Corneille's outraged hero laments for some sixty lines, believing Célidée to love Dorimant, but it is in terms which are certainly not pathetic in their impact. There are suggestions of comic overstatement on the hero's part as he creates a vast scene of carnage brought about by his own desperate rage:

> *Il faut que, sans esgard, ma rage impitoyable*
> *Confonde l'innocent avecque le coupable,*
> *Que, dans mon desespoir, je traite esgalement*
> *Celidée, Hippolite, Aronte, Dorimant . . .* (1225–8)

an imagined scene whose grand effect is undermined noticeably by the presence of Aronte, his own servant. The theatricality of the outburst is underlined even further by Lysandre's subsequent moments of self-irony, his sudden return to calm and the touching avowal of his unvanquishable love, expressed simply and without exaggeration. The violent jealousy is abandoned, and behind it is revealed the face of a character in love:

> *Celle que nous aimons jamais ne nous offence,*
> *Un mouvement secret prend tousjours sa deffence:*
> *L'amant souffre tout d'elle, et dans son changement,*
> *Quelque irrité qu'il soit, il est tousjours amant.* (1245–8)

Such discreet charm is apparent again in the same character's lament of Act V Scene 1. The audience is distant from the violent passions which Lysandre evokes, and an ironical light is cast on the language used. The hero contemplates the death of Dorimant, but realises his folly in a moment of crushing self-awareness:

> *Indiscrette vangeance, imprudentes chaleurs,*
> *Dont l'impuissance adjoute un comble à mes malheurs,*
> *Ne me conseillez plus la mort de ce faussaire,*
> *J'aime encor Celidée, et n'ose luy déplaire:*
> *Priver de la clarté ce qu'elle aime le mieux,*
> *Ce n'est pas le moyen d'agréer à ses yeux.* (1495–500)

The banality of the last two lines cuts right through the impact of the heroic apostrophe. Furthermore, however, Corneille's stress on the hero's renewed love for Célidée is exploited as the necessary preparation for the comic encounter with Dorimant which follows. At the end of the monologue, Lysandre has again adopted a familiar heroic attitude, speaking traditional lines of despair:

> *Je tarde trop: allons, ou vaincre ses refus,*
> *Ou me vanger sur moy de ne luy plaire plus,*
> *Et tirons de son coeur, malgré sa flame éteinte,*
> *La pitié par ma mort, ou l'amour par ma pleinte,*
> *Ses rigueurs par ce fer me perceront le sein.* (1527–31)

It is this stance which is carefully ridiculed in the next scene.

In this encounter, Corneille exploits further than in *Mélite* the potential for comedy in the confrontation of rival lovers, deliberately underlining the misunderstanding which deceives both characters, the false conviction that they love the same girl. For both heroes, a duel to the death is both imminent and desirable: Lysandre's challenge is quite categorical:

> *Vous voulés seul à seul cajoler Celidee,*
> *Nous en aurons bien tost la querelle vuidée:*
> *Ma mort vous donnera chés elle un libre accés,*
> *Ou ma juste vengeance un funeste succés,* (1541–4)

but such heroic sentiments serve to suggest folly, not courage. Even when the truth is spoken, and each character protests anew his love for his designated partner, nothing will shake off the mask which blinds them. Instead of leading to recognition, the truth only takes the heroes further into confusion and mistrust:

> Dorimant: *Le Ciel, le juste Ciel, ennemy des ingrats,*
> *Qui pour ton chastiment a destiné mon bras,*
> *T' aprendra qu'à moy seul Hyppolite est gardée.*
> Lysandre: *Garde ton Hyppolite.*
> Dorimant: *Et toy, ta Celidée.*
> Lysandre: *Voila faire le fin, de crainte d'un combat.* (1551–5)

Corneille clearly delights here in the comic transformation of drama, presenting two characters who are made to underline quite inadvertently the ridiculousness of their stance. They are simply eager to fight, whether there is a reason for it or not: '*Laissons à part les noms, disputons la maistresse, / Et pour qui que ce soit montre icy ton adresse*' (1557–8). The dramatist takes his protagonists to the heights of absurdity. They are no longer two heroes involved in the struggle over a mistress, touchingly beset by fears that they may be unloved, but two actors, quite careless of dramatic context, determined to act out their roles.

3

> Toutefois un desdain esprouvera ses feux:
> Ainsi de tous costez j'auray ce que je veux;
> Il me rendra constante, ou me fera volage:
> S'il m'aime, il me retient; s'il change, il me desgage.
> Suivant ce qu'il aura d'amour ou de froideur,
> Je suivrai ma nouvelle ou ma premiere ardeur.[7]

It is in Célidée, however, that Corneille's particular sensitivity is clearly apparent. It is not uncommon in plays before *La Galerie du Palais* for girls to feign indifference for the ones they love. In *Silvanire*, Mairet's heroine is forced by her father to give no indication of her love for Aglante, and in Act II Scene 1 she laments the violence which she must do to her heart. Beneath apparent coldness, the dramatist shows the warmth of her love, juxtaposing mask and face, role and reality for striking dramatic effect:

> Ah! si comme le front ce coeur t'était visible,
> Ce coeur qu'injustement tu nommes insensible,
> Voyant en mes froideurs et mes soupirs ardens
> La Scythie au dehors et l'Afrique au dedans,
> Tu dirais que l'Honneur et l'Amour m'ont placée
> Sous la zone torride et la zone glacée. (547–52)

Set against this background, the heroine's rejection of Aglante in Act III Scene 2 suggests not the absence of love, but the touching plight of a daughter whose happiness is threatened: 'N'importe, la franchise est un bien si parfait / Que je hais de l'amour et le nom et l'effet' (1041–2).

Other dramatists use the theme for simple comic ends. A girl may delight in a momentary teasing of the hero, hearing him rage a little in jealousy before she reassures him that all is well. In Rotrou's *Amélie*,[8] Act IV Scene 5, the heroine proposes such a *feinte*, which will provide simple and harmless amusement for all concerned:

> Ce divertissement ne vous déplaira pas;
> Vous entendrez souvent invoquer le trépas;

> *Nous ferons un jaloux, et son cruel martyre,*
> *Nous fournira ce soir un beau sujet de rire.* (III, p. 332)

Again, the impact of the role is determined by the context, carefully prepared by the dramatist. Attention is fixed on the hero in Act V Scene 2, as Amélie professes with absolute conviction her sudden attraction for another:

> *Eh bien, je l'avoûrai, cet infidèle coeur*
> *S'est affranchi des lois de son premier vainqueur:*
> *J'aime cet etranger, de secrètes puissances*
> *Lui donnent mes desirs et forcent mes défenses.* (p. 338)

In other plays again, the motivation is left quite vague. In Coste's *Lizimène*, Act V, the heroine is suddenly and quite inexplicably aloof: 'Voicy mon Berenis, je ne veus pas qu'il sçache, / Que je l'ayme si fort, il faut que je le cache' (p. 63), and in Scudéry's *L'Amour caché par l'amour*, Act IV Scene 5, Melisée admits herself that she does not know why she had earlier feigned indifference for Pirandre: 'Ma passion voyant la sienne mutuelle, / Sans raison en l'aimant, je me feignois cruelle' (890–1).

In these examples, different as they are from each other, the audience is aware of a sharp division between the expressions of aloofness and the true feelings of the heroine, aware indeed that words of indifference are just a role which bears no relation to reality; no investigation of the speaker's love is implied. With Célidée, however, this is not the case. Quite free from all parental pressure, the heroine is suddenly led to hesitate about her love for Lysandre which she has been so confident to proclaim; she feels an incomprehensible but equally pleasurable attraction for Dorimant:

> *Mon coeur a de la peine à demeurer constant,*
> *Et pour te descouvrir jusqu'au fonds de mon ame,*
> *Ce n'est plus que ma foy qui conserve ma flame.* (512–14)

Célidée can only love with certainty if she knows that she also is loved. For her, the *feinte* is a test not only of Lysandre's affection, but also, by extension, of her own; the lines which head this section express her determination to carry out this curious experiment.

The apparent self-control which is implied in the project, however, is constantly undercut by suggestions of insecurity and doubt. In Act II Scene 5 she protests to Hippolyte that she plans to

disguise her feelings for Lysandre, claiming for herself that
absolute mastery over her emotions which characterises the other
heroines referred to:

> J'armeray de rigueurs jusqu'à la moindre oeillade,
> Et regleray si bien toutes mes actions
> Qu'il ne pourra juger de mes intentions. (558–60)

It is quite clear, however, that these intentions are as hidden to
Célidée as they will be to the hero. Ambiguity is revealed in the
monologue which ends the scene, as the heroine outlines her
doubts and struggles to define her feelings for Lysandre:

> Quel estrange combat! Je meurs de le quitter,
> Et mon reste d'amour ne le peut mal-traiter . . .
> Mon ame veut et n'ose, et bien que refroidie,
> N'aura trait de mespris si je ne l'estudie. (571–2, 577–8)

The lines are fascinating. Corneille suggests not now the temporary replacement of passion with indifference, but the subtle
coexistence of the two. He creates a character who is neither in love
nor aloof with complete certainty; Célidée feels herself distant
from Lysandre, and yet she cannot articulate this feeling with total
spontaneity. At the end of the speech, she prepares herself for the
role she is about to play, the actress picking up the mask which is
destined to cover her face completely and conceal all her feelings:
'Prepare-toy, mon coeur, et laisse à mes discours / Assez de liberté pour
trahir mes amours' (587–8). The verb trahir suggests at first sight that
mask of indifference and inscrutability which will betray the love
she has professed for Lysandre. Furetière gives the following
definition:[9] 'On dit qu'un home trahit ses sentimens, quand il parle
contre sa propre conscience.' And yet it is significant that the word
carries too, in the rhetoric of love, suggestions of inadvertent
expression and revelation: 'Un amant dit que ses yeux et ses souspirs
ont trahi son amour.' The double force is particularly suggestive
here, underlining Célidée's own uncertainty about her feelings
and motives. Her language of indifference is intended both to
cover up continued love for Lysandre and to express a new truth,
inspired by her attraction to Dorimant; the character both plays and
is. The mask which Célidée adopts is there to protect her face, to
determine her own emotions and to give her that sense of security
in love which she so earnestly seeks. Corneille's originality here is
quite remarkable.

Such complexities are sustained in the lovers' meeting of Act
II Scene 6, as Célidée speaks lines of studied ambiguity, playing
a role and yet ignorant herself as to how far it corresponds to the
truth. She expresses impatience at Lysandre's courtship of her:
'*Quelque forte que soit l'ardeur qui nous consomme, / On s'ennuye
aisément de voir tousjours un homme*' (593–4), but irony is never far
from the surface, as she follows this remark with a telling
protestation of sincerity and earnestness; nowhere is she less
convinced of what she says than in these lines:

> *Ne vous flattez point tant que ce soit raillerie,*
> *Ce que j'ay dans l'esprit, je ne le puis celer,*
> *Et ne suis pas d'humeur à rien dissimuler.* (602–4)

Lysandre's assertions of love reawaken Célidée's passion, and
from this initial ambiguity in language Corneille now suggests a
solid base of love beneath the *feinte*. The more the heroine
protests that her love is dead, the more the audience is aware of
her own delight in the affection she has inspired in the hero,
and which she is now only too happy to reciprocate:

> *Tout cela n'est qu'autant de propos superflus,*
> *Je voulus vous aimer, et je ne le veux plus;*
> *Mon feu fut sans raison, ma glace l'est de mesme,*
> *Si l'un fut excessif, je rendray l'autre extreme.* (611–14)

The force of these lines is particularly interesting, revealing
again in the heroine a blend of spontaneity and deception. On
one level, the words reflect that doubt and inconstancy which
was apparent earlier in Act II Scene 5 when, indeed, the change
of affection seemed quite sudden, arbitrary, '*sans raison*'. But at
the same time, the lines imply the renewed passion of the
speaker. Célidée is certain now of Lysandre's love and of her
own, and this new found confidence in her feelings gives her
the courage to see earlier hesitation in terms of complete self-
mastery.

This scene of indifference is, however, not the only occasion
on which Célidée resorts to play-acting. More than any other
heroine of the time, this character's constant recourse to a role is
given particular psychological suggestiveness. In Act III Scene 4,
delighted by her success, Célidée resolves to prove to Hippolyte
the intensity of Lysandre's passion, preening herself on the
power she so obviously exercises over the hero:

> *Je presumois beaucoup de ses affections,*
> *Mais je n'attendois pas tant de submissions.*
> *Jamais le desespoir qui saisit son courage*
> *N'en pût tirer un mot à mon desadvantage,*
> *Il tenoit mes desdains encor trop precieux,*
> *Et ses reproches mesme estoient officieux.* (823–8)

The heroine now sees herself as the omnipotent controller, proposing to continue the *feinte* for just a moment longer, to seem harsh so that the love which she will then reveal to Lysandre will be all the more intensely felt by him. However, what so often characterises the establishment of comic order, the revelation of harmony and joy beneath apparent sorrow, is here cast in an ironical light. Corneille deliberately sows the seeds of a happy *dénouement* in the third Act, only to avert it at once. Lysandre has been persuaded to feign indifference on his own account, and Célidée's plan is foiled as she is taken in by the more convincing performance of her lover: '*Adore qui voudra vostre rare merite, / Un change heureux me donne à la belle Hippolite*' (865–6).

The jealousy which Corneille subsequently suggests in Célidée is particularly discreet. In a similar situation in du Ryer's *Amarillis*, Act III Scene 1, the heroine is persuaded that the hero loves her rival Callirée; her consequent suffering is quite openly expressed in words of violent accusation:

> *Infidele Berger, où la mesme malice,*
> *Fait luire ouvertement son funeste artifice!*
> *Deloyal, inconstant, que tes affections*
> *Tromperent doucement mes jeunes passions!* (p. 53)

Célidée however, is much less spontaneous. She tries to persuade Lysandre that she is quite unmoved by his infidelity, adopting once more her role of aloofness and taking refuge behind this linguistic façade. She insists on her indifference for the hero, severing all links with him:

> *Tant s'en faut que je prenne une si triste gloire,*
> *Je chasse mes desdains mesme de ma memoire,*
> *Et dans leur souvenir rien ne me semble doux,*
> *Puisque, le conservant, je songerois à vous.* (873–6)

The lines may express scorn, but beneath them the character's suffering is quite clear. Her eagerness to forget the disdain of the previous encounter is inspired not only by her lost love for Lysandre, but also by her regret at this ill-fortuned experiment. It

is only in the last line, with the bold effort of the *puisque*, that
Célidée manages to redirect words which only barely conceal her
love. Such feelings are finally implied in the explosion which
marks her exit, the adoption of any excuse to flee from a scene in
which she can no longer play her part: *'Viens avec moy, Florice: /J'ay
des nippes en haut que je te veux monstrer'* (906–7). It is not
uncommon in plays of this time for heroines to lament that they
cannot sustain reproval of their loved ones. In Mareschal's *La
Généreuse Allemande*, Act I Scene 3, for instance, Camille remarks
thus how anger constantly gives way to love:

> *Si mon esprit medite un discours rigoureux,*
> *Ma bouche n'a pour luy que des mots amoureux,*
> *Et découvrant le vray dans l'oubly de ma feinte*
> *Je luy parle d'amour au plus fort de ma plainte.* (p. 20)

In Célidée, however, Corneille does not simply describe this
charming persistence of love, but actually suggests it through the
very language she uses.

Corneille's particular subtlety is apparent, too, in Act IV Scene
3 when Célidée is seen to court Dorimant. The depiction on stage
of a girl offering her heart to a man who does not love her is not
uncommon in plays of the time. In Rayssiguier's *La Bourgeoise*,
Act III Scene 5, the scheming *bourgeoise* offers herself to Acrise,
having persuaded him that his love for Cloris is vain. The
speaker's cynicism and lack of nobility are stressed in these lines,
as she proposes a cowardly change of affection, rather than
suicide, as the answer to the hero's despair:

> *Ce dessein imprudent offence un honeste homme,*
> *Cherchez d'autre remede au mal qui vous consomme.*
> *Un amour par un autre aïsément se détruit,*
> *Recevez mon conseil, vous en aurez le fruict.* (p. 63)

Similarly, in Rotrou's *Filandre*, Act II Scene 7, Cephise's proposal
to Celidor is presented in an atmosphere of light-hearted villainy.
Having persuaded the hero that his beloved Nerée is unfaithful,
she now proceeds to tempt him in her direction, using the
traditional logic of the *inconstante*, for whom such changes are
quite natural:

> *Mais vivons, Celidor, et vivons satisfaits:*
> *Fuis ce que tu chéris, aime ce que tu hais;*
> *Reconnois la fidèle, et punis l'inconstante;*
> *Rends Nerée enragée, et Céphise contente.* (II, p. 560)[10]

Corneille's use of the encounter, however, is quite particular. While the words of the other heroines express their love for the one they address, Corneille suggests in Célidée a greater complexity of feeling. On one level, her attraction to Dorimant is quite genuine and reflects her earlier inclination of Act II, but at the same time her declaration is motivated by a certain amount of personal frustration. She tries to turn Dorimant away from Hippolyte in lines which imply coldness and calculation:

> Son objet, tout aimable et tout parfait qu'il est,
> N'a des charmes pour luy que depuis qu'il vous plaist,
> Et vostre affection, de la sienne suivie,
> Monstre que c'est par là qu'il en a pris envie,
> Qu'il veut moins l'acquerir que vous la desrober, (1127–31)

but whereas both the *bourgeoise* and Cephise simply put their feelings into words, Célidée's lines suggest more than they say. She seemingly offers herself to Dorimant here, but in the lines is apparent, too, her persistent sense of hurt over Lysandre's infidelity and a stubborn refusal to accept the power of Hippolyte's beauty. Her words may be intended partly to turn Dorimant's affection away from her rival, but they imply also an attempt to convince herself that Lysandre has no genuine love for the girl, nor she any influence over him. She argues as much for her own benefit as for Dorimant's and her love for the hero is clear, even at this point when she seemingly abandons him.

Further discreet comedy is suggested at the end of Act IV, as the hesitating heroine is assured by her father of Lysandre's continued love. The irony implied in a girl's resistance to a proposed partner not because of genuine incompatibility but out of *dépit* is found already in Rotrou's *Diane*. Filemon happily proposes to join together his daughter Orante with Ariste, unaware that they both suspect each other of infidelity. In Act IV Scene 2, he persuades her that Ariste's accusations are born of love: 'Simple, tout ce mépris prouve un amour extrême, / Et vous devez l'aimer pour son offense même' (I, p. 310), but the scene ends with the heroine's charming lament, clearly still hurt by her jealousy: 'Dure et fâcheuse loi qu'impose la naissance, / De soumettre nos voeux à notre obéissance' (p. 310).

In *La Galerie du Palais*, Act IV Scene 8, Pleirante similarly casts aside his daughter's doubts, assuring her of Lysandre's love:

> *Folle, il n'aima jamais que toy dessous les Cieux,*
> *Et nous sommes tous prests de choisir la journée*
> *Qui bien tost de vous deux termine l'Hymenée.*
> *Il se plaint toutefois un peu de ta froideur,*
> *Mais pour l'amour de moy, montre luy plus d'ardeur,* (1368–72)

and like Rotrou's heroine, Célidée is left alone to reflect. She sees herself as the victim of her father's tyranny, compelled to marry the partner whom she claims not to love:

> *Dures extremitez où mon sort est reduit!*
> *On donne mes faveurs à celuy qui les fuit;*
> *Nous avons l'un pour l'autre une pareille haine,*
> *Et l'on m'attache à luy d'une eternelle chaisne.* (1407–10)

Like Rotrou, Corneille suggests here the persistence of love beneath a hesitating obedience to parental authority, but he goes much further than this. As the speech progresses, all dramatic pretence is dropped, and there is revealed beneath it that feeling of uncertainty and the need for protective stability which have been constantly apparent in the presentation of this character. Célidée is always one to take refuge in a role, to protect herself from others and her own feelings behind a mask which she can only uncomfortably uphold. Behind the heroic outbursts of this speech, Corneille reveals the troubled mind of a girl whose insecurity is suggestively mingled with pride:

> *Je ne sçay quoy me flatte, et je sens déja bien*
> *Que mon feu ne dépend que de croire le sien.*
> *Tout-beau, ma passion, c'est déja trop paroistre:*
> *Attends, attends du moins la sienne pour renaistre.* (1415–18)

There is a clarity of insight in this speech, a revelation of confused and complex feelings which merges with a hint of self-irony. Célidée is aware of her love for Lysandre; she may be loath to admit it to herself, yet it is apparent even in her most wilful heroic fury:

> *L'ingrat cherche ma peine, et veut par sa malice*
> *Que la rigueur d'un pere augmente mon supplice.*
> *Rentrons, que son objet presenté par hazard*
> *De mon coeur ébranlé ne reprenne une part:*
> *C'est bien assez qu'un pere à souffrir me destine,*
> *Sans que mes yeux encor aident à ma ruine.* (1421–6)

4
> Celidée, il est vray, je te suis desloyale;
> Tu me crois ton amie, et je suis ta rivale:
> Si je te puis resoudre à suivre mon conseil,
> Je t'enleve et me donne un bon-heur sans pareil.[11]

Most critical attention is focused on Célidée and the particular complexity of her feelings; little time is spent on Hippolyte. Her role in the action is technically that of mere villainess, the *amie rivale*, a role familiar in plays of the time. In du Ryer's *Amarillis*, Callirée tries to separate Amarillis and Philidor, by telling the heroine that her beloved also loves her, and the same part is played by Rayssiguier's *bourgeoise*, who, from the first scene in the play is quite open about her plans:

> En ce cas on met tout au rang des ennemis,
> Il n'est crime en aymant, qui ne nous soit permis,
> Pour obtenir le bien où nostre flamme aspire,
> Pourveu que nous rions n'importe qui souspire. (pp. 6–7)

In the presentation of Hippolyte's villainy, however, Corneille demonstrates a sensitive interest in her motives and possible suffering. In Act II Scene 4, she may protest her treacherous intentions to steal Lysandre from Célidée but far from suggesting a simple dramatic *déclic*, there is a hint already of that complex search for happiness in love which so characterises her.

To some extent, the character falls into the tradition of the *fille gaie*, the girl who is untouched by love and who can happily control importunate suitors. In Act II Scene 1, for instance, she exhibits a charming vanity as she silences the pleading Dorimant:

> Ce grand et prompt effet m'asseure puissamment
> De la vivacité de vostre jugement.
> Pour moy, que la nature a faite un peu grossiere,
> Mon esprit, qui n'a pas cette vive lumiere,
> Conduit trop pesamment toutes ses fonctions
> Pour m'advertir si tost de vos perfections. (375–80)

Such a type appears in other plays of the time, and dramatists are certainly alive to possible suggestions of tension between words of *gaieté* and actual suffering. In Rotrou's *Céliane*, for example, Julie speaks lines of delightful unconcern as she comforts a lamenting lover spurned by the one he loves:

> M'as-tu vue autrefois conserver un souci?
> Que tu serois content si tu vivois ainsi!

> *Veux-tu joindre les noms d'heureux et de fidèle?*
> *Il faut que mon humeur te serve de modèle . . .* (II, p. 305)

but later in the scene the dramatist reveals that this *désinvolture* only serves to disguise the heroine's hopeless love for the one she has been comforting:

> *En l'état où je suis que cette crainte est vaine,*
> *Et que je veux en vain dissimuler ma peine!*
> *C'est un foible moyen envers cet inconstant*
> *Que de me plaindre peu lorsque je souffre tant.* (p. 307)

In Hippolyte, however, Corneille suggests greater complexity than that implied in this simple juxtaposition of different moods.

In Act III Scene 5, for instance, she finds herself courted by Lysandre. The hero's feigned effusions have a primary comic function, of course, insofar as they deliver an appropriate punishment for Célidée, hoist with her own petard. Corneille is interested, too, however, in the implications of the *feinte* as far as Hippolyte is concerned: in Act III Scene 6, the performance continues, even when Célidée has left the stage. Hippolyte's initial reaction implies on one level her consummate villainy as she encourages the hero in this courtship of her, by carefully insisting on his former love for Célidée:

> *Allez, Lisandre, allez, c'est assez de contraintes;*
> *J'ay pitié du tourment que vous donnent ces feintes,*
> *Suivez ce bel objet dont les charmes puissants*
> *Sont et seront tousjours absolus sur vos sens.* (909–12)

And yet these words suggest at the same time the speaker's own disbelief at the effectiveness of her scheming; jealousy of Célidée is touchingly implied here as she acknowledges to herself her rival's power over the hero. She is quite unable to tell whether Lysandre is feigning love or not.

The scene is a fascinating variation of Hippolyte's earlier meeting with Dorimant in Act II Scene 1 which again brought together passionate declaration and cold response. Here, a similar scene is acted out, but between a lover who clearly has no love at all, and an aloof lady whose indifference is only feigned. Hippolyte rejects the effusions of her suitor for the conventional reasons of their exaggeration and illogicality. She plays her part to perfection, underlining the folly of the words addressed to her:

> *Espargnez avec moy ces propos affettez,*
> *Encor hier Celidée avoit ces qualitez,*
> *Encor hier en merite elle estoit sans pareille,*
> *Si je suis aujourd'huy cette unique merveille,*
> *Demain quelque autre objet, dont vous suivrez la loy,*
> *Gaignera vostre coeur et ce tiltre sur moy,* (939–44)

just as she had rejected Dorimant's declaration in the earlier scene:

> *Cessez aussi, Monsieur, de vous l'imaginer,*
> *Veu que, si vous m'aymez, ce ne sont pas merveilles.*
> *J'ay de pareils discours chaque jour aux oreilles,*
> *Et tous les gens d'esprit en font autant que vous.* (364–7)

But again her words imply more than they say, more than just the traditional criticism of valueless rhetoric, which was seen in the first chapter to be a popular comic scene in plays of the time. Corneille takes a traditional theme and uncovers beneath it a more suggestive complexity of motive. Behind Hippolyte's aloofness is implied an intense attraction and longing for love; it is not Lysandre's passion which she rejects, but rather the language with which it is expressed, language which carries with it the possibility of infidelity and suffering which she is so eager to avoid.

Victims of feigned courtships are not uncommon in plays before this. In Claveret's *L'Esprit fort*, Orante is deceived by Orilame but is quite able to forget her love for him when the deception comes to light in Act IV Scene 3:

> *Se vanter que je l'ayme, & me joüer ce traict?*
> *Le perfide qu'il est n'aura plus mon portraict . . .*
> *Qu'en faveur d'Angelie il exerce sa veine,*
> *Je me riray de voir son esperance vaine . . .* (pp. 83–4)

Similarly, in Mairet's *Les Galanteries du duc d'Ossonne*, Act V Scene 11, Flavie is quick to plot revenge when she learns that the duke has only feigned love for her: '*Ha! si comme je pense il m'a joué ce tour, / Foi de femme irritée, à beau jeu, beau retour . . .*' (1328–9). Such a character appears twice also in early plays of du Ryer. In *Lisandre et Caliste*, Act IV Scene 4, the deceived heroine reflects on the trickery of Lisandre which has clearly hurt her:

> *Le traistre languissant pour une feinte playe*
> *Dans mon coeur amoureux en a fait une vraye,*
> *Et ce perfide auteur de mon premier ennuy*
> *Me vint offrir un coeur qui n'estoit plus à luy . . .* (p. 112)

and in *Alcimédon*, the credulous Rodope moves from a reaction of violent anger in Act III Scene 4 to a more suggestive desire to deceive herself, prepared to act out scenes of love with the hero, however insincere she knows him to be:

> *Le courroux d'une amante à peine dure un jour,*
> *Et venant de l'amour, c'est un signe d'amour.*
> *Ayme ailleurs, feins pour moy, j'arresteray mes larmes,*
> *La feinte qui nous flatte a mesme quelques charmes.* (pp. 107–8)

What characterises all these heroines is the clarity of their realisation and the emotional flexibility they exhibit in coming to terms with it. Corneille, however, suggests Hippolyte's consciousness of this deception in more subtle ways, as she is seen constantly to struggle against the truth, unable to face up to the fact that she is not loved. In Act IV Scene 1, she learns from Aronte that Lysandre loves none other than Célidée, and when she meets the hero again in Act IV Scene 5 she tries to have him admit the cause of his suffering:

> *Ce visage enflammé, ces yeux pleins de colere,*
> *Me sont de vostre peine une marque assez claire.*
> *Encor qui la sçauroit, on pourroit adviser*
> *A prendre des moyens propres à l'appaiser.* (1265–8)

On one level, Hippolyte plays here the traditional role of comforter who elicits a lament from a desperate lover. However, for this character who knows only too well that Lysandre suffers out of love for her rival, this conventional act of mercy suggests a more fascinating form of self-punishment. At the end of the scene, she makes a final protestation of power over the one who had courted her so fluently in the previous Act:

> *Vous faites le secret, mais je le veux sçavoir,*
> *Et par là sur vostre ame essayer mon pouvoir.*
> *Hier vous m'en donniez tant que j'estime impossible*
> *Que pour me contenter rien vous soit trop sensible.* (1271–4)

Her lines contain strained and barely concealed irony, for while they express on the surface a continued belief that the hero loves her, they reflect on a deeper level the realisation that her suit is vain and all hope of happiness lost. Behind claims of control lies a clear admission of her own powerlessness.

Hippolyte's subsequent meeting with Célidée in Act IV Scene 6 is one of several such scenes in comedy of the time when female

rivals encounter each other and attempt to disguise the fact that
they love. In Mareschal's *L'Inconstance d'Hylas*, Act II Scene 5,
Florice and Dorinde meet and both claim absolute indifference to
the faithless Hylas:

Dorinde:	*La voix n'est que du vent, il parle, & ce langage*
	Ne sçauroit estre pris pour un noeud qui l'engage.
Florice:	*Les pieds suivent le coeur où l'on va chaque jour,*
	On ne s'entretient pas si souvent sans amour. (p. 52)

And in Claveret's *L'Esprit fort*, Act III Scene 1, the rival sisters
Orante and Celirée both have an assignation with Orilame, and
each tries to send the other away on a hastily invented errand:

> *Va, cours, tu trouveras de l'ombrage au Chasteau;*
> *Ma soeur ne sçais tu pas que faute d'exercice*
> *Une fille amoureuse a souvent la jaunisse,*
> *Et que le travail aide à la digestion?*
> *Prens pour toy ce conseil de mon affection.* (p. 49)

In both scenes, the comic effect derives from the obvious
discrepancy between the love which the speakers feel and their
awkward attempts to express indifference. Corneille's meeting of
rivals is, however, more suggestive than this.

Hippolyte has lines of scarcely disguised aggression, counter-
ing the earlier vanity of Célidée by now preening herself on the
attentions of Lysandre:

> *Il ne tient pas à luy que je ne sois un Ange,*
> *Et quand il vient aprés à parler de ses feux,*
> *Aucune passion jamais n'approcha d'eux.*
> *Par tous ces vains discours il croit fort qu'il m'oblige,*
> *Mais non la moitié tant qu'alors qu'il te neglige.* (1302–6)

The role of the *fille gaie* is here played with deliberate intent to
arouse her rival's jealousy, her protestations of friendship being a
covert but cruel reminder that Lysandre had abandoned Célidée
for her. Had the lines been spoken after the first interview of
Hippolyte and Lysandre in Act III Scene 6, the comic impact
would have been thus quite unambiguous. However, placing it
after Hippolyte's second meeting with the hero in Act IV Scene 5,
Corneille gives greater suggestiveness to the speech. What she
says about Lysandre's attentions no longer corresponds to the
truth. She suffers no less than Célidée here, and her lines reflect
another attempt to convince herself of what she knows to be false:

that Lysandre is in love with her. Suffering is suggested behind
the aggressive role she plays.

A new order is sketched out in this scene, as Célidée proposes
the exchange of lovers which was seen to be so effortless in plays
of the time. Harmony seems to be possible:

> *Si Lisandre te plaist, possede le volage,*
> *Mais ne me traite point avec desadvantage,*
> *Et si tu te resous d'accepter mon amant,*
> *Relasche moy du moins le coeur de Dorimant.* (1313–16)

But in this formulation, Corneille is not simply reproducing a
traditionally flexible attitude to love. Behind Célidée's words of
rejection Corneille hints at her persistent feelings of affection,
and although she may try here to persuade herself that the hero
means nothing more to her, the telling phrase *'mon amant'*
suggests that this love cannot be so easily quelled. And indeed, in
Hippolyte's reaction to this proposal there are further hints of
self-deception. She may continue to hurt Célidée by damning
Lysandre, and yet, as before, she is clearly eager to persuade
herself of his possible love for her:

> *Je te repute heureuse apres l'avoir perdu.*
> *Que son humeur est vaine, et qu'il fait l'entendu!*
> *Mon Dieu! qu'il est chargeant avec ses flatteries!*
> *Qu'on est importuné de ses affetteries!*
> *Vrayment, si tout le monde estoit fait comme luy,*
> *Je pense avant deux jours que je mourrois d'ennuy.* (1323–8)

The scene is comic, of course, on one level. Each character speaks
words which the audience knows not to correspond to the truth
of her feelings, each acts out a role for the benefit of the other. Yet
emphasis on these masks is intended by Corneille to suggest not
only simple comic discrepancies, but to indicate the feelings
which lie behind them. The two heroines try to see and present
themselves as other than they are and know themselves to be, yet
they fail to convince.

5

tant y a qu'avant que nous séparer nous fusmes tellement remis en nostre bon
sens, ainsi le faut-il dire, que nous recogneusmes le peu de raison qu'il y avoit de
nous soupçonner les uns les autres.[12]

Tales of jealousy and suspicion among lovers are certainly popular
at this time, but by the final scenes order is always happily re-
established. In an early story from *L'Astrée*, Astrée herself tells
how she and Phillis had suspected each other of attempting to steal
each other's lover; the misunderstanding, however, came to light,
and the characters were returned to their former tranquillity and
'*bon sens*', unhurt by the incident. Such trouble-free reconciliations
are a characteristic of many plays of the period. In Scudéry's *Le
Trompeur puny*, Act III Scene 5, Nérée forgets at once her angry
suspicion of the hero as soon as it is revealed that a villain lay
behind the deception:

> Cette preuve suffit, & n'est que trop certaine.
> Allez vous retirer, voicy venir la Reine,
> Et chassez le passé de vostre souvenir, (p. 67)

and even when actual infidelity has taken place, the transition to
order is swift and effortless. In Rotrou's *Céliane*, Act V Scene 8,
Florimant's temporary faithlessness to the heroine leads swiftly to
repentance: '*Un secret repentir me rend mes premiers fers; / Celiane est
sensible aux maux que j'ai soufferts*' (II, p. 334), and in Mairet's *Les
Galanteries du duc d'Ossonne*, Act V Scene 6, the duke expresses the
feelings of unconditional forgiveness shared by all four protagonists as they forget their earlier trickery of each other:

> Comte, donnons-leur donc, pour éviter querelle,
> Cette légère faute au sexe naturelle;
> Ou bien, puisque entre nous le scandale est égal,
> Entreconcédons-nous un pardon général. (1644–7)

In the *dénouement* of *La Galerie du Palais*, however, Corneille seeks
to suggest a greater complexity of feelings which, although it may
not affect the aesthetic framework of the play, implies a keenness
of analysis which is rare in plays of this time.

Act V Scene 4 depicts the final reconciliation of Célidée and
Lysandre, the gradual peeling away of pretence and illusion, and
the spontaneous expression of mutual love. The hero is presented
in a charming light as he speaks the violent language of the tragi-
comic lover, still believing that Célidée is unfaithful to him:

> Vous lirez dans mon sang, à vos pieds respandu,
> La valeur d'un amant que vous aurez perdu,
> Et sans vous reprocher un si cruel outrage,
> Ma main de vos rigueurs achevera l'ouvrage. (1575–8)

Such discreet deflation of words of despair is apparent, too, in du Ryer's *Alcimédon*, Act II Scene 3, in which the hero longs for death at the hands of his beloved, quite unaware that she loves him:

> *Ouvre, ouvre-moy le sein, arrache-moy le coeur,*
> *Et le porte sanglant aux yeux de son vainqueur,*
> *Et si pour ce dessein tu manques de courage,*
> *Je presteray ma main à ce funeste ouvrage.* (p. 40)

In Célidée's reply, Corneille suggests the heroine's touching refusal to believe what she most fervently wishes to be true; behind lines of protested disbelief, love is everywhere apparent:

> *Moy, du pouvoir sur vous! vos yeux se sont mépris,*
> *Et quelque illusion qui trouble vos esprits*
> *Vous fait imaginer d'estre auprés d'Hyppolite.*
> *Allez, volage, allez où l'amour vous invite.* (1583–6)

This charming mixture of doubt and delight is found in several *dénouements* of the time, when characters catch a glimpse of happiness and yet hesitate to believe it. In Beys' *Le Jaloux sans sujet*, Act IV Scene 2, the heroine Arthémise is similarly reluctant to believe that Erace is still faithful to her:

> *Pour t'ouïr souspirer, ne crois pas que je pleure,*
> *Je ne crains point icy de causer ton trespas,*
> *Ton deuil est faux, je sçay que tu n'en mourras pas.*
> *Le traistre sçait bien feindre un amoureux martire,* (pp. 71–2)

and in Rotrou's *Diane*, Act V Scene 3, Orante is unwilling to accept the evidence of Ariste's love in his anguished self-accusations, longing, yet fearing to believe that she is still worthy of his affection:

> *Je connois mes défauts, et sais que l'amitié*
> *De qui daigne m'aimer est digne de pitié;*
> *Je ne vous crois, Monsieur, aveugle ni coupable;*
> *Je ne condamne point un discours véritable,*
> *Et vous n'avez failli qu'en ce point seulement*
> *Que vous m'avez traitée encor trop doucement.* (I, p. 326)

It is a form of reconciliation in which discretion and charm replace the bombast and rhetorical excess of so many heroes and heroines; feelings of love are suggested, rather than mightily proclaimed.

Corneille, however, takes this charm further than his contemporaries, suggesting greater depth behind the words his lovers use. Célidée is led to reproach Lysandre for his credulity and doubt, affirming that her initial indifference was only feigned:

> Volage, falloit-il, pour un peu de rudesse,
> Vous porter si soudain à changer de maistresse?
> Que je vous croyois bien d'un jugement plus meur!
> Ne pouviez vous souffrir de ma mauvaise humeur?
> Ne pouviez vous juger que c'estoit une feinte
> A dessein d'éprouver quelle estoit vostre atteinte? (1617–22)

The lines are in themselves quite traditional. In Claveret's *L'Esprit fort*, Act V Scene 4, Angelie accounts thus for her earlier indifference to the hero:

> Orilame il est vray que vos perfections
> Ont tousjours peu beaucoup sur mes affections;
> Et j'ay feint à dessein de l'amour pour un autre
> Affin de juger mieux de la grandeur du vostre, (p. 126)

and the same attitude is expressed by Melisée in a similar situation in Scudéry's *L'Amour caché par l'amour*, Act V Scene 4:

> Trop amoureux Berger sçaches que ma rigueur
> Ne fut jamais d'accord au sentiment du coeur.
> Pour esprouver le tien, je me feignois cruelle,
> Et je bruslois pourtant d'une ardeur mutuelle. (1156–9)

Finally, in Scudéry's *Le Fils supposé*, Act V Scene 5, Luciane reproaches the jealous Oronte for being foolish enough to doubt her love:

> Et bien jaloux Oronte, estiez-vous raisonnable?
> Vostre faute commise est elle pardonnable?
> Ce soupçon mal fondé n'est-il pas criminel?
> Et n'en aurez-vous point un remords eternel? (p. 118)

Célidée's words, however, are more suggestive than these, as they bring together a curious blend of falsehood and truth. What she says about Lysandre is appropriate equally to her own behaviour in the play; behind this traditional role of self-justification, Corneille suggests also his heroine's self-reproach at her own mistaken belief in the hero's feigned indifference and her hurried change of affection. Célidée, no less than Lysandre, was not certain enough of their love, and she knows it.

This implied insecurity is more apparent in the lines which
follow these, as she makes a statement which is clearly false:

> *Les Dieux m'en soient témoins, et ce nouveau sujet*
> *Que vos feux inconstants ont choisi pour objet,*
> *Si jamais j'eus pour vous de dédain veritable*
> *Avant que vostre amour parust si peu durable!* (1623–6)

Here, as before, Célidée seeks to convince herself of the
assurance of her feelings. She plays the part of one in absolute
control in order to disguise from herself the uncertainty which so
characterised her in the earlier scenes, and she attempts here to
re-write the sequence of events so that she may have the power
over both the action and herself which, in reality, she so
manifestly lacked. Not only does she underestimate now the
complexity and vagueness of her motives in the initial *feinte*, but
she also seeks to deny the love which caused her such suffering in
moments of what she now claims to have been '*dédain véritable*'.

This uncertainty finally spills out as Célidée implies that she is
as much to blame as Lysandre, and that a lesson has been learnt
by the incident:

> *Si nous avons failly de feindre l'un et l'autre,*
> *Pardonnez à ma faute, et j'oublieray la vostre.*
> *Moy-mesme je l'advoüe à ma confusion,*
> *Mon imprudence a fait nostre division.*
> *Tu ne meritois pas de si rudes alarmes:*
> *Accepte un repentir accompagné de larmes.* (1641–6)

The characters have been changed a little by their experience, and
they are unable just to shrug it off with amused irony. And
indeed, at the end of the scene, Corneille hints again, with the
very lightest of touches, at the insecurity of his heroine. Hurt
pride and fear merge suggestively as she hurries off the stage on
the arrival of Dorimant and Hippolyte; having accepted her role
as Lysandre's beloved, she is eager to avoid all subsequent
pressure on herself:

Lysandre: *Vous craignez qu'à vos yeux cette belle Hyppolite*
           N'ait encor de ma bouche un hommage hypocrite?
Célidée: *Non, je fuy Dorimant qu'ensemble j'apperçoy;*
           Je ne veux plus le voir, puis que je suis à toy. (1665–8)

The lovers leave the stage reconciled, as they should be, and yet
this reconciliation has taken place in no facile way. In Célidée's

acceptance of Lysandre, Corneille suggests not simply her spontaneous expression of affection, but a refuge, a role which she plays in order to protect herself from her own frailty.

The meeting of Hippolyte and Dorimant which immediately follows this scene, seemingly continues the familiar movement towards harmony and order, presenting the expected softening of the aloof girl to the persistent and unridiculous suit of her lover. Although she may still love another, it is suggested that she is not absolutely insensitive to Dorimant's charms. The union of this second couple, hinted at already in Lysandre's observation of Act II Scene 3, '*Tu verras sa froideur se perdre tout d'un coup*' (460), is taken a stage further here:

> *Vous devez presumer de vos perfections*
> *Que si vous attaquiez un coeur qui fut à prendre,*
> *Il seroit malaisé qu'il s'en peust bien defendre;*
> *Vous auriez eu le mien, s'il n'eust esté donné.* (1704–7)

Hippolyte is given lines which suggest the kind of emotional flexibility so typical of characters at this time, whose feelings can be re-channelled anywhere in the interests of harmony. She speaks words characteristic of the secondary figure, contemplating a possible change of affection and making a familiar promise to the patient adorer:

> *Je cheris sa personne, et hay si peu la vostre,*
> *Qu'ayant perdu l'espoir de le voir mon espoux,*
> *Si ma mere y consent, Hyppolite est à vous.* (1718–20)

Her lines echo the promises of Philène to Dorise in Mairet's *Sylvie*, Act V Scene 1, or this of Clorifée to Caliante in La Croix, *Climène*,[13] Act III Scene 1, who proposes to forget her love of Silandre:

> *Si Silandre ne veut oublier sa Climène,*
> *Et si mon coeur un jour peut mespriser sa haine,*
> *Changeant d'affection je recevray vos voeus*
> *Pour vous rendre à la fin content & bien heureus.* (pp. 38–9)

Corneille continues on this traditional path, suggesting the apparent immunity to suffering of his character. In Act V Scene 6, Lysandre simply disowns the love he has feigned for Hippolyte, underlining the order which is expected of comedy and leaving the way open for the double marriage which will be inevitable.

All notions of jealousy, conflict and hurt are held to be out of
place, as he assures Dorimant that he loves Célidée alone:

> *Dissipe, cher amy, cette jalouse atteinte,*
> *C'est l'objet de tes feux, et celuy de ma feinte.*
> *Mon coeur fut tousjours ferme, et moy je me dédis*
> *Des voeux que de ma bouche elle receut jadis.* (1733–6)

For many victims of feigned courtships in plays of the time
such transitions are indeed quite effortless or unambiguous. In
Claveret's *L'Esprit fort*, Act IV Scene 6, the deceived Orante
happily forgets Orilame, whom she had once loved, in order to
accept the suit of another lover: *'Ma soeur, de tres bon coeur je te cede
Orilame, / Une plus noble ardeur triomphe de mon âme'* (p. 94), and in
du Ryer's *Alcimédon*, Act V Scene 5, Rodope gives up her love for
the hero in a noble gesture of generosity:

> *Joüissez, chers amans, des voluptez du calme,*
> *Joignez à vostre Mirthe une agreable Palme,*
> *Je cede sans regret, & de ma volonté,*
> *Ce qu'un autre rendroit à la necessité.* (p. 135)

In *Lisandre et Caliste*, the movement is slightly more complex as du
Ryer inserts in Act V Scene 1, a scene of angry accusation between
Hippolyte and her deceiver Lisandre:

> *J'accuseray tousjours vos discours criminels*
> *Dont la feinte me plonge en des maux éternels,*
> *Et qui ne peuvent rendre à mon âme asservie*
> *La douce liberté que vous m'avez ravie,* (p. 124)

but from this dramatic outburst emerges total and unconditional
reconciliation as the heroine accepts the husband proposed for
her with no explicit or implicit suggestion of self-sacrifice; she
obeys royal command, and acknowledges the greater importance
of her rival's happiness:

> *Le respect que je doibs à vostre Majesté*
> *M'a fait tousjours fléchir sous vostre volonté,*
> *Et le bien qui finit les ennuis de Caliste*
> *Rend mon coeur plus content, qu'il n'avoit esté triste.* (p. 137)

In *La Galerie du Palais*, however, Corneille presents a far more
suggestive acquiescence. In Act V Scene 7, Hippolyte, like du
Ryer's heroine, is given words of accusation as she suffers from
the deception of others:

> *Qu'auray-je cependant pour satisfaction*
> *D'avoir servy d'objet à vostre fiction?*
> *Dans vostre different je suis la plus blessée,*
> *Et me trouve, à l'accord, entierement laissée.* (1747–50)

Célidée speaks words of reconciliation, suggesting the harmony and forgiveness which is expected at this stage:

> *N'y songe plus, ma soeur, et pour l'amour de moy,*
> *Trouve bon qu'il ait feint de vivre sous ta loy.*
> *Veux-tu le quereller lors que je luy pardonne?*
> *Le droit de l'amitié tout autrement ordonne,* (1751–4)

but Hippolyte, although coaxed into forgiveness, disavows at this very moment her implied love of Dorimant which had seemingly suggested her happy acceptance of this role:

> *A vous dire le vray, j'ay fait une folie;*
> *Je le croyois encor loing de se rëünir,*
> *Et moy, par consequent, bien loing de la tenir.* (1774–6)

Such a disavowal is not without parallel in plays of the time. In Rayssiguier's *La Bourgeoise*, Act IV Scene 3, the heroine makes a promise to her lover Climant:

> *Quand cela sera faict, asseurez-vous Climant*
> *Que je travailleray pour vostre allegement.*
> *Adieu, vivez content apres cette promesse* . . . (p. 84)

only to retract it as soon as he has gone:

> *De ton maistre, & de toy les desseins traversez,*
> *Par mes inventions se verront renversez:*
> *J'avois desja de loin preveu cette menée:*
> *Mais ils ne sont pas près de voir cet hymenée.* (p. 84)

The parallel is interesting, but it throws into relief Corneille's particular sensitivity. Whereas Rayssiguier's heroine is cast largely as the hypocritical schemer, insincere with other characters but quite open with the audience, Hippolyte is both more complex and more touching. Her retraction of a promise does not simply suggest an admission of villainous intent, but reflects more clearly the ambiguity of her feelings. The transference of her affections from Lysandre to Dorimant, which had seemed so convincing to the audience because it was so traditional, is revealed now to be merely a role which is played with reluctance and uncertainty.

In the final scene it is noticeable that, unlike her namesake in du Ryer's play, she does not accept her partner directly. Crysante, her mother, is quite adamant in her refusal to impose a partner on her daughter:

> *Il me souvient encor de tous mes déplaisirs,*
> *Lorsqu'un premier Hymen contraignit mes desirs,*
> *Et sage à mes dépens, je veux bien qu'Hyppolite*
> *Prenne ou laisse, à son choix, un homme de merite,* (1795–8)

and yet Hippolyte is equally insistent that the decision should be taken for her; for one so uncertain, necessity is preferable to choice:

> *Madame, un mot de vous me mettroit hors de peine.*
> *Ce que vous remettez à mon choix d'accorder,*
> *Vous feriez beaucoup mieux de me le commander.* (1802–4)

Nothing may be read into the words themselves, no suggestions of coercion, so traditional are they in their formulation. In Rayssiguier's *Tragi-comédie pastorale*, Act V Scene 4, for instance, Leonide quite happily accepts the suit of Ergaste with reference again to the authority of a parent: '*Monsieur, dont le pouvoir est absolu sur moy,* / *Outre vostre merite, en a donné la loy*' (p. 144). And yet this very conventionality is perhaps the most suggestive part of the *dénouement*. Hippolyte, whose feelings have been apparent beneath the roles she has played throughout the play, becomes at this point absolutely inscrutable; the mask she adopts here is totally opaque. The aesthetic order is seemingly left quite undisturbed, but at the end of the play Corneille suggests again that more may lie behind such familiar formulae, alluding to the traditional and apparently arbitrary nature of the happy ending in comedy. At Florice's suggestion that Pleirante marry Crysante, the mother replies: '*Outre l'aage en tous deux un peu trop refroidie,* / *Cela sentiroit trop sa fin de Comedie*' (1825–6). This parodic observation has been seen simply to indicate Corneille's ironical detachment from the easy harmonies of comedy, his refusal to create marriages for their own sake;[14] such an attitude was seen already in the ending of *Mélite*. In the context of the previous scenes, however, the lines have a greater significance. They embody again what has been implied in the *dénouement* as a whole, suggesting that order is not established with such effortlessness, and that the hearts of characters may not conform so easily to the demands of comic convention.

It is here that the originality of Corneille is most suggestively apparent. In the first chapter, a certain detachment of characters from their roles was examined in the *dénouement* of Rotrou's *Filandre*; in this play, however, such discrepancies were suggested rather than analysed, appended rather arbitrarily to a conventional plot. In *La Galerie du Palais,* on the other hand, such detachment is made apparent throughout the reconciliation of both couples, discreet, but nevertheless sustained. It is not just an ironical undercurrent, but informs the very nature of the *dénouement,* reflecting more subtly a complexity of feeling in the characters which has been examined in the course of the comedy, and of which it is the logical consequence.

6

De six Comedies qui me sont eschappées, si celle-cy n'est pas la meilleure, c'est la plus heureuse.[15]

In many ways, *La Galerie du Palais* suggests a completely new departure for Corneille in his comic writing. Here is little of that sustained and sophisticated deflation of tragi-comic scenes and characters which had been the hallmark of *Mélite* and *La Veuve,* little delight in the ridiculing of foolish and incompetent villains. Instead, there is a more obvious internalisation of drama and the careful investigation of the heart in search of itself. Nevertheless, its development from the earliest plays is clear. Here comic effects derive again from language which is given its full significance through the audience's awareness of context and speaker. In the laments of Lysandre, and in the encounter of the two rival heroes, discrepancies between the character and his role lead to a delightful distance from drama and laughter at the expense of lovers taking up inappropriately heroic stances. In the presentation of the two heroines, these same techniques are then developed for more subtle effects. Behind masks so readily adopted Corneille reveals characters who seek either to protect themselves from disturbed and largely uncontrollable emotions or from the probing of others. If *Mélite* and *La Veuve* exploited the comic relationship of the actor and his role, *La Galerie du Palais* looks more closely now at the actor and his feelings.

Like his earliest plays, *La Galerie du Palais* has many features in common with other comedies and tragi-comedies of the period:

topical allusions, the use of the *feinte*, the interest in the nature of love and lovers. Corneille certainly does not innovate here in his choice of subject-matter, and yet, once again, the originality of his experiment with such traditional themes is clear. Immediately striking is the unity of the comedy, which brings together to a degree not yet achieved by any of his contemporaries a localised setting and a discreet investigation of feelings. The drama which so often bursts quite obtrusively into other plays is here noticeably absent. More important, though, is Corneille's great sensitivity in the depiction of his protagonists and his ability to suggest through the ambiguities of language the particular complexity of their feelings. Plays of the time frequently present girls who feign indifference or jealously seek their own happiness in love: none, though, has the suggestive depth of either Célidée or Hippolyte. And in the *dénouement*, by tradition so smooth and unproblematical, Corneille implies a final and most suggestive ambiguity. Within the conventional framework of comedy he gives glimpses of hidden or dormant tensions, a look of pain or uncertainty behind the mask which smiles.

V

La Suivante
'Une voix demi-gaie
et demi-serieuse'

1

les fourbes et les intrigues sont principalement du jeu de la Comedie, les passions n'y entrent que par accident.[1]

La Suivante[2] has aroused different reactions among critics. Some dismiss it completely as a comedy which fails either to move or to amuse, and it is often held to be the weakest of Corneille's early plays.[3] Others, however, take it particularly seriously, and highlight in their analyses the curious cruelty implied in the plot[4] or the materialism of the characters,[5] seeing here the presentation of a disturbing social conflict[6] or of tensions between the worlds of money and rank.[7] In general, it is a play which is held not to be essentially comic, and Lancaster's remark (I 2, 609), that it is *'one of the least amusing of Corneille's early comedies'*, crystallises what is implied, if not explicitly stated, in so many critical readings.

Nevertheless, the comedy suggests in its presentation of plot and character a certain comic virtuosity which is largely overlooked by commentators in their thematic studies. From the start of the play, Corneille develops and refines scenes already exploited for comic effect in his earliest works. The relationship of Theante and Florame, for instance, is clearly moulded on that of Eraste and Tirsis in *Mélite*. In the opening scene, Theante explains to Damon how he proposes to undermine the arguments of the *esprit fort*, Florame, by introducing him to his mistress: *'Florame, dis je alors, ton ame indifferente / Ne tiendroit que fort peu contre mon Amarante'* (41–2). However, a project which was a manifestation of incompetence in Eraste, is intended here to be proof of superior guile: Theante proposes thus to rid himself of Amarante in order to have time to court Daphnis, her mistress, whom he really loves. For both schemers, though, the gesture leads to failure and frustration. By introducing Florame to Amarante, Theante gives him access also to Daphnis, with whom inevitably he falls in love; the villain has succeeded only in creating for himself a rival.

When these two characters meet in Act I Scene 3, Corneille develops a sophisticated adaptation of the comic encounter of lover and anti-lover. Each claims that he is more honest and heroic than his counterpart in the earlier comedy: Florame, unlike Tirsis, admits that he is no longer quite insensitive to love, and Theante, unlike Eraste, expresses generous respect for his rival's feelings. And yet, beneath this openness, the true motive of the speakers is made comically apparent.

At the start of the scene, Florame outlines to Theante the irresistible charms of Amarante which threaten to overcome him:

> *Mais l'objet d'Amarante est trop embarassant,*
> *Ce n'est point un visage à ne voir qu'en passant;*
> *Un je ne sçay quel charme aupres d'elle m'attache,*
> *Je ne la puis quitter que le jour ne se cache:*
> *Encor n'est-ce pas tout, son image me suit,*
> *Et me vient au lieu d'elle entretenir la nuit,*
> *Elle entre effrontément jusques dedans ma couche,*
> *Me redit ses propos, me presente sa bouche.* (139–46)

It is a fine evocation of the haunting effect of beauty, but these lines, studied and theatrical as they may be, contain also a second, more spontaneous meaning. Florame's inability to detach himself from Amarante reflects on one level the burgeoning of love, but it expresses, too, the hero's real frustration that he is thus prevented from courting Daphnis. He plays a part for the benefit of his interlocutor, but beneath these words of passion is revealed his own comic annoyance.

The ambiguity here is complemented by that of Theante, resolved to have Florame persist in his courtship of Amarante. His protestations of generosity in the event of defeat hide beneath them his desire that he be 'supplanted' by his rival:

> *Je ne m'en prendray lors qu'à ma seule imprudence,*
> *Et demeurant ensemble en bonne intelligence,*

> *En despit du mal-heur que j'auray merité*
> *J'aimeray le Rival qui m'aura supplanté.* (165–8)

As the scene progresses, the masks adopted by both characters become less and less opaque, their attempts to couch their true motives in heroic and noble terms less and less effective. From accomplished and controlled ambiguity, the characters' language is reduced to that of barely disguised frustration, until finally Florame avows his desire to see Daphnis in a gesture of only slightly convincing self-sacrifice:

> *Separer davantage une amour si parfaite!*
> *Continuer encor la faute que j'ay faite!*
> *Elle n'est que trop grande, et pour la reparer*
> *J'empescheray Daphnis de plus vous separer.* (173–6)

That Corneille is here taking advantage of techniques already used in earlier comedies is clearly underlined in the interview of Theante and Amarante in Act II Scene 12, a scene in which florid, amorous language is seen to express the sheerest contempt and indifference, just as it had done in the meeting of Doris and Alcidon in *La Veuve*. Theante, like Alcidon, is a buffoon, outplayed in his witty game by the versatile servant, who wishes defeat and frustration on her lover in the most longing and loving terms:

> *Tu sçais (et je le dis sans te mésestimer)*
> *Que quand bien ma maistresse aura sceu te charmer,*
> *Vostre inesgalité mettroit hors d'esperance*
> *Les fruits qui seroient deubz à ta perseverance:*
> *Pleust à Dieu que le Ciel te donnast assez d'heur*
> *Pour faire naistre en elle autant que j'ay d'ardeur!* (595–600)

This ridiculing of the ineffectual villain is pursued throughout the comedy; Theante is the comic coward, in the same mould as Philandre, carefully put into situations which cause him to struggle in his uneasily maintained role of generous and sincere friend. In Act IV Scene 6, he tries to lure Florame into a duel with Clarimond, arguing that this other suitor of Daphnis is a serious threat to his friend's love, and yet aiming thus to clear a path for himself; Florame, however, is not deceived. Coward and hero are juxtaposed as they had been in the encounter of Tirsis and Philandre in *Mélite*, Act III Scene 2, but here Corneille sharpens the comic focus. Like Tirsis, Florame is eager to draw swords with this apparent rival, but his expression of anger does not so much reflect the dignity of the hero as the skill of the trickster who carefully lulls his enemy into a false sense of security. In words which barely conceal his villainous intentions, Theante encourages Florame in his plan:

> *Et sans t'espouventer d'une vaine fortune*
> *Qu'il soustient laschement d'une valeur commune,*
> *Ne fais de son orgueil qu'un sujet de mespris,*
> *Et pense que Daphnis ne s'acquiert qu'à ce prix.*
> *Adieu, puisse le Ciel à ton amour parfaite,*
> *Accorder un succez tel que je le souhaite,* (1193–8)

only to find that he has inadvertently committed himself to take part in the fight as his 'friend's' second. Corneille's ridicule of the struggling coward is significantly refined here as Theante is made to revoke all his previous arguments in favour of armed combat, the comic reversal of his attitude being carefully underlined and crystallised in a crescendo of stychomythic exchanges:

Florame: *Clarimond n'eut jamais qu'une valeur commune.*
Theante: *La valeur aux duëls fait moins que la fortune.*
Florame: *C'est par là seulement qu'on merite Daphnis.*
Theante: *Mais plustost de ses yeux par là tu te bannis.* (1225–8)

The villain's fear is beautifully stylised here, his lack of courage matched by superb linguistic and intellectual agility; it is this which is finally stressed above all:

> *Il en parle des mieux, c'est un jeu qui luy plaist,*
> *Mais il devient fort sage aussi tost qu'il en est,*
> *Et montre cependant des graces peu vulgaires*
> *A battre ses raisons par des raisons contraires.* (1239–42)

Two other incidents in these early Acts suggest Corneille's particular comic accomplishment. The first is the sequence of scenes beginning at Act II Scene 4, which present the courtship of Florame and Daphnis, comically interrupted by the servant. A heroine's attempt to rid herself of an unwanted third party is a popular source of comedy at this time. The meeting of Orante and Cellirée in Claveret's *L'Esprit fort* has already been discussed, and in Rotrou's *Cléagenor et Doristée*, Act III Scene 2, Dorante tries frantically to dismiss her servant, Diane, before resorting finally to the blunt command: '*Faites ce qu'il vous plaît, mais tirez-vous d'ici*' (I, p. 213). However, whereas these exchanges between rivals are simply brief interludes before the meeting of lovers, Corneille has Amarante constantly interrupt the protagonists. Her importunity is stylised to a fine degree in a series of mechanical, seemingly inexorable intrusions which elicit from the heroine ever more desperate pretexts to send her away, firstly to another room: 'Amarante, allez voir si dans la galerie / Ils ont bien tost tendu cette tapisserie' (409–10), and finally to another part of the town:

> A propos de Clarine, il m'estoit echappé
> Qu'elle a depuis long temps à moy du point-coupé,
> Allez, et dites-luy qu'elle me le renvoye. (471–3)

However, comedy does not simply derive from the juxtaposition of the unwanted servant and the passionate exchanges of hero and heroine; the conversation of the lovers themselves is viewed in an ironical light. Florame insists that he will declare his feelings in a confident, unselfconscious way, mocking that reticence seen in certain aspiring suitors:

> . . . Je ry de ces amants
> Dont l'importun respect redouble les tourments,
> Et qui pour les cacher se faisant violence
> Pensent fort avancer par un honteux silence. (423–6)

If Philiste was seen to take the advice of d'Urfé's Daphnis, Florame here follows naturally in the path of Hylas, whose advice to Clorian is similarly uncompromising: 'Il faut que celuy qui veut faire ce mestier, ose, entreprenne, demande, et supplie, qu'il importune, qu'il presse, qu'il surprenne, voire qu'il ravisse' (L'Astrée, II 3, p. 116). And yet, having thus announced his position, Florame falls into the most ponderous circumlocution, seemingly quite unable to make the declaration he had so boldly prefaced:

> Sans affront je la quitte, et luy préfere un autre,
> Dont le merite esgal, le rang pareil au vostre,
> L'esprit et les attraits egalement puissants
> Ne devroient de ma part avoir que des encens. (441–4)

His eventual avowal of love does not lead to the lyrical exchange one would expect, but to protestations of incredulity on both sides. Daphnis' lines are those of disarming coyness, her love clearly apparent beneath the words of reproof and doubt:

> *Sans me faire rougir il vous devoit suffire*
> *De me taire l'objet dont vous aimez l'empire,*
> *En nommer un au lieu qui ne vous touche pas*
> *N'est que faire un reproche à son manque d'appas.* (453–6)

These are answered by a complementary speech of disbelief from Florame, which not only contrasts again comically with his earlier claims of confidence, but also underlines the inability of both characters to express their true feelings:

> *Veu le peu que je suis vous dedaignez de croire*
> *Une si malheureuse et si basse victoire;*
> *Mon coeur est un captif si peu digne de vous*
> *Que vos yeux en voudroient desadvouër leurs coups.* (457–60)

External intrusions complement and highlight the lovers' difficulty in finding spontaneity; from a popular comic situation, Corneille develops an encounter of hesitation and charm.

Further comic virtuosity is apparent in the meeting of Daphnis and her importunate suitor, Clarimond, in Act III Scene 2. The rejection of a sighing lover by an aloof lady is an incident which often gives rise to great poetic stylisation in pastoral, the most celebrated instance of this being the accomplished *Dialogue* in Mairet's *Sylvie*, Act I Scene 3, in which the heroine spurns the pleading but unridiculous Philène in an exchange of rhyming couplets lasting some eighty lines:

> Philene: *Comme avecque le temps toute chose se change,*
>   *De même ta rigueur un jour s'adoucira.*
> Sylvie: *Ce sera donc alors que d'une course étrange*
>   *Ce ruisseau révolté contre sa source ira.* (145–8)[8]

In his scene, Corneille demonstrates similar technical mastery, but his purpose is more obviously comic as he emphasises the ineffectuality of a suitor in the face of superior wit; the ironical retorts of Daphnis reveal all that is colourless and banal in Clarimond's pleas:

> Clarimond: *Me quittez vous si tost sans me vouloir guerir?*
> Daphnis: *Clarimond sans Daphnis peut et vivre et mourir.*
> Clarimond: *Je mourray toutesfois si je ne vous possede.*
> Daphnis: *Tenez vous donc pour mort s'il vous faut ce remede.* (739–42)

The comic force of the encounter is further underlined in the fool's subsequent meeting with Amarante. His monologue of despair at this unrequited love ends in a mock-heroic crescendo:

'*Adieu, cruelle ingratte, Adieu, je fuy ces lieux / Pour desrober mon ame au pouvoir de tes yeux*' (759–60), a stance which is then effectively punctured by Amarante's entry and her opening lines of banal and bathetic understatement:

> *Monsieur, Monsieur, un mot. L'air de vostre visage*
> *Tesmoigne un déplaisir caché dans le courage,*
> *Vous quittez ma maistresse un peu mal satisfait.* (761–3)

The comic juxtaposition of bombast and litotes is complemented by Amarante's brilliantly misleading interpretation of the previous scene, as she persuades Clarimond that Daphnis' disdain is not to be taken at face value:

> *Elle vous fait tandis cette galanterie*
> *Pour s'acquerir le bruit de fille bien nourrie,*
> *Et gaigner d'autant plus de reputation*
> *Qu'on la croira forcer son inclination.*
> *Nommez cette maxime ou prudence ou sottise,*
> *C'est la seule raison qui fait qu'on vous mesprise.* (793–8)

The argument is in itself traditional. In Pichou's *Filis de Scire*, Act III Scene 3, Nérée comforts the hero with a similar and just explanation of his apparent rejection by the heroine:

> *Ne desespere point, tu verras que son ame*
> *Dessous un froid mépris cache une ardante flame,*
> *Et que cette Beauté dont tu crains la rigueur*
> *A la haine à la bouche & l'amour dans le coeur.* (p. 66)

However, where in Pichou there is emphasis on drama and conflict both in hero and heroine, in Corneille the focus is purely comic. Amarante wishes to use this suitor in her own scheme for stealing Florame from Daphnis, but his role as the instrument of the *suivante's* villainy is quite subordinate to his more obvious comic function as the credulous dupe. In the monologue which ends the encounter, it is not Amarante's joy at a successful ruse which is stressed, but her amused astonishment at the gullibility of the fool she has deceived:

> *Clarimond est bien vain, ensemble et bien credule*
> *De se persuader que Daphnis dissimule,*
> *Et que ce grand dédain déguise un grand amour,*
> *Que le seul choix d'un pere a droit de mettre au jour.*
> *Il s'en pâme de joye, et dessus ma parole*
> *De tant d'affronts receus son ame se console.* (813–18)

2

> *Accorde qui pourra le pere avec la fille,*
> *Ils ont l'esprit troublé dedans cette famille.*[9]

Corneille's development of comic situations is most obviously
sustained, however, in the scenes of confusion which dominate
the second half of the play. Hero and heroine are first led falsely
to believe that their love has been authorised, and then, equally
falsely, that they are to be forced apart. The untimely suggestion
of order which was a significant feature of both *La Veuve* and *La
Galerie du Palais* is here extended over three scenes in Act III; the
traditional language of reconciliation and enlightenment is cast in
an ironical light. In her attempt to separate the lovers, Amarante
persuades Geraste that his daughter, Daphnis, loves Clarimond.
The old man believes this at once, and his encouragement of Act
III Scene 7 is as heavy with irony as Pleirante's had been free of it
at the beginning of *La Galerie du Palais*. Not only is Geraste comic
for being completely out of touch with the truth, he is further
ridiculous for being able to use such noble language with
reference to a character whom the audience has seen to be a
credulous fool:

> *Ma fille, c'est en vain que tu fais la discrette,*
> *J'ay découvert en fin ta passion secrette,*
> *Je ne t'en parle point sur des advis douteux.*
> *N'en rougy point, Daphnis, ton choix n'est pas honteux.* (873–6)

Ironically, Geraste omits to mention the name of the suitor he
has in mind. Daphnis, predictably, misunderstands her father's
meaning and the scene is followed by a monologue of delight, in
which she evokes, as Clarice had done before her, the exaltation
felt as love seemingly triumphs over all obstacles and can be
freely reciprocated and expressed:

> *Florame, il m'est permis de te recompenser,*
> *Et sans plus déguiser ce qu'un pere autorise*
> *Je me puis revancher du don de ta franchise,*
> *Ton merite le rend, malgré ton peu de biens,*
> *Indulgent à mes feux, et favorable aux tiens . . .* (888–92)

Here expressed is the familiar defeat of tyranny and materialism,
the victory of pure love and the establishment of order. However,
the inappropriateness and hollowness of this language is

carefully underlined. The traditional expression of doubt which, in the mouth of Pyrandre, for instance, in Boisrobert's *Pyrandre et Lisimène*, Act V Scene 3, suggests absolute delight at unspeakable happiness: *'Non, je ne veille point, ce seroit trop de croire, / Que ma Princesse encor fust temoin de ma gloire'* (p. 94), becomes, for Daphnis, a more ironically apt intimation of the truth:

> *Mais est-il vray mes sens? m'estes vous bien fidelles?*
> *Mon heur me rend confuse, et ma confusion*
> *Me fait tout soupçonner de quelque illusion.* (894–6)

This comic distortion of conventional themes is taken to its logical conclusion in the subsequent interview of hero and heroine, in which joy at reconciliation is expressed through praise of the omnipotent god of Love who has thus brought about victory for the lovers in distress:

> *Les advis d'Amarante en trahissant ma flame*
> *N'ont point gaigné Geraste en faveur de Florame,*
> *Les ressorts d'un miracle ont un plus haut moteur,*
> *Et tout autre qu'un Dieu n'en peut estre l'autheur.* (937–40)

The only god at work here is the dramatist, and his omnipotence directed towards the creation not of order, but of comic disorder, in which the traditional themes of *comédie* are systematically deflated.

But if the language of hero and heroine is thus distorted, the misunderstanding serves also to mete out comic punishment on Amarante, confused completely by the course of events. The 'reunion' scene of Act III Scene 9 is comic in its own right, but it looks forward to a further comic encounter with the servant:

> *Si je puis tant soit peu dissimuler ma joye,*
> *Et que dessus mon front son excés ne se voye,*
> *Je me joüeray bien d'elle et des empeschemens*
> *Que son adresse apporte à nos contentemens.* (953–6)

Having believed that her plan to fool both Clarimond and Geraste had succeeded, Amarante is suddenly confronted with apparent failure. Far from being desperate at the thought of marriage with one she does not love, Daphnis is seen to radiate with delight. The servant's bewilderment of Act III Scene 11 is total:

> *Florame, Clarimond, ces deux noms ce me semble*
> *Pour estre confondus n'ont rien qui se ressemble.*
> *Le moyen que jamais on entendist si mal*
> *Que l'un de ces amants fust pris pour son rival?*
> *Parmy de tels détours mon esprit ne voit goute*
> *Et leurs prosperitez le mettent en deroute.* (1013–18)

With a fine sense of comic balance, Corneille then reverses this forward movement towards harmony, replacing inappropriate joy with inappropriate despair. Geraste loves Florame's sister, Florise, and yet he can only hope to win her if the hero marries Daphnis. Unaware of his daughter's misunderstanding, the old man is compelled to make her retract her earlier promise.

The reaction of the lovers to this 'news' is carefully tinged with irony. In Florame's anger, Corneille underlines the hero's comically violent jealousy of himself:

> *Le nom de cet amant dont l'indiscrette envie*
> *A mes ressentimens vient aporter sa vie?*
> *Le nom de cet amant qui par sa prompte mort*
> *Doit au lieu du vieillard me reparer ce tort . . .* (1257–60)

and the heroine's reply is similarly ambiguous as her assertions of love for Florame reflect also the reaction she would have, did she but know the identity of the partner proposed for her: *'Je n'aime pas si mal que de m'en informer, / Je t'aurois fait trop voir que j'eusse peu l'aimer'* (1263–4). In the following scene, the hero rages for a while in confusion, but his anger and despair are soon dispelled by the arrival of Celie, Geraste's *confidente*, whose delight throws into comic relief Florame's misplaced grief:

> *. . . Et bien Celie? en fin elle a tant fait*
> *Qu'à vos desirs Geraste accorde leur effet.*
> *Quel visage avez-vous? vostre ayse vous transporte . . .* (1339–41)

Greater comic emphasis is placed, however, on Geraste in these scenes. In Act IV Scene 2, he takes back his earlier promise to Daphnis with words of authority and assertion, but his claims of absolute insensitivity to his daughter's feelings are quite unconvincing: they are followed at once, and unexpectedly, with words of tenderness. Geraste cannot be the despot he would like to be:

> *Vous soupirez en vain, vos soupirs et vos larmes*
> *Contre ma volonté sont d'impuissantes armes,*
> *Rentrez, je ne puis voir qu'avec mille douleurs*
> *Vostre rebellion s'exprimer par vos pleurs.* (1057–60)

These struggles become the centre of comic attention in the prelude to and encounter of Act V Scene 7. Still believing Daphnis to reject Florame's suit, the old man protests fidelity to his promise and absolute control over his rebellious daughter: he will serve Florame's cause to the end:

> *. . . Et moy trop de courage*
> *Pour manquer où l'amour, l'honneur, la foy m'engage.*
> *Va donc, va le chercher, à ses yeux tu verras*
> *Que pour luy mon pouvoir ne s'espargnera pas,*
> *Que je maltraitteray Daphnis en sa presence*
> *D'avoir pour son amour si peu de complaisance.* (1541–6)

The speech is comic on several levels. The foolishness of Geraste is underlined, as he mistakenly believes that Daphnis refuses to marry the hero she loves. Furthermore, he is seen to protest here a control which he knows he can exercise only imperfectly; such words are indeed less a declaration of intent than an attempt at self-deception. And, perhaps most significantly of all, this honourable insistence that he keep his promise to Florame only thinly disguises the true motive of the old man's outburst, namely a ridiculous mixture of fear and frustration at this apparent threat to his passion for Florise. Misunderstanding is carefully used here to bring out comic tensions between genuine feeling for his daughter and his own uncontrollable desires. Stress lies not so much on the possible suffering of Daphnis or on the curious attraction to a young girl, but on the discomfiture of the old man. Out of the traditional figures of tyrannical father and *vieillard amoureux*, Corneille creates a character of particular comic complexity.

The meeting of father and daughter in Act V Scene 7 is a comic transformation of what is a typical scene in many plays of the time, juxtaposing an assertive father, adamant in his authority, and a helpless daughter. In Scudéry's *Le Trompeur puny*, Act IV Scene 1, for instance, the king is quite absolute in his decree: '*Ne m'interrogez plus en tirant vos cheveux, / Car ma raison consiste à dire, je le veux* (p. 76).[10] Geraste, on the other hand, is far more hesitant and uncertain. At the start of the scene, he recalls his earlier weakness in the role, and looks forward to the encounter with a certain trepidation:

> *Geraste, sur le champ il te falloit contraindre*
> *Celle que ta pitié ne pouvoit ouyr plaindre,*
> *Tu n'as peu refuser du temps à ses douleurs*
> *Ton coeur s'atendrissoit de voir couler ses pleurs* . . . (1553–6)

When he begins his speech of authoritative command, he falls quickly into pleas and questions:

> *Faudra-t'il que de vous je reçoive la loy,*
> *Et que l'aveuglement d'une amour obstinée,*
> *Contre ma volonté regle vostre Himenée?* . . .
> *Mais sçachez qu'il falloit, ingrate, en vos amours*
> *Ou ne m'obeyr point, ou m'obeyr tousjours,* (1560–2; 1567–8)

and his logic begins to falter. He is fully aware that his own change of mind is arbitrary, and he seeks now to find inconsistency in the behaviour of his daughter.

Daphnis, however, is more than a match for her father. In no sense the oppressed victim, she has the confidence and self-assurance which Geraste so obviously lacks, revealing to him quite categorically the absurdity of his remarks:

> *Quoy que mette en avant vostre injuste courroux*
> *Je ne veux opposer à vous mesme que vous.*
> *Vostre permission doit estre irrevocable,*
> *Devenez seulement à vous mesme semblable,*
> *Il vous falloit, Monsieur, vous mesme, en mes amours*
> *Ou ne consentir point, ou consentir tousjours.* (1571–6)

Such certainty in the validity of her arguments characterised also the heroine in Gombauld's *Amaranthe*, who similarly defended the love which she had sworn to the hero in Act V Scene 2:

> *J'ay donné ma parole, & je la veux deffendre.*
> *Je n'ay plus desormais d'autre conseil à prendre* . . .
> *Sa deffense est ma gloire, & mon contentement:*
> *Et ce n'est plus honneur que de faire autrement,* (p. 144)

but the dramatic force of the scene is clearly different. In Gombauld's play, the heroine's resistance increases the play's tension, and is seen as a terrifying and dangerous lack of concern for the oracle's decree which seemingly forbids this union of lovers:

> Crain Diane, Amaranthe, & la parolle expresse
> Dont son ire aujourd'huy nous menasse, & nous presse;
> Ne luy resiste point. (p. 144)

In Corneille's scene, however, the defiance of Daphnis places comic attention on the increasing desperation of Geraste. His only response is a sequence of questions, as logic completely breaks down under this severe attack on a position he knows to be untenable. Roles are reversed in the scene, as father, not daughter, is seen to struggle under relentless pressure:

> Qui le doit emporter ou de vous ou de moy?
> Et qui doit de nous deux plustost manquer de foy?
> Quand vous en manquerez mon vouloir vous excuse.
> Mais à trop raisonner moy mesme je m'abuse,
> Il n'est point de raison valable entre nous deux,
> Et pour toute raison il suffit que je veux. (1587–92)

His final stance of authority is only very shakily adopted. Its impact is not that of the powerful tyrant, assured of his force, but that of the comic character, trying to persuade himself and others of the control he does not possess.

As before, the misunderstandings which torment the protagonists culminate in the particular confusion of Amarante. Like Ménèchme Ravy in Rotrou's *Les Ménèchmes*, she finds herself caught in a seemingly absurd world where reactions are illogical and unpredictable. According to her earlier scene with Daphnis, Florame is the husband her father proposes, and yet according to Geraste, the heroine seemingly resists this partner at all costs. In Rotrou's play, Act IV Scene 6, the hero is left to doubt the balance of his own mind: '*Aurois-tu, ma raison, oublié ton usage? / Il faut que je sois fou si tout le monde est sage*' (I, p. 576), and at the end of Act V Scene 4, Amarante gives similar expression to her bewilderment. Is she insane, or are they?

> Sous un tel embarras je me trouve accablée,
> Eux ou moy nous avons la cervelle troublée,
> Si ce n'est qu'à dessein ils veuillent tout mesler,
> Et soient d'intelligence à me faire affoler.
> Mon foible esprit s'y perd, et n'y peut rien comprendre. (1489–93)

3   *Où les conditions n'ont point d'égalité*
                     L'amour ne se fait guere avec sincerité.[11]

For all its comic versatility, however, *La Suivante* is clearly much
more than just a well-constructed *comédie d'intrigue*, and Corneille's use of this particular form suggests a daring and original
treatment of certain important themes.

Critics have often remarked on the dramatist's presentation of
Florame, an apparently ignoble hero,[12] and these attitudes are
clearly inspired by such passages as Damon's speech in the
opening scne of the play, which could not be more explicit:

> *Sa richesse l'attire, et sa beauté le blesse,*
> *Elle le passe en biens, il l'esgalle en Noblesse,*
> *Et cherche ambitieux par sa possession*
> *A relever l'esclat de son extraction.*
> *Il a peu de fortune et beaucoup de courage,*
> *Et hors cette esperance il hait le mariage:*
> *C'est ce que l'autre jour en secret il m'apprit.* (73–9)

The lines reverse the traditional sentiments of lovers, devoted to
one lady alone; love of virtue and beauty is now replaced by
simple and undisguised attraction to wealth.

However, such self-seeking heroes were not uncommon at this
time. In Mairet's *Les Galanteries du duc d'Ossonne*, Act IV Scene 3,
for instance, Octave is quite open about the motives which
inspire him in his affairs, happy to court Stephanile for his own
pleasure, and nothing more:

> *La fille pauvre et belle, à mon avis, est née*
> *Pour la réjouissance, et non pour l'Hyménée*
> *Qui, selon le proverbe, est pire que l'enfer,*
> *Quand au lieu d'être d'or ses chaînes sont de fer,* (1132–5)

and in Rotrou's *La Pèlerine amoureuse*, Act II Scene 2, Filidan
characterises thus the traditional lover of the day:

> *Les plus fins, en ce temps, épousent les trésors,*
> *Et n'examinent point ni l'esprit ni le corps.*
> *L'ayant, n'aurez-vous pas quelque objet qui vous plaise?*
> *Une femme enrichit, et la maîtresse baise.* (II, pp. 458–9)

Furthermore, attitudes apparent in these essentially episodic
characters are manifestly shared by certain protagonists, particularly in Rotrou's plays. In his *Diane*, Act I Scene 1, the heroine
laments that she has been abandoned by a faithless lover in
search of his own fortune: '*L'avare faim de l'or a rompu ses promesses,*

/ *Une riche ennemie attire ses caresses'* (I, p. 270), and in Act II Scene 3, the hero in question reflects on a custom to which he himself has readily submitted:

> *La grâce et la vertu ne sont plus adorées,*
> *On ne s'enchaîne plus qu'en des chaînes dorées;*
> *Possédant beaucoup d'or on a beaucoup d'appas,*
> *Et ce métal rend beau tout ce qui ne l'est pas.* (p. 286)

Similar feelings are expressed by Lucidor in *La Pèlerine amoureuse*, Act I Scene 1, who readily admits why he finds Célie so attractive: *'Tous n'aiment que sa grâce, et moi que sa fortune; / Elle n'est à mes yeux qu'une beauté commune'* (II, p. 444).

What is significant in *La Suivante*, clearly, is not so much the theme itself as the use Corneille makes of it. Not only are these remarks made by a third party and not once intimated in the actual behaviour of the protagonist, but also they contribute primarily to the undeceiving of the foolish Theante who learns thus that he has failed to keep Daphnis for himself. In the following scene, the audience is left not so much with thoughts about the cynical motives of Florame, as with Theante's frustrated self-reproaches, angry at his own incompetence:

> . . . *Par quel mal-heur fatal*
> *Ay-je donné moy mesme entrée à mon rival?*
> *De quelque trait rusé que mon esprit se vante*
> *Je me trompe moy-mesme en trompant Amarante.* (87–90)

Doubt is cast on the motives of the hero not in scenes of accusation and confession, but it is suggested more surreptitiously in a comic context.

This particular form of irony is apparent, too, in Act III Scene 1, when Florame outlines to Celie his plans for his sister to marry Geraste in exchange for the hand of Daphnis:

> *Elle se sacrifie à mes contentemens,*
> *Et pour mes interests contraint ses sentimens.*
> *Asseure donc Geraste, en me donnant sa fille,*
> *Qu'il gaigne en un moment toute nostre famille.* (687–90)

A similar situation arises in Rayssiguier's *Palinice, Circeine et Florice*, in which the hero, Alcandre, is quite happy to make his sister marry an old man, Arimant, in return for this latter's niece. He expresses his willingness in Act II Scene 4 with curious unconcern:

> *Je sçay quelle est l'ardeur qui vous brûle le sein,*
> *Florice n'oseroit en cela me deplaire,*
> *On sçait l'autorité que doit avoir un frere,*
> *Votre dessein l'honore, & je puis l'engager.* (p. 39)

The theme is again not particular to Corneille, but his treatment of it is suggestive. Out of Florice, Rayssiguier makes a *fille gaie*, quite able to cope with the amorous longings of a ridiculous old man, and contemplating him with amused detachment in Act IV Scene 5: '*Que ce vieil amoureux a de belles saillies, / Et je serois subjette à toutes ses follies!*' (p. 80). In Corneille's play, however, Florise never appears. Her vulnerability is suggested by Celie, who makes a calm plea on her behalf:

> *Quoy qu'elle s'en rapporte à vous entierement,*
> *Vous luy feriez plaisir d'en user autrement,*
> *Les amours d'un vieillard sont d'une foible amorce.* (683–5)

Florame, however, is quite adamant, and in response, Celie is given a single line whose ironical implications are penetrating. As she seemingly approves of the union of hero and heroine, she alludes to the importance of spontaneous affection in the pairing of couples, and thus highlights again the suggestions of coercion and self-interest on which this particular marriage is based: '*Plaisez-vous à Daphnis? c'est là le principal*' (695). Order and disorder, harmony and tension are suggestively held side by side.

Much of the comedy's complexity derives certainly from Amarante, but the nature of this should be carefully analysed. Corneille's *suivante*, vainly struggling to satisfy her love for Florame, is not the first character to see herself at odds with a social order, regretting her poverty and resorting to ruse in order to win a husband. In Rayssiguier's *La Bourgeoise*, the heroine tries every trick to capture the heart of Acrise, determined not to be held back by arbitrary distinctions as early as the opening scene:

> *La Noblesse à Paris, est tellement confuse,*
> *Que pour la discerner, le plus sage s'abuse,*
> *Et puis je sçauray bien esviter finement,*
> *Ce qui sera contraire à mon contentement.* (p. 2)

Her role is that of the traditional villainess, attempting to separate perfect lovers, and ultimately failing.

Amarante's aims and fate are similar, but her presentation is less straightforward. As has been seen in the analysis of certain scenes already, she has an essentially comic function, causing great discomfort to both Florame and Theante, importuning the lovers with her presence and manifesting considerable skill in the duping of Geraste and Clarimond. Her depiction, however, is more complex than this, and its particular nature is suggested in the opening scene when Theante recounts how she had deliberately kept him away from Daphnis:

> Elle usoit de ses droits, et toute imperieuse,
> D'une voix demy-gaye et demy-serieuse,
> Quand j'ay des serviteurs c'est pour m'entretenir,
> Disoit-elle, autrement je les sçay bien punir. (25–8)

This particular blend of gaiety and seriousness is carefully created in Amarante's scenes with the hero and heroine.

Florame's first interview with the *suivante* in Act I Scene 5 is seemingly one of unequivocal comedy. The hero's frustration at her importunity is expressed in speeches of carefully prepared ambiguity, lines of apparent heroic dignity in love disguising the spontaneous expression of annoyance at the obstacle to his happiness which Amarante represents:

> Mais, helas! je vous sers, je vy sous vostre empire,
> Et je ne puis pretendre où mon desir aspire:
> Theante (ah! nom fatal pour me combler d'ennuy)
> Vous demandez mon coeur et le vostre est à luy!
> Et mon sterile amour n'aura que des suplices!
> Trouvez bon que j'adresse autrepart mes services,
> Contraint manque d'espoir de vous abandonner. (213–19)

The audience sees behind the heroic mask, as role and reality are again superimposed the one on the other.

Amarante, however, is not taken in by this ploy; unlike Alcidon or Theante, she is no dupe, and realises that the hero's protestations of love are feigned and ironical. This knowledge may be the source of further comic effects, as the *suivante* refuses to play into Florame's hands, deliberately taunting him by herself acting out a role, that of the *fille gaie* for whom such noble arguments have no meaning:

> Aprenez que chez moy c'est un foible avantage
> De m'avoir de ses voeux le premier fait hommage!

> *Le merite y fait tout, et tel plaist à mes yeux*
> *Que je negligerois pres d'un qui valust mieux.* (221–4)

By the end of the scene, however, there are suggestions of strain beneath this comic exchange as Amarante abandons this role and underlines the artificiality of all that has gone before, revealing tension and hurt beneath apparent flippancy: *'Peut-estre, mais en fin il le faut confesser, / Vous vous trouveriez mieux aupres de ma maistresse'* (228–9).

A similar mood is evoked in Daphnis' meeting with Amarante in Act I Scene 8. It is not unusual for dramatists of this time to depict tensions between a mistress and a servant. The rivalry of Dorante and Diane in Rotrou's *Cléagenor et Doristée* has already been referred to, and in Gougenot's *Comédie des comédiens*,[13] Act III Scene 6, Flaminie suffers at the hands of Caliste, her mistress, as she tries to urge a particular suitor on her, much to the heroine's annoyance: *'Vostre condition doit borner vos discours: / Vous n'estes pas à moy pour regler mes amours'* (1440–1). In Corneille's scene, however, the suggestions of tension are more subtle. There is a certain charm in the presentation of the heroine, as she plays the part of benevolent mistress, trying to warn her *suivante* of the risk she runs by having Florame court her, but only half disguising her own pangs of jealousy:

> *Cette assiduité de Florame avec vous*
> *A la fin a rendu Theante un peu jaloux.*
> *Aussi de vous y voir tous les jours attachée*
> *Quelle puissante amour n'en seroit pas faschée?* (283–6)

Amarante, however, refuses again to be deceived; she rejects the suit of Theante, and taunts Daphnis by going straight to the heart of her unease:

> *Je luy veux quelque bien puis que changeant de flame*
> *Vous voyez par pitié qu'il me laisse Florame,*
> *Qui n'estant pas si vain a plus de fermeté.* (309–11)

The lines clearly have a double edge and a double function. On one level, they are deliberately comic in effect, used to discomfort the heroine and to put her in a position of charming disarray, as she struggles to conceal her own feelings beneath protestations of impartiality:

> *Amarante, apres tout, disons la verité,*
> *Theante n'est si vain qu'en vostre fantaisie,*

> *Et toute sa froideur naist de sa jalousie.*
> *C'est chose au demeurant qui ne me touche en rien,*
> *Et ce que je vous dis n'est que pour vostre bien.* (312–16)

But, on another level, the lines suggest the ironical feelings of
Amarante, aware both of Daphnis' reciprocated love for the hero
and of her own role as the victim of his *feinte*. Emphasis on the
charm of the heroine's love does not totally conceal the
suggestions of hurt and bitterness beneath the surface, feelings
sensed again in the *suivante*'s monologue which ends the Act:

> *Que m'importe de perdre une amitié si feinte?*
> *Dois-je pas m'ennuyer de son discours moqueur,*
> *Où sa langue jamais n'a l'adveu de son coeur?*
> *Non, je ne le sçaurois, et quoy qu'il m'en arrive*
> *Je feray mes effors afin qu'on ne m'en prive . . .* (334–8)

It is at the height of the comic confusion that these tensions are
felt in their most suggestive way. In Act III Scene 10, for instance,
Daphnis delights in accusing Amarante of betraying her love for
Florame; she believes that her passion has been approved, and
can thus play with great enthusiasm the role of outraged
mistress:

> *Quoy! souffrir un moment l'entretien de Florame,*
> *Vous le nommez bien tost une secrette flame!*
> *Cette jalouse humeur dont vous suivez la loy*
> *Vous fait en mes secrets plus sçavante que moy.*
> *Mais passe pour le croire, il falloit que mon pere*
> *De vostre confidence apprist ceste Chimere?* (977–82)

There is again the purest comedy on one level, of course, as
Daphnis' misunderstanding is quite evident. She believes herself
in control, her love assured, whereas, in fact, the reverse is true.
Moreover, the more she accuses Amarante of betraying her love
for Florame to Geraste, the greater the *suivante*'s confusion who
cannot understand her mistress' accusations: '*Si touchant vos
amours on sçait rien de ma bouche, / Que je puisse à vos yeux devenir une
souche*' (1001–2). Corneille exploits again that same double focus
which he has developed since *La Veuve*. Daphnis' allegations of
villainy are true, yet misdirected, and Amarante's protestations
of innocence reflect not only the studied hypocrisy of the
schemer, denying her disruptive intent, but also the spontaneous
and bewildered expression of innocence with regard to a crime
which she did not in fact commit.

However, beneath the comic confusion are clear suggestions of tension. Daphnis, in her mistaken joy, may only feign anger at Amarante, but this pose of detachment conceals an equally committed aggression: she still means what she says:

> *Amarante, vrayment vous estes fort jolie,*
> *Vous n'égayez pas mal vostre melancolie,*
> *Dans ce jaloux chagrin qui tient vos sens saisis,*
> *Vos divertissemens sont assez bien choisis.* (965–8)

And in Amarante's genuine protestation of innocence are hidden equally spontaneous jibes at her mistress, and scorn at the love which she knows her to feel for Florame:

> *S'il croit que vous l'aimez, c'est sur quelque soupçon*
> *Où je ne contribuë en aucune façon,*
> *Je sçay trop que le Ciel, avecque tant de graces,*
> *Vous donne trop de coeur pour des flames si basses,*
> *Et quand je vous croirois dans cet indigne choix*
> *Je sçay ce que je suis, et ce que je vous dois.* (983–8)

There is more than just humorous confusion in these lines; the juxtaposition of spontaneity and pretence which characterised the particularly sophisticated comic language of Corneille's earliest plays is here used to suggest more subtly the tense rivalry of mistress and servant.

Similar ambiguities are sensed in the fascinating encounter of Florame and Amarante in Act V Scene 3. Again, there is a simple level of comic misunderstanding in the scene, as each character thinks the other mad: Amarante is astonished to hear Florame lament that he has a rival in love, and Florame no less so to hear Amarante insist that Daphnis alone is the obstacle to his happiness. The *suivante* answers the hero's pleas with her own assertions:

> *Ce vous deust estre assez de m'avoir abusée*
> *Sans faire encor de moy vos sujets de risée.*
> *Je sçay que le vieillard favorise vos feux,*
> *Et que rien que Daphnis n'est contraire à vos voeux,* (1465–8)

and her confusion is complemented by the bewilderment of Florame, as hopelessly out of touch with events as ever, who believes this news to be just another ploy:

> *Vois-tu, ne t'en ry plus, ta seule jalousie*
> *A mis à ce vieillard ce change en fantaisie,*

> Ce n'est pas avec moy que tu te dois joüer,
> Tu redoubles ton crime à le desavoüer . . . (1473–6)

Misunderstanding makes comic the accusations of these two characters, but it does not totally disguise the expression of aggressive feelings underneath the confusion, the final dropping of pretence which had been hinted at from the beginning of the play. The tenseness of this relationship between the hero who has only feigned love and the *suivante* whose feelings of hurt are mingled with ironical self-awareness is now presented, significantly, not in a dramatic confrontation, but in a scene of the purest comedy; the ambiguity of comic language is here taken to its most suggestive lengths.

4

S'ils sont sages tous deux, il faut que je sois folle.[14]

As was the case in *La Galerie du Palais*, tensions sensed in the course of the comedy culminate in quite perceptible strain in the final establishment of order. In *La Suivante*, the comic mechanism is familiar, as lovers, separated through villainy and brought into conflict with parental authority, are reunited in an atmosphere of harmony; and yet these themes are curiously distorted.

Dénouements with their own particular strain are not uncommon before *La Suivante*, and in certain plays money is seen to replace love as the ultimate source of harmony and happiness for the protagonists. In du Ryer's *Vendanges de Suresne*, Tirsis, defeated in his suit of the heroine, laments that he has been vanquished not by a superior lover, but by the hero's propitious inheritance of wealth, an accusation which Polidor, in Act V Scene 3, does not contradict: *'Lors que l'or & l'Amour se meslent d'une chose / On peut bien esperer tout ce qu'on s'en propose'* (p. 119). Similarly, in Rotrou's *Diane*, the heroine wins back the affections of her faithless lover by pretending that she has been bequeathed a fortune. In the final scene, this illusion is turned quite miraculously into reality, and she can address Lysimant with these ironical words:

> Enfin, heureux amant, le soin des destinées
> A-t-il avec mes maux tes froideurs terminées?
> Et la soeur de Lysandre a-t-elle plus d'appas
> Que celle, que tous ceux d'un sort abject et bas? (I, p. 339)

Detachment from pastoral ideals is clear, but what is in these two plays an ironical presentation of love's dominion, becomes in *La Suivante* a much more suggestive and profound tension.

Immediately striking is the way in which Corneille gives traditional roles to characters with whom they are not normally associated. The final dramatic stress lies not so much with the reconciliation of hero and heroine, joyful after their temporary separation, but on the happiness to which the old man aspires: '*Allons donc la treuver, que cet eschange heureux / Comble d'aise à son tour un vieillard amoureux*' (1639–40). Words of blissful expectation, normally spoken by the young protagonists are now spoken by Geraste, and Florame adopts instead the stance of mellow experience, commenting on the ardour felt by those in love:

Geraste: *Le temps en sera long à mon affection.*
Florame: *Tousjours l'impatience à l'amour est meslée.* (1656–7)

This peculiar reversal of roles is particularly striking, indeed, in the fate which Corneille accords to his *vieillard amoureux*. It is traditional for the amorous old man to be mocked for a passion which runs counter to normal and expected patterns of behaviour. In du Ryer's *Amarillis*, Act II Scene 1, the elderly Thelamon is ridiculed, as is Trasile in Gougenot's *Comédie des comédiens*, Act VI Scene 4, and in Rayssiguier's *Palinice, Circeine et Florice*, Act V Scene 6, Sileine thus upbraids Arimant as he proposes to defend his ridiculous passion: '*Remettez vostre espée, & vous montrez plus sage, / L'amour est importun aux hommes de vostre age*' (p. 99). An old man's attempt to play the part of a young lover is seen as foolish and inappropriate.

This is not the case, however, in *La Suivante*. Here, Geraste is not mocked, but his passion is seen as yet another shining example of love's great power, as Florame explains to Daphnis:

> *Mon coeur, s'il t'en souvient, je t'avois advertie*
> *Qu'un grand effet d'amour avant qu'il fust long temps*
> *Te rendroit estonnée et nos desirs contens.* (1642–4)

The hero's lines are significant. This unusual attitude towards the amorous old man goes hand in hand with an evident concern for his own happiness, and such words of understanding thus throw into doubt, without going any further, the authenticity of the principal harmony.

But that is not all. In the fate of the two villains, Corneille again suggests curious discords and tensions. At the beginning of Act V, Theante, the coward comically defeated, resolves to leave the country, his aim being:

> A les laisser en paix et courir l'Italie
> Pour divertir le cours de ma melancolie,
> Et ne voir point Florame emporter à mes yeux
> Le prix où pretendoit mon coeur ambitieux. (1405–8)

It would not have been unusual if Corneille had paired off Theante with Amarante at this point: the marriage of villains was quite common in comedy of the time. In Rotrou's *Filandre*, as has been seen in another context, the co-schemers Filandre and Cephise are joined at the end of the play, and in du Ryer's *Vendanges de Suresne*, Florice and Tirsis forget their respective love for the hero and heroine and move where happiness is to be found. For Florice, the transition is quite natural, as she remarks in Act IV Scene 1: '*Peux-tu donc me blasmer de me voir inconstante / Si je ne veux changer que pour estre contente?* (p. 83). Corneille is clearly conscious of this tradition, and at various stages of the play Theante gives hints of his attraction to the *suivante* which would seemingly prepare for their eventual union. In the opening scene, he is in no doubt about his feelings for her: '*Quelques puissans appas que possede Amarante, / Je treuve qu'apres tout ce n'est qu'une Suivante*' (9–10), and this attitude persists until his last appearance in Act V Scene 1:

> Bien que j'adore encor l'excez de son merite,
> Florame ayant Daphnis de honte je la quitte:
> Le Ciel ne nous fit point et pareils et rivaux
> Pour avoir des succés tellement inegaux. (1413–16)

Yet it is not love, but ambition which finally vanquishes, and the villain leaves the stage alone.

Theante's role here clearly has a double function. Not only does this obstinacy suggest a refusal by Corneille to create harmony just for the sake of harmony, an ironical distance from tradition which has been evident in his work as early as *Mélite*, but also this very hiatus in the establishment of order is connected quite explicitly with the distortion implied in the harmony of the protagonists. Theante's self-imposed exile from the happy lovers does not imply here the greater authority of their values, as traditionally it was seen to do; on the contrary, it throws them into doubt. It is in this light also that must be seen the strange monologue of Amarante which ends the play.

The final speech of the *suivante* evokes a wealth of suggestions in critics; it is seen to express the rancour of an embittered villainess,[15] the pathetic lament of one who suffers innocently[16] or the amusing anger of a ridiculous servant.[17]

Amarante clearly belongs to that tradition of characters who fail to win the affection of the one they love, a type which, as was seen in the earlier analysis of Hippolyte, exerted some fascination on dramatists of the time. That a heroine should express frustration in her defeat is not in itself unusual. In du Ryer's *Vendanges de Suresne*, Act II Scene 4, Florice laments thus the first failure of her plan to separate the protagonists:

> *Toute notre industrie à moy seule fatale*
> *Luy donne une maistresse, à nous une rivale,*
> *Et nostre invention n'a servy seulement*
> *Qu'à le combler de bien comme moy de tourment.* (p. 41)

On one level, Amarante's role as a comic character is certainly clear. Like Florice, she looks ironically at her own defeat, recalling the confusion which she has reaped as a reward for her scheming:

> *Je le perds sans avoir de tout mon artifice*
> *Qu'autant de mal que luy, bien que diversement,*
> *Veu que pas un effet n'a suivy ma malice*
> *Où ma confusion n'egalast son tourment.* (1661–4)

Furthermore, at certain points, Corneille clearly gives a more obviously comic force to what, in other characters of the time, are penetrating and violent displays of passion. In Rayssiguier's adaptation of *Aminta*, for instance, Elpin is seen to lament that the avarice of his beloved prevents him from finding happiness with her:

> *De là j'ay bien jugé que c'est ma pauvreté,*
> *Et non pas mes deffauts qui m'ostent sa beauté,*
> *O Ciel, dont je ressens l'influence barbare,*
> *Puis qu'il falloit qu'un jour j'adorasse un avare.* (p. 31)

Here is clearly expressed the theme familiar in pastoral that wealth and not virtue is prized by man in his present state of corruption. The theme occurs in Amarante's speech, too, but here the lament suggests not only insight into the hero's motives, but also a certain amount of frustrated self-congratulation, a desire to protect her already injured vanity:

> Daphnis me le ravit, non par son beau visage,
> Non par son bel esprit, ou ses doux entretiens,
> Non que sur moy sa race ait aucun advantage,
> Mais par le seul éclat qui sort d'un peu de biens. (1669–72)

The centre of attention here is not so much Florame as Amarante herself, trying to find a flattering explanation for her defeat.

A similar comic dimension is apparent in the final curse. In Beys' *Le Jaloux sans sujet*, Act V Scene 2, Belanire learns that the heroine has only feigned love for him, and reacts to this news with a passionate malediction of the protagonists:

> Qu'aussi tost que l'Hymen vous aura joints ensemble,
> La discorde chez vous ses machines assemble,
> Qu'en tous les lieux du monde elle suive vos pas,
> Qu'elle mesle du fiel dans vos plus doux repas,
> Et qu'elle fasse enfin par des ruses nouvelles,
> De deux parfaicts amans deux espous infideles. (p. 87)

Belanire looks forward to the disturbing collapse of ideal love, but Amarante's anger is more obviously situated in a tradition of farce. Her vision of adultery suggests inventiveness rather than despair, as she evokes the guile of a young wife, duping an old and ridiculous husband:

> Puisse enfin ta foiblesse et ton humeur jalouze
> Te frustrer desormais de tout contentement,
> Te remplir de soupçons, et cette jeune épouse
> Joindre à mille mespris le secours d'un amant! (1697–700)

For the audience familiar with the *Chansons* of Gaultier-Garguille, such references would evoke a host of farcical associations.

There is obvious comedy, then, in the presentation of this heroine and in her attitude to characters and events, and yet, through this comic angle of vision, Corneille creates particularly subtle and complex suggestions. In her acknowledgement of the inevitable course of the plot, Amarante parodies grimly that traditional acceptance of superior values which is expected from the defeated villainess:

> Ouy, Ciel, il le falloit, ce n'est pas sans justice
> Que cet esprit usé se renverse à son tour:
> Puisqu'un jeune amant suit les loix de l'avarice,
> Il faut bien qu'un vieillard suive celles d'amour, (1681–4)

and yet this comically distorted vision has a curious aptness: it
corresponds exactly to the distortions clearly apparent in the
dénouement. The ridiculing of the old man, so conspicuously
absent in the final scenes, is now put into the mouth of the
rejected servant, and the ambiguities suggested in the hero's
bland manipulation of his sister, glossed over by the protagonists
themselves, are finally brought to the surface. It is here that the
unity and suggestiveness of the play is ultimately captured.
Throughout the comedy of confusion, Amarante voices comic
astonishment at the apparent illogicality of the other characters'
reactions, wondering if she or they are insane. The same question
is implied in this final statement of bewilderment, but now the
implications are more far-reaching. The *suivante* is banished from
the charmed circle of young lovers, who traditionally embody the
values of the audience, and yet, in her comic and wholly justified
isolation, she alone highlights the unique reversal of roles which
has been seen to characterise this creation of order. Is her
interpretation of events simply a figment of an embittered and
frustrated imagination, or is this servant the only sane member of
a curious cast who each play each other's parts? Corneille leaves
the play open with this final question mark. Irony and tension in
the order of comedy could not be given a more perplexing and
original expression.

5

*Je vous presente une Comedie qui n'a pas esté également aymée de toutes sortes
d'esprits: beaucoup, et de fort bons, n'en ont pas fait grand estat, et beaucoup
d'autres l'ont mise au dessus du reste des miennes.*[18]

On the surface so simple and unsubtle, *La Suivante* is a comedy of
fascinating complexity. On one level, Corneille's adaptation of
the *comédie de confusion* suggests a significant reduction of interest
in the feelings of his protagonists. Whereas in *La Galerie du Palais*
the lovers are separated through misunderstanding of themselves and each other, here the obstacle to happiness is a largely and
outrageously improbable event, *'un nom tu par hasard'* (1633). For
Corneille, this plot provides the opportunity to derive entertainment from the ridiculing of villains, the gullibility and discomfort
of an old man and the confusion of a servant; in such scenes as
these the dramatist's refinement and sophistication of techniques

already exploited in his earliest work is clearly apparent. It is moreover significant that at the time of *La Suivante*, only two other such *comédies de confusion* had been written in French, both by Rotrou and both adaptations of a foreign text: *La Bague de l'oubly* taken from a play by Lope de Vega, and *Les Ménèchmes* adapted from Plautus. Corneille, however, works from no known source, and seeks obviously to create the maximum confusion for his characters and the maximum pleasure for his spectators. Taken on its own terms, therefore, it suggests again the dramatist's particular comic versatility and accomplishment.

More than this, however, Corneille exploits his comic plot in a way quite unparalleled in comedies of the time, using it to suggest tension in relationships and ambiguity in attitudes. Themes such as the cynical self-seeking of lovers, the suffering of girls who fall victim to hypocritical suitors, the tyranny of fathers and brothers are frequently found in plays at this period, and yet, in *La Suivante*, the dramatist analyses their implications in a more suggestively comic way. The misunderstandings and confusion which characterise the plot both shroud and intensify the underlying problems. It is this fascinating and perplexing depth in the comic vision which is at the heart of the play's originality, this curious '*voix demy-gaie et demy-serieuse*' which lies behind the diversity of critical reactions to it from the time of its creation.

VI

La Place Royale
The comedy of fear

1

Et je puis avec joye accepter tous maris.[1]

The disturbing qualities of *La Place Royale* are those most frequently alluded to by critics. The curious anti-heroic actions of Alidor who constantly mistreats Angelique in his attempts to overcome his love for her are seen to make of this play a particularly dark comedy. Lemonnier (p. 55) stresses the cruelty of the world it presents, Rousset (p. 209) evokes in it the basic instability of human feelings, Rivaille (p. 760) points out the play's '*aspect sinistre*', Nadal (p. 79) underlines the moving nature of the plot, and for Stegmann, the comedy: '. . . *témoigne des adieux contraints de Corneille à un genre qu'il ne parvient plus à renouveler*' (II, 574). As was the case with *La Suivante*, however, the isolation of certain elements may lead to a distortion of the text and such conclusions as those noted above imply too cursory a consideration of features whose impact is quite clearly comic.

As in *La Galerie du Palais* and *La Suivante*, Corneille deliberately creates in the opening scenes of his next comedy an atmosphere of order and good humour. The initial debate of Angelique and her friend Philis follows the course of many confrontations of ideal and inconstant love, of fidelity and infidelity, scenes whose immediate pastoral predecessors are to be found in adaptations of *Aminta* and *Silvanire*. Noticeable in Corneille's scene, though, is the tone of charm and relaxation, the encounter having none of the moral seriousness of a great debate. Angelique defends her love for Alidor against Philis, who urges her to give up such ideals and to show interest in Doraste, her brother. Each character is endowed with delightful good humour, smiling indulgently at the apparent extravagance of the other. Philis' reaction to her friend's protestations: *'Dans l'obstination où je te voy reduite / J'admire ton amour & ris de ta conduite'* (45–6) is followed at once by a similar retort from Angelique: *'Ce grand flux de raisons dont tu viens m'attaquer, / Est bon à faire rire, & non à pratiquer'* (87–8).

In Philis, Corneille creates a heroine who demonstrates all the qualities of the *fille gaie*, happily detached from her feelings. The character was becoming increasingly popular in comedies of this period. In Claveret's *L'Esprit fort*, Act I Scene 4, Orante protests her ability to love on demand: *'Mon foible esprit se plaist à vivre en liberté / En quelque aimable lieu qu'il se soit aresté'* (p. 16), a claim which is justified by the end of the play, and in du Ryer's *Vendanges de Suresne*, Act II Scene 4, Lisete is seen to argue that happiness is not to be found in total subservience to a single lover:

> *Moy, je suis d'une humeur un peu plus difficile,*
> *Je n'en aurois pas trop quand j'en aurois dix mille.*
> *Lors qu'on a ce mal-heur de n'avoir qu'un Amant,*
> *La crainte de le perdre afflige incessamment.* (p. 45)[2]

Philis follows clearly in this tradition, content to respond to anyone who may court her:

> *Pour moy j'ayme un chacun, & sans rien negliger*
> *Le premier qui m'en conte a dequoy m'engager,*
> *Ainsi tout contribuë à ma bonne fortune,*
> *Tout le monde me plaist, & rien ne m'inportune.* (63–6)

Her function in the comic structure of the play is significant. Through her particular *désinvolture*, Corneille suggests that absence of tension which he carefully seeks in the early stages of his comedy. Her brother courts Angelique in vain, but his frustration is kept firmly in perspective by the cheerful remarks of the *fille gaie* who in Act I Scene 2 banishes all thoughts of suffering and refuses to be drawn into scenes of lament:

> *Contraindre mon humeur me seroit un supplice,*
> *Qui me rendroit moins propre à te faire service,*
> *Vois-tu? par tous moyens je te veux soulager,*
> *Mais j'ay bien plus d'esprit que de m'en affliger . . .* (133–6)

What is true of her attitude to others' problems is true also of her attitude to her own. Cleandre feigns love for her in an attempt to be near Angelique, but unlike either Hippolyte or Amarante, Philis is given neither to despair nor self-pity. Quite aware of her suitor's true feelings, she can reproach Cleandre for his infidelity with witty indifference in Act II Scene 7:

> *Quoy donc, c'est tout de bon que tu me veux quitter?*
> *Tu ne dis mot, resveur, & pour toute replique*
> *Tu tournes tes regards du costé d'Angelique,*
> *Est-ce là donc l'objet de tes legeretez?*
> *Veux-tu faire d'un coup deux infidelitez . . .* (564–8)

If she expresses concern here, it is not on her own account, but because she seeks to protect her brother. Amarante's comic importuning of the lovers in *La Suivante* is taken in this play to further sophisticated lengths, as the girl stubbornly, but gaily refuses to leave Cleandre's side, frustrating his plans to reach Angelique and demonstrating a charming eloquence in her role:

> *Si tu sçais t'en aller je sçauray bien te suivre,*
> *Et quelque occasion qui t'amene en ces lieux,*
> *Tu ne luy diras pas grand secret à mes yeux.*
> *Je suis plus incommode encor qu'il ne te semble.*
> *Parlons plustost d'accord & composons ensemble . . .* (606–10)

In Philis, indeed, Corneille develops a character who not only provides a comic focus in individual scenes, but whose very nature suggests an affirmation of the order, solidity and lack of tension which is expected and found in comedy.

2

Etrange humeur d'Amant![3]

The particular comic atmosphere embodied in Philis is sustained in the presentation of Alidor, the *amoureux extravagant*. This character is often taken in earnest by critics. His struggles for self-domination are frequently seen to indicate a courageous search for permanence in love,[4] a resolute quest to subordinate emotions to the will in the manner of later tragic heroes,[5] a conflict which is the mark of a noble, aristocratic mind.[6] Nadal speaks in his analysis of the '*étrange beauté dans son combat*' (p. 114), and Brunon makes explicit an attitude tacitly held by many others when he stresses the dramatic seriousness of the hero's character: he sees in his behaviour: '*Non de cette inconstance comique et frivole qui est pur désir de changement, mais d'une inconstance réfléchie et presque tragique, fondée sur le devoir de liberté'* (p. 23). If comedy is seen in Alidor, it is held to lie in a discrepancy between the ideals, which are essentially noble and worthy, and the pettiness of the one who propounds them. Morel sees the hero as another Matamore, the *'poète des exploits qu'il ne pourra jamais accomplir'*,[7] and Maurens describes him as a *'personnage franchement comique par la contradiction entre l'idéal dont il se réclame et la réalité du caractère.'*[8]

Alidor embodies certain characteristics of two distinct, but connected types, both essentially comic and both popular in plays of the time: the *amant inconstant* and the *esprit fort*. D'Urfé's Hylas is certainly a model for the faithless lover, the one who will not tolerate the suffering associated with fidelity in love, seeking only his own pleasure in amorous adventures and avoiding all responsibilities. He is one who provides much entertainment for the shepherds in *L'Astrée*, as he argues with great conviction the validity of his selfish and extravagant ideals:

Véritablement, respondit Tamire, je ris des raisons que tu rapportes pour approuver ta volage humeur, et je croy qu'il n'y a personne de la trouppe qui n'en fasse autant que moy, et que, peut-estre, Hylas mesme, si ce n'est en apparence, ne laisse pas d'en rire en son coeur, estant bien mal-aisé de s'en empescher en semblable sujet. (IV 5, pp. 231–2)

The hero appears in several plays adapted from d'Urfé's novel – Mairet's *Silvanire*, Rayssiguier's *Tragi-comédie pastorale* and Mareschal's *L'Inconstance d'Hylas* – and he is clearly the inspiration of several other incidental comic roles: Fernant in Pichou's *Folies de Cardenio*, Ardilan in Auvray's *Dorinde*, Dorandre in Rayssiguier's *Les Thuilleries*.

The *esprit fort* is the character who despises everything to do with love, the one who may play the social game of courtship but who never allows personal feelings to enter a relationship. The type has its origins in the aloof hunters of Italian pastoral (Silvia in *Aminta*, Silvio in *Il Pastor Fido*), and these essential traits of complete self-sufficiency are frequently found either in the comic banter of a cynical servant – Fabrice in Rotrou's *Bague de l'oubly* – or in the flippant remarks of characters such as Corneille's own Tirsis or Claveret's *L'Esprit fort*, described thus in Act II Scene 2: *'Ce rafiné Criton est un homme à la mode, / Dont le seul entretien vaut bien qu'on s'incommode'* (p. 36). For the

onlooker, the aspirations of a hero such as this are as ridiculous as
those of Hylas:

> *Ne songer qu'au present, n'avoir soin que de soy,*
> *Enfin estre à soy mesme & son juge & sa loy,*
> *C'est en quoy ces esprits qui n'ont rien que l'escorce,*
> *Dans leur sotte foiblesse establissent leur force.* (p. 61)

Like many of these characters, Alidor lays claim to total control
over his feelings, proudly outlining his philosophy to Cleandre in
Act I Scene 4:

> *Je le hay s'il me force, & quand j'aime je veux*
> *Que de ma volonté dépendent tous mes voeux,*
> *Que mon feu m'obeïsse au lieu de me contraindre,*
> *Que je puisse à mon gré l'augmenter, & l'éteindre,*
> *Et tousjours en estat de disposer de moy,*
> *Donner quand il me plaist, & retirer ma foy.* (215–20)

These claims are indeed traditional. At the beginning of Beys' *Le
Jaloux sans sujet*, Belanire is similarly absolute in his assertions:

> *Je suis maistre absolu sur toutes mes puissances,*
> *A mon gré seulement je gouverne mes pleurs,*
> *Et je n'impute point leur honte à mes douleurs,*
> *Sans mon consentement aucun souspir ne monte,*
> *Je les tire moy-mesme & les donne par conte,* (p. 3)

and in *L'Astrée*, I 1, Hylas can happily take his leave of a mistress
when he needs to:

> *Et prenons de nous-même un congé volontaire.*
> *Nous le vaincrons ainsi, cest Amour indompté,*
> *Et ferons sagement de nostre volonté*
> *Ce que le temps en fin nous forceroit de faire.* (p. 31)

Corneille's hero, however, is quite distinctive. Whereas
Belanire and Hylas have the power they profess, Alidor has not;
the traditional *esprit fort* loves none of the girls he courts, but
Alidor is helplessly in love with Angelique. This fundamental
difference is clearly suggested in a comparison of the language
used by each lover. The confident assertions of Belanire and
Hylas reflect their sustained mastery of themselves, but with
Alidor claims to self-control are dependent on the verb *'je veux'*.
Each character refers to a notion of *'volonté'*, but for Alidor it
implies not so much the supreme domination of the heart by the
will, but a more feeble desire to be other than he knows himself to

be. His very next lines reveal indeed that such self-mastery is simply an illusion: *'Pour vivre de la sorte Angelique est trop belle, / Mes pensers n'oseroient m'entretenir que d'elle'* (221–2), and he is reduced to an outburst of flailing petulance, angry at his own evident weakness: *'J'ay honte de souffrir les maux dont je me plains, / Et d'éprouver ses yeux plus forts que mes desseins'* (227–8). The extravagance of Alidor does not reside in the fact that he is an *esprit fort*, but that he fancies and wishes himself to be one.

Corneille's exploitation of this particular folly for comic effects is most clear in Alidor's first interview with Angelique in Act II Scene 2 where he sets out to turn the heroine against himself by pretending to be unfaithful. The scene is often held to be particularly disturbing, and yet in comedy of the time encounters between angry heroines and insolent suitors are not unusual. In Rotrou's *Les Ménechmes*, Act IV Scene 1, for instance, Orazie rages at Ménechme Sosicle, believing him to be her faithless husband, Ménechme Ravy. Her language has all the violence of the *femme en furie*:

> *Homme le plus brutal qui respire en ces lieux,*
> *Oses-tu désormais te montrer à mes yeux?*
> *Ma plainte, déloyal, est-elle légitime,*
> *Maintenant que tu tiens la preuve de ton crime?* (I, p. 558)

but its impact is clearly comic as it stands in stark opposition to the confusion of Sosicle. As the hero denies all knowledge of Orazie, fury shades into bewilderment:

Sosicle: *Quoy je suis ton mari? que je plains ta manie!*
Orazie: *Voyez de ce gausseur l'impudence infinie.*
   Il ne me connoît pas! (p. 560)

This juxtaposition of dramatic ravings and insolent unconcern lies also behind the comic force of a similar meeting in Mareschal's *L'Inconstance d'Hylas*. When Hylas meets Dorinde in Act III Scene 2, the extravagant matter-of-factness of the hero quite relaxes all tension; the more the deceived heroine rails, the more the madman's calmness is thrown into relief:

Dorinde: *Horreur de tous les yeux, & des ames la peste,*
   De ta déloyauté viens voir ce qui me reste,
   Voy comme tu changeas ma douceur en poison,
   Que ma facilité reproche à ma raison;
   Et tu ne rougis point? & je puis vivre encor?
Hylas: *Et vous pouvez traiter ainsi qui vous adore?* (p. 62)

Similarly here, Alidor plays a part of gracelessness and indifference which captures the audience's attention:

Angelique: *Aprens, perfide, aprens que je suis hors d'erreur,*
             Tes yeux ne me sont plus que des objets d'horreur,
             Je ne suis plus charmée, & mon ame plus saine
             N'eut jamais tant d'amour qu'elle a pour toy de haine.
Alidor: *Voila me recevoir avec des compliments.* (351–5)

There is sympathy for the heroine in this scene, not so much in her suffering, but in the confusion and astonishment she expresses at the extravagant behaviour of her lover: '*Aprés mille serments il me manque de foy,* / *Et me demande encor si c'est là tant dequoy!*' (371–2). Corneille clearly follows in an established comic tradition, but there is an important difference between his scene and the others. Whereas both Ménèchme Sosicle and Hylas act spontaneously, their insolence being the consequence either of a complete misunderstanding or of a naturally inconstant nature, Alidor is seen simply to pretend. It is this element of pretence which lies behind the originality of the scene.

The letter which apparently proves Alidor's infidelity to the heroine has that brutality which is characteristic of several of Hylas' missives. When he rids himself of Dorinde in Mareschal's play, Act III Scene 6, he is quite unsparing in his insults:

> *Apprenez que mon coeur, qui rit à vos dépens,*
> *Ne vous a point aymée, ou que je m'en repents?*
> *Et que pour vous porter à ce nom de cruelle,*
> *Hylas n'est pas si sot, ni Dorinde assez belle.* (p. 79)

What is significant about Alidor's letter, however, is not so much that it disparages Angelique, but that it insults even more the fictitious recipient:

> *Ce n'est qu'une Idole mouvante,*
> *Ses yeux sont sans vigueur, sa bouche sans appas,*
> *Quand je la crûs d'esprit je ne la connus pas,*
> *Et de quelques attraits que le monde vous vante,*
> *Vous devez mes affections*
> *Autant à ses defauts qu'à vos perfections.* (363–8)

Such lines as these reveal not so much the mind of an *inconstant*, but of one who tries to play such a part; Alidor follows a traditional path, but he is less competent and convincing than his model.

This comic presentation of Alidor the role-player is crystallised in the hero's sarcastic rebuff of Angelique's expression of despair. As the heroine muses on the mirror which reflects the imperfections of her face, Alidor is quick to step in with an ironical observation:

Angelique: Il m'en donne un advis sans me les reprocher,
             Et me les découvrant, il m'aide à les cacher.
Alidor: Vous estes en colere, & vous dites des pointes! (399–401)

This form of stylisation which in its precious word-play suggests an oddly intellectualised reaction to suffering, was subject to much criticism at the time, as was seen in an earlier chapter. D'Alibray, for instance, in his preface to *Aminte* saw such language as quite incapable of expressing deeply felt emotions: 'Car comment une personne vrayment touchée auroit-elle de semblables pensées, qui tant s'en faut qu'elles percent, qu'elles ne piquent pas seulement, mais ne font que nous chatoüiller l'ame, & nous exciter à rire en nous mesmes . . .' That Alidor should echo this current theatrical criticism is significant. He clearly regards Angelique not as a heroine who may suffer, but as an actress whose language is *invraisemblable*. So conscious is he of himself as an actor that he conceives the entire encounter as a dramatic performance in which feelings are not deeply felt, neither his nor Angelique's.

3

> Que pour ton amitié, je vay souffrir de peine!
> Desja presque eschappé je rentre dans ma chaine,
> Il faut encore un coup m'exposant à ses yeux,
> Reprendre de l'amour afin d'en donner mieux . . .[9]

More than just an aspiring *esprit fort*, however, Alidor has a comic complexity as a lover which is suggested particularly in his relationship with Cleandre. From their first meeting in Act I Scene 4, it is clear that he identifies with his friend's aspirations to love Angelique, and he speaks the language of many a hero prepared, out of friendship, to give up his beloved. This is a theme current in plays of the time, and it lies at the centre of Rayssiguier's *Célidée*, in which Oronte resolves to give up the heroine for the sake of Alidor, who dies of unrequited love for her:

> *Quelqu'amour que mon ame ayt encore pour elle,*
> *Il ne doit pas mourir pour aymer ceste belle.*
> *Je veux que mon amour cede à mon amitié,*
> *Qu'en sa faveur je sois contre moy sans pitié.* (I 2, p. 6)

Similarly, in Rotrou's *Céliane*, Act III Scene 3, Pamphile tries to persuade Nise that she should transfer her affections to Florimant, in whose favour the hero renounces his love:

> *Un seul de vos baisers charme tous mes esprits,*
> *Et je ne songe plus au nectar sans mépris,*
> *Mais souffrez que mon ame, esclave de la votre*
> *Les prenne désormais par la bouche d'un autre,*
> *D'un ami sans exemple, et que je tiens si cher,*
> *Que par lui je croirai vous voir et vous toucher . . .* (II, p. 291)

Alidor makes the same sacrifice with regard to Cleandre, but in his case it suggests not an act of courageous self-denial but reflects a more complex comic personality. He acts thus, not because he prefers his friend to himself, but because he fears to love on his own account; his gesture is less a spontaneous act of strength, but an attempt to disguise his own weakness:

> *Si ce joug inhumain, ce passage trompeur,*
> *Ce supplice éternel ne te fait point de peur,*
> *A moy ne tiendra pas que la Beauté que j'aime*
> *Ne me quitte bien tost pour un autre moy-mesme.* (279–82)

This curious relationship is given greater depth in the second half of the comedy. The hero's first scheme to have Cleandre replace him in Angelique's affections is a failure: Doraste steps in and takes advantage of the heroine's temporary *dépit*. For Alidor seeking merely to rid himself of this love, such a failure should have been of no consequence; his avowed aim was to avoid the ties of marriage, and in this he has been successful. Clearly, however, this particular outcome does not satisfy him, and when he learns the news in Act III Scene 4, the complexity of his attitude towards Cleandre and his love becomes apparent:

> *Que je serois heureux si je ne t'aimois point!*
> *Cet Hymen auroit mis mon bonheur à son point.*
> *La prison d'Angelique auroit rompu la mienne,*
> *Quelque empire sur moy que son visage obtienne,*
> *Ma passion fust morte avec sa liberté . . .* (715–19)

Cleandre is something of a second persona for Alidor, the hero through whom he wishes to satisfy the love he fears to satisfy himself. Alidor clearly loves Angelique, and his true aim is not so much to forget her as to fulfil his love from a safe distance. By a curious paradox, the *amoureux extravagant* seeks happiness with Angelique even as he seems to reject her, and this happiness depends quite literally on Cleandre's:

> A ces conditions mon bon heur me desplaist,
> Je ne puis estre heureux, si Cleandre ne l'est,
> Ce que je t'ay promis ne peut estre à personne,
> Il faut que je perisse, ou que je te le donne. (731–4)

In Alidor's second scheme, Corneille suggests this particular ambiguity in his character. The hero proposes to re-win Angelique's love, persuade her to elope with him and then to substitute Cleandre for himself at the last moment. In Act III Scene 6, he returns to the heroine, playing the part of the repentant lover; it is a scene of reconciliation which is fascinating in its implications.

Alidor's role as the self-justifying hero is a traditional one. In Rayssiguier's *Célidée*, Act IV Scene 3, Oronte urges the heroine to believe that he still loves her, in spite of his apparent desire to see another marry her:

> Mais si vous me voulez escouter un moment,
> Vous sçaurez que je suis tousjours fidelle Amant,
> Vous verrez que ma flame est tousjours toute entiere,
> Que je n'ay rien perdu de mon ardeur premiere,
> Que j'aime Calirie, & que ce que j'ay fait
> N'est que de mon malheur un miserable effet . . . (p. 83)

For Corneille's hero, this role suggests a curious blend of falsehood and truth, of calculation and spontaneity. As he protests his innocence to Angelique, he has an ulterior intention to deceive, and yet what he says is factually true; he acts a part here, and yet, in a certain way, the part he plays is that of himself:

> Mais demeurez du moins tant que vous ayez sceu
> Que par un feint mépris vostre amour fut deçeu,
> Que je vous fus fidelle en dépit de ma lettre,
> Qu'en vos mains seulement on la devoit remettre,
> Que mon dessein n'alloit qu'à voir vos mouvements,
> Et juger de vos feux par vos ressentiments. (815–20)

Alidor's delight in the performance is clear as he launches himself into his role, nobly renouncing all claims to his mistress in favour of the rival suitor:

> *Aussi ne viens-je pas pour regaigner vostre ame,*
> *Preferez moy Doraste, & devenez sa femme,*
> *Je vous viens par ma mort en donner le pouvoir.*
> *Moy vivant vostre foy ne le peut recevoir* . . . (837–40)

The theatricality is evident; his lines are quite conventional, and in their formulation they echo those of many a hero who returns to his beloved to seek death at her hands. Clitophon speaks thus in du Ryer's *Clitophon*, Act IV Scene 10, and in Pichou's *Filis de Scire*, Act V Scene 3, Nise addresses the heroine with these words:

> *Je cherche le supplice, & non pas le pardon,*
> *Quand mesme tu voudrois m'obliger de ce don:*
> *Et quoy que la raison apporte à ma defence,*
> *Je veux par mon trespas reparer mon offence.* (p. 114)

Alidor's performance is comic on an obvious level, of course, insofar as it is quite clear that he has not the slightest intention of dying. The audience's knowledge of context suggests a comic discrepancy between the speaker and the role, in just the same way as the protestations of Artoclise, for instance, in the anonymous *Capitan*,[10] Act V Scene 2, however polished on their own terms, are seen to be an accomplished performance designed to dupe the gullible Pirgopolinice:

> *Je veux à ses genoux implorer sa clemence:*
> *Et si ce beau vainqueur neglige ma souffrance,*
> *Un poignard fera voir en me privant du jour,*
> *Et son ingratitude, & mon fidelle amour.* (p. 109)

The comedy, however, extends further than this. As was the case in Corneille's earlier plays, studied theatricality is seen to suggest both simultaneously and paradoxically the spontaneous expression of feelings. The affection of hero for heroine has been apparent from the start and through his mask of lover which Alidor so comically adopts is suggested the image of his face. By acting the role of himself he can reconcile the fundamental discrepancy in his character, between his love for the heroine and his unwillingness to express it directly; he is now able to protest his affection in traditional terms, but in such a way as to convince himself that he is only playing a part. When Tirsis reads out his sonnet of love to Cloris in *Mélite*, he wishes to persuade her that '*je est un autre*', and Corneille suggests the comic failure of this performance as an astute sister sees through the ruse. Here, the dramatist suggests in his hero a more subtle form of attempted deception, not simply of another, but also of himself.

As the scene progresses, the hero's lines reveal this complex double force. Like the amusing villain, he enthuses in the performance of his role, and his fears that his plan may be frustrated are comically reflected in the ever-increasing violence of his language:

> Puis que vous consentez plustost à vos suplices,
> Qu'à l'unique moyen de payer mes services,
> Ma mort va me vanger de vostre peu d'amour,
> Si vous n'estes à moy, je ne veux plus du jour. (861–4)

And yet, behind this evocation of annoyance Corneille suggests Alidor's more complex personal frustration as a lover, seemingly unable to win back the affection of a girl whom he still loves.

Throughout this encounter the dramatist implies a dual focus on the actor who both speaks for another and for himself, on the character who both plays and is. The hero's final speech of triumph suggests on one level, indeed, the villain who gloriously boasts his skill in deception. When Ardilan feigns love for Darinée in Auvray's *Dorinde*, Act II Scene 1, he is delighted at the accomplishment of his performance: '*J'ay fort bien fait mon role, & le meilleur Acteur / Ne sçauroit mieux que moy contrefaire le flateur*' (p. 35). This same element of self-congratulation is found in Alidor's reaction:

> Cleandre elle est à toy, j'ay flechy son courage.
> Que ne peut l'artifice, & le fard du langage!
> Et si pour un amy ces effets je produis,
> Lors que j'agis pour moy, qu'est ce que je ne puis? (905–8)

but there are suggestions here, too, of fascinating self-deception. By acting, Alidor is able to project and perform the role of himself as lover which he longs, and yet fears to fulfil. It is significant that his protestations of control, the assertions that he has spoken purely on behalf of Cleandre, should thus go hand in hand with references to himself and to the pleasure which such a performance can bring.

Corneille develops these particularly subtle comic ambiguities in his presentation of the abduction itself. The complexity of Alidor's role is suggested in the opening monologue of Act IV. As he waits for Angelique to appear, he welcomes the darkness of night which promises to favour his plans. This reaction is traditional in tragi-comedy of the time, an expectation of success which is voiced by both heroes and villains alike. In Rotrou's *Les Deux Pucelles*,[11] Act I Scene 1, the hero Don Antoine speaks thus as he looks forward to an amorous assignation: '*Dieux! que le ciel ce soir couvre d'un voile obscur / Le lambris étiolé de sa voûte d'azur!*' (II, p. 463),[12] and in Scudéry's *Le Trompeur puny*, Act I Scene 7, the scheming Cleonte prays in this way as he plans a more violent encounter: '*O Nuict, obscure nuict, favorable aux trompeurs, / Double bien ton manteau de ces noires vapeurs . . .*' (p. 25).[13] That Alidor should voice these same feelings is, in itself, suggestive, underlying what is both traditionally heroic and villainous in his nature. And, in the very terms of his reaction, Corneille suggests the curious paradox in the character of one who only acts the part of himself, and whose happiness is to be experienced from a distance:

> *Enfin la nuict s'avance, & son voile propice*
> *Me va faciliter le succés que j'attends*
> *Pour rendre heureux Cleandre, & mes desirs contents.* (934–6)

It is at this point of calm self-examination that Corneille uncovers in his hero a fascinating awareness of his own frailty and foolishness. His love for Angelique emerges again in all its intensity, and he hints that his fear of its dominion over him is simply a figment of his imagination:

> *Quel excés de plaisirs gousta mon imprudence*
> *Avant que s'adviser de cette violence!*
> *Examinant mon feu qu'est-ce que je ne pers!*
> *Et qu'il m'est cher vendu de cognoistre mes fers!* (957–60)

Alidor's weakness here is clear, and the more he moves to protest his strength, the more evident becomes his dependence on love. He is quite unable to play convincingly his self-appointed role of *esprit fort*, and his powerlessness is made explicit, even at the point of his most confident self-assertion:

> *Amour, que ton pouvoir tasche en vain de paroistre!*
> *Fuy, petit insolent, je veux estre le maistre,*

> *Il ne sera pas dit qu'un homme tel que moy*
> *En despit qu'il en ait obeisse à ta loy.* (993–6)

Banality and petulance deflate the character's heroic protestations here, and his claims of control and self-mastery are undermined literally from within, as he admits, in the final line, that he is simply and hopelessly in love.

The abduction attempt is a fiasco. Philis, not Angelique, is swept away by Cleandre, and Alidor is left alone once more, unaware that Angelique is still in the house. For a moment, the hero is overcome again with passion, and prepares to fulfil his role as the faithful suitor:

> *Escoute ses souspirs, considere ses larmes,*
> *Et laisse toy gaigner à de si fortes armes,*
> *Cours apres elle, & voy si Cleandre aujourd'huy*
> *Pourra faire pour toy ce que tu fais pour luy.* (1065–8)

His defeat here is total, and yet, within the space of a few lines, he disavows once more the feelings he has. For Alidor, weakness is again translated into strength as he banishes all thought of tenderness:

> *Suis-je encor Alidor apres ces sentiments?*
> *Et ne pourray-je en fin regler mes mouvements? . . .*
> *Temeraire avorton d'un impuissant remors,*
> *Va, va porter ailleurs tes debiles efforts . . .*
> *Pour un meschant souspir que tu m'as desrobé*
> *Ne me presume pas encore succombé.*
> *Je sçay trop maintenir ce que je me propose,*
> *Et souverain sur moy rien que moy n'en dispose.* (1075–6; 1079–80; 1083–6)

The singleness of identity which the hero seeks is suggested in this telling reference to his name, and yet the self-deception it implies is clear. Following as it does the passage of spontaneous and loving remorse, such claims to self mastery carry less than total conviction. Alidor, the *esprit fort*, is only one side of the complex comic personality already known to the audience. Furthermore, the hero is no more able to rid himself of Angelique in his deeds than he is in his words. She is present in his mind even as he claims to reject her, and she is even more comically present in person at the precise moment when he believes her to be far away. The farcical failure of his abduction plan highlights in a striking way the comic vacillations in a hero who tries vainly to persuade himself that he can fall out of love.

4

Le caractère d'Angelique sort de la bienseance, en ce qu'elle est trop amoureuse . . .[14]

Although Corneille devotes much time to Alidor, he gives also to Angelique an important and complex dramatic function. In many respects, this character falls into the tradition of the deceived heroine whose love continues even after apparent infidelity. In Act II Scene 3, her anger at Alidor's curious rejection of her has a charming comic force as outrage gives way to particular tenderness:

> *Que je m'anime en vain contre un objet aimable!*
> *Tout criminel qu'il est il me semble adorable,*
> *Et mes souhaits qu'estouffe un soudain repentir*
> *En demandant sa mort n'y sçauroient consentir,* (449–52)

and indeed, when the hero returns to her in Act III Scene 6, her love comes again to the fore. This capacity for forgiveness is not unusual in heroines of the time. In Rayssiguier's *Les Thuilleries*, Act II Scene 1, Daphnide confesses that her anger at the faithless hero could only be shortlived:

> *Je ne puis l'oublier, & ma facillité*
> *Me feroit pardonner son infidellité,*
> *Si l'ingrat revenoit par quelque foible excuse,*
> *Asseurer mon esprit qu'un faux soupçon l'abuse,* (p. 26)

and in Rotrou's *La Pèlerine amoureuse*, Act V Scene 8, Angelique is quite open about her inability not to forgive the lover who has betrayed her: '*Pour traiter froidement un traître qui m'outrage, / J'ai trop d'affection et trop peu de courage*' (II, p. 520). In *La Place Royale*, however, as in *La Galerie du Palais*, Corneille gives a sensitive dramatic portrayal of what other writers simply describe, revealing in Angelique's words of aggravation her vain attempt to conceal continued love. As the hero kneels silently before her in Act III Scene 6, all anger dissolves into an avowal of forgiveness and longing:

> *Pour triompher de moy, veux tu pour toutes armes*
> *Employer des soupirs, & de muettes larmes?*
> *Sur nostre amour passé c'est là trop te fier,*
> *Du moins dy quelque chose à te justifier,*
> *Demande le pardon que tes regards m'arrachent,*
> *Explique leurs discours, dy moy ce qu'ils me cachent.* (801–6)

The heroine's resurgence of love here and her willingness to flee with Alidor is often seen as a sign of moral weakness and culpability.[15] Corneille himself argues in this way, and yet such a desire to elope is certainly not an indicator of wantonness in lovers of the time. Amélie resolves to follow her beloved in Rotrou's *Amélie*, Act III Scene 3, as do Belise in Scudéry's *Le Fils supposé*, Act I Scene 5 and Amarillis in du Ryer's *Amarillis*, Act IV Scene 6, and in the latter dramatist's *Clitophon*, Act I Scene 8, Lucipe acknowledges the omnipotence of love which inspires her in her flight:

> *Brisons là Clitophon; l'amour m'a resolue*
> *Et je cede à la fin à sa force absolue.*
> *Je veux suivre par tout tes pas et tes desirs,*
> *J'aurai part à tes maux ainsi qu'à tes plaisirs.* (p. 82)

It is in these terms exactly that Angelique justifies her own action:

> *Dessus mes volontez ta puissance absoluë*
> *Peut disposer de moy, peut tout me commander.*
> *Mon honneur en tes mains prest à se hazarder,*
> *Par un trait si hardy, quelque tort qu'il se fasse,*
> *Y consent toutefois . . .* (866–70)

Such absolute commitment to love is not the mark of an extravagant idealism but a quite conventional response to one's lover. In the opening scene of the play, Angelique expresses pride in her devotion to Alidor:

> *Vois-tu, j'ayme Alidor, & cela c'est tout dire;*
> *Le reste des mortels pourroit m'offrir des voeux,*
> *Je suis aveugle, sourde, insensible pour eux . . .* (34–6)

lines which, far from setting her apart, situate her in a tradition of heroines with a similar conception of love and its demands. Astrée herself has no less passion, and expects no less from Celadon: '*Il faudra servir, souffrir, et n'avoir des yeux, ny de l'amour que pour moy; car ne croyez point que je veuille avoir à partir avec quelque autre, ny que je reçoive une volonté à moitié mienne*' (I 3, p. 67), and these same feelings are echoed by Rotrou's heroine in *La Pèlerine amoureuse*, Act IV Scene 7, who sees her own love as exemplary:

> *J'aime seule ardemment, et, de toutes les âmes*
> *Capables de porter des chaînes et des flammes,*
> *J'ai seule de l'amour senti les vifs accès,*
> *Seule aimée sans réserve, et seule dans l'excès.* (II, p. 499)

However, Corneille does far more than simply present a conventional heroine; the traditional elements which he deliberately reproduces here serve a particular purpose in the comic structure of the play.

It has been seen how, in the first meeting with her lover, her expression of confusion and disbelief highlights the comic extravagance of the hero. Similarly, in the final stages of the hero's attempted abduction, her sudden appearance is exploited by Corneille as a further source of discomfort for Alidor. The force of the comedy is crystallised in her opening line of Act IV Scene 6, whose very simplicity, not to say banality, underlines the crushing blow delivered to the hero by this unexpected entry: '*Je demande pardon de t'avoir fait attendre*' (1090). In this encounter, stress is not given to the pathetic vulnerability of Angelique but to the comic struggles and surprise of the hero. Words of suspicion and accusation are spoken, but not by an outraged heroine. As Alidor realises the mistake which has been made, he uses the language of attack in an attempt to cover up his own defencelessness:

> *Quel soudain repentir, quelle crainte de blasme,*
> *Et quelle ruse en fin vous desrobe à ma flame?*
> *Ne vous suffit-il point de me manquer de foy,*
> *Sans prendre encor plaisir à vous joüer de moy?* (1101–4)

Angelique continues to embarrass the hero, chastising him for his ridiculous inertia. Her expression of fear at the prospect of marriage to a man she does not love, traditional as it is in its formulation, emphasises not so much her potential misery, as the absurdity of the hero. No drama is felt here, no parental tyranny exercising its force on a powerless heroine; the focus of attention is Alidor himself, unable to play the role of lover:

> *L'hymen (ah! ce penser desja me fait mourir)*
> *Me va joindre à Doraste, & tu le peux souffrir!*
> *Tu me peux exposer à cette tyrannie!*
> *De l'erreur de tes gens je me verray punie!* (1135–8)

Her confusion and frustration in the face of an abductor curiously rooted to the spot throws into relief the hero's vacillations and it reaches a fine comic climax as she uncovers in telling lines what has been seen throughout to be the fundamental frailty and weakness behind her lover's extravagance:

> *Tu manques de courage aussi bien que d'amour,*
> *Et tu me fais trop voir par cette resverie*
> *Le chimerique effet de ta poltronnerie.*
> *Alidor (quel amant!) n'ose me posseder.* (1148–51)

Significantly, through this presentation of the heroine, Corneille carefully builds up the expectations of the audience, prefiguring thus the traditional happy ending of comedy. Angelique is seen to have a capacity for love which is part of her particular dramatic appeal. Apparent anger constantly gives way to forgiveness, and through this Corneille suggests all the charm of a lover's *dépit* whose effects can only be temporary. Similar expectations are aroused by the heroine's comic relationship with Alidor. Not simply a touching figure created in isolation, Angelique constantly throws into relief the absurd behaviour of her lover, highlighting by her own devotion the folly of the hero's inept attempt to disguise and control his own. Her capacity for tenderness suggests indeed that Alidor's fears are all groundless, and that his extravagance, like a bout of madness, will ultimately be cured. It is against this background of particularly sophisticated comedy that the unique force of the *dénouement* may be fully appreciated.

5

A ce mot Hylas luy rebaisa la main, et Stelle, après avoir fait semblant de ne vouloir plus de luy, fut enfin contrainte de le remettre en grace, toute la compagnie l'ayant condamnée à cela.[16]

The opening of the last Act prepares the way for such expected reconciliations. Cleandre is to marry Philis whom he has spurned for so long, the reversal of his intentions expressed in a speech of gratuitous virtuosity, as the lover piles contrast upon contrast:

> *Avez vous jamais veu dessein plus renversé?*
> *Quand j'ay la force en main, je me trouve forcé,*
> *Je crois prendre une fille, & suis pris par un autre,*
> *J'ay tout pouvoir sur vous & me remets au vostre . . .* (1280–3)

The creation of order is here so effortless and unproblematical that it can be reduced to the stylised exhibition of verbal acrobatics and a shameless delight in the improbable. Yet, at the same time, this easy creation of harmony is slightly distorted. At

the end of Act V Scene 1, Philis suggests quite calculating
motives behind her parents' acceptance of her suitor: '*Le monde
vous croit riche, & mes parens sont vieux*' (1313), and in Act V Scene
5, she stresses, arbitrarily perhaps, that although she will gladly
obey her father's wishes, she has no particular feelings of
affection for her designated partner:

> *Il fait tous ses efforts pour gaigner mes parens,*
> *Et s'il les peut flechir, quant à moy je me rends,*
> *Non pas, à dire vray, que son objet me tente,*
> *Mais mon pere content je suis assez contente.* (1444–7)

This curious awkwardness is sustained in the reaction of
Doraste to the attempted abduction, where again a traditional
movement is deliberately warped. Doraste is cast in the same
mould as Beys' Belanire in *Le Jaloux sans sujet*, who, as was seen
in the last chapter, reacts angrily and bitterly to the discovery
that his suit of the heroine is vain. In Beys' play, the disappointed lover is ultimately brought back into the order of the
principals, unable to remain angry until the end, and in Act V
Scene 5, falling in love with the sister of the one who had
rejected him:

> *Je retourne chez vous, je ne vous puis quitter;*
> *Ces aimables appas me viennent d'arrester,*
> *J'aime dans cette soeur la moitié de vous mesmes.* (p. 107)

For Doraste, however, scorn remains to the last, its force being
all the greater since its object is to bring together the hero and
heroine. Words of forgiveness are spoken, but in a way which is
strikingly unforgiving; in Act V Scene 4, he is quite incapable of
believing Angelique's innocence in her proposed flight:

> *Et tiens sa trahison indigne à l'advenir*
> *D'occuper aucun lieu dedans mon souvenir.*
> *Qu'Alidor la possede, il est traistre comme elle,*
> *Jamais pour ce sujet nous n'aurons de querelle.* (1404–7)

In Act V Scene 6, Cleandre requests in traditional terms that the
past be forgotten: '*Ne me refusez point un oubly du passé*' (1468),
but in his reply, Doraste's personal feelings of acrimony are
again apparent. He welcomes his brother-in-law to be not as a
fitting partner for Philis, but as the one who has enlightened
him about the faithless nature of Angelique:

> *Vous m'avez obligé de m'oster Angelique,*
> *Rien de ce qui la touche à present ne me picque,*
> *Je n'y prens plus de part apres sa trahison,*
> *Je l'aimay par malheur, & la hay par raison.* (1478–81)

Finally, as he urges hero and heroine together in Act V Scene 7, the smooth movement towards the expected harmony is warped again by the tone of his encouragement. He is inspired in his lines not by generosity, by humility before the higher and principal order of love which the protagonists traditionally embody, by forgiveness, but, quite simply, by contempt:

> *Satisfaites sans crainte à vos intentions,*
> *Je ne mets plus d'obstacle à vos affections,*
> *Si vous faussez desja la parole donnée*
> *Que ne feriez-vous point apres nostre Hymenée?*
> *Pour moy, mal aisément on me trompe deux fois,*
> *Vous l'aimiez, aimez-le, je luy cede mes droits.* (1500–5)

What is most striking, however, is that Doraste's total inability to forgive is complemented by Angelique's own. Her reaction to Alidor's final deception is quite categorical: '. . . *Desloyal, cesse de me poursuivre, / Si je t'aime jamais je veux cesser de vivre*' (1510–11), and she simply expresses the desire to retreat to a convent, unable now to love again:

> *Un Cloistre desormais bornera mes desseins,*
> *C'est là que je prendray des mouvements plus saints,*
> *C'est là que loing du monde & de sa vaine pompe*
> *Je n'auray qui tromper, non plus que qui me trompe.* (1524–7)

Such a reaction is not in itself unusual, of course. Indeed, in many plays of the time deceived heroines swear to renounce all love and seek security elsewhere. Angelique recalls Arthenice, the heroine of Racan's *Bergeries*, who, in Act II Scene 4, makes a similar resolution when convinced of her lover's treachery:

> *Quant à moi désormais le seul bien que j'espère*
> *Est de passer ma vie en un désert austère,*
> *Où sage à mes dépens, je veux à l'avenir*
> *Au seul amour du Ciel mes volontés unir,* (989–92)

or Célidée in Rayssiguier's *Célidée*, Act III Scene 1, who expresses her despair that Oronte should be able to sacrifice her to another:

> *Mon esprit détrompé ne sera plus capable*
> *De croire rien en moy qui me peut rendre aimable,*

> *Ainsi me defiant des hommes desormais,*
> *Je vivray tousjours libre, & n'aimeray jamais.*[17] (p. 52)

In all these cases, however, despair is ultimately controlled and cured. Infidelity is either revealed to have been an illusion, or, where it has actually taken place, forgiveness is always forthcoming. In Rotrou's *Florimonde*, Act V Scene 5, for instance, Cleonie takes back the villainous Timante:

> *Je souffre ta présence apres ta perfidie!*
> *Traître, tu m'as charmée, il faut que je le die;*
> *Gouverne mes desseins, dispose de mes voeux,*
> *Et prends comme il te plaît le pardon que tu veux.* (V, p. 488)

Such lines reflect that same ability to forget the past which was seen to be a characteristic of many heroines in plays of the time.

This solidity in the framework of comedy is frequently embodied in the character of the *fille gaie*, the voice of reason and common sense who firmly controls suffering and warns about the dangers of taking life too seriously. Such a figure has its origins in the sound advisors who abound in *L'Astrée*, who are able to pass equitable judgements and settle disputes. Diane is such a one, chosen, it seems, by the gods to ensure that no harm comes to the characters whose problems lead them to the brink of chaos, and who is welcomed thus:

Et puis que les dieux vous ont choisie parmy tous ceux qui sont en cette contrée, pour nous remettre dans le repos, dont par mal-heur nous sommes sortis, et que nous ne pouvons retrouver sans vous, il ne faut point douter, qu'ensemble ils ne vous ayent donné et la puissance et la capacité de le faire. (IV 2, p. 55)

The character is particularly frequent in Rotrou's comic world, where all longing for isolation and death is firmly put into perspective. In *Céliane*, Act IV Scene 6, Julie thus dissuades Nise from taking poison: *'Dieux! les plaisans effets dont votre coeur se pique! / C'est bien traiter l'amour à la façon antique . . .'* (II, pp. 310–11), and in *Clorinde*, Act IV Scene 2, Lysante similarly controls the heroine's despair, her irony delicately but surely maintaining the comic order:

> *On eût prisé jadis l'ardeur qui vous transporte,*
> *Mais le siècle n'est plus d'aimer de telle sorte;*
> *Représentez-vous point ces reines des romans,*
> *Qui ne l'ont pas été des coeurs de leurs amans,*
> *Dont l'amour fut ingrate, et la constance vaine,*
> *Et qu'au théâtre même on souffriroit à peine . . .* (III, p. 230)

In *La Place Royale*, Corneille clearly casts Philis in this same mould, having her underline what has already been seen to be implicit in Angelique herself and what is deeply rooted in the tradition of comedy: the fact that forgiveness is possible and to be desired. As early as the opening scene of the play she claims for herself this ability to dispel all suffering: '*Il n'est point de douleur si forte en un courage / Qui ne perde sa force auprès de mon visage . . .*' (137–8). For her, a *dépit amoureux* must not assume tragic proportions, and as she leaves the stage she offers this advice and encouragement to the heroine:

> *Je croy qu'un bon dessein dans le Cloistre te porte,*
> *Mais un despit d'amour n'en est pas bien la porte,*
> *Et l'on court grand hazard d'un cuisant repentir*
> *De se voir en prison sans espoir d'en sortir. . . .*
> *Adieu, par mon exemple apprends comme il faut vivre,*
> *Et pren pour Alidor un naturel plus doux.* (1546–9; 1551–2)

Against this background of reassuring good sense, the final resolution of Angelique to flee to a convent is felt with even greater force. Corneille builds up conventional expectations in order to throw more sharply into relief his departure from tradition. The framework of comedy which, in *L'Astrée*, is such that Hylas is returned to fidelity and Stelle to forgiveness, crumbles totally in this play. Angelique acknowledges no such restraint; for her there can be no simple changes of heart, and her only course is to leave the comic scene:

> *Ma foy qu'avoit Doraste engageoit ma franchise,*
> *Et je ne voy plus rien puis qu'il me l'a remise*
> *Qui me retienne au monde, ou m'arreste en ce lieu.*
> *Cherche un autre à trahir, & pour jamais, Adieu.* (1558–61)

Such an unexpected separation of hero and heroine is not without parallel in plays of the time. In Pichou's *L'Infidèle Confidente*, Lisanor betrays Lorise and subsequently marries his new mistress; in Act V Scene 4, however, the deceived fiancée is happy to forget her first love and accept the suit of another:

> *Ainsi vostre malheur treuve un allegement*
> *Dedans les voluptez d'un heureux changement,*
> *Et son affection reparant son outrage*
> *Vous fera mieux gouster le calme apres l'orage.* (p. 116)

Similarly, in Rayssiguier's *Les Thuilleries*, the heroine Daphnide is forsaken by her lover, and the couple are never united; she again,

though, willingly transfers her affections and forgets the past in
Act V Scene 4:

> *Il est vray, je l'ay fait pour vanger une injure,*
> *Qu'avoit à mon amour fait cette ame parjure.*
> *Mais le ressentiment de ce coeur effacé*
> *Je vous prie oublions tout ce qui s'est passé.* (p. 100)

Comparison with these two plays is revealing. In the texts of both
Pichou and Rayssiguier, the heroine's love for the hero is finally
extinguished, but this separation is happily accepted. For
Angelique, however, the same transition from love to indifference is far more complex and suggestive. Her rejection of Alidor
does not entail the exchange of one lover for another, implying a
rather arbitrary change of attitude, but it is more carefully
motivated, bringing together suggestions of continued love and
fear.

   Although indicating on one level a categorical refusal of Philis'
final advice, Angelique's determination to retreat to a convent
suggests in a significant way her reminiscence of an earlier
conversation with her friend. It is one of the roles of the *fille gaie* to
perceive the true nature of a character's heart, and in Act II Scene
4 Philis' astute remark that Angelique will forgive Alidor in spite
of his treachery is proved right by events. In that same scene,
however, she voices a warning that such facility in forgiveness
may be the heroine's undoing:

> *Mais j'en crains un progrés à ta confusion,*
> *Qui change une fois, change à toute occasion,*
> *Et nous verrons tousjours, si Dieu le laisse vivre,*
> *Un change, un repentir, un pardon s'entresuivre,*
> *Ce dernier est souvent l'amorce d'un forfait,*
> *Et l'on cesse de craindre un courous sans effet.* (487–92)

In this early scene, the outraged heroine had dismissed the very
possibility of her forgiving Alidor, but, in so doing, she added a
qualification whose significance here is paramount:

> *Et si je presumois que mon trop de bonté*
> *Peust jamais se resoudre à cette lascheté,*
> *Qu'un si honteux pardon peust suivre cette offense,*
> *J'en previendrois le coup, m'en ostant la puissance.* (495–8)

In Act III, Angelique's confident protestations of self-control
were proved wrong, and pardon was readily granted; in Act V,

however, this is no longer the case. Angelique has learned much
about herself in the course of the play, about her willingness to
forgive and about her inability to control her love. Such self-
knowledge is typical of several heroines of the time, as has been
seen, but for Angelique the consequences of it are far more
suggestive. She fears future deceptions, future disappoint-
ments, and sees herself embarked on that cycle of reactions
which Philis had so pertinently described. Behind this final
gesture, Corneille suggests not so much a simple transition from
love to hatred, but the heroine's ultimate awareness of her own
frailty.

In his presentation of Angelique, Corneille manipulates the
expectations of the audience in order to throw into relief the
originality of his heroine, suggesting particularly complex motives behind an action which comes as a complete surprise. His
depiction of Alidor in these final scenes follows a similar
pattern.

In Act V Scene 3, it seems that Alidor has finally returned to
his senses, and that the madness which had characterised his
actions in the play has finally been cured. It is a traditional
transition which suggests a comic form of poetic justice; as with
Tirsis, Criton or Hylas, his protestations as an *esprit fort* are
ultimately to be proved vain. It is Alidor the spontaneous lover
who now appears before the audience, rejecting his earlier
extravagance and accepting the role which he has resisted for so
long. Confusion has ceased, and love has vanquished:

> Que l'amour pour nous vaincre a de chemins divers,
> Et que mal aisément on rompt de si beaux fers!
> C'est en vain qu'on resiste aux traits d'un beau visage,
> En vain à son pouvoir refusant son courage
> On veut esteindre un feu par ses yeux allumé,
> Et ne le point aimer quand on s'en voit aimé. (1360–5)

Like Silvandre, in Rayssiguier's *Tragi-comédie pastorale*, Alidor
commits himself to the love which he had struggled in vain to
cast off; his language is no less absolute than that of the pastoral
hero in whose steps he treads:

> Amour pour eviter les traits dont tu nous blesses,
> Que la raison humaine a de grandes foiblesses:
> Helas qu'elle est fragile, & que facilement
> Le regard d'un bel oeil force le jugement. (p. 46)[18]

In Alidor, however, this renewed commitment to love is less than total. Whereas Tirsis, for instance, moved from being the cynical to the ideal lover in a single, abrupt and unconditional gesture, Alidor retains his extravagance at the point when he would appear to be most sane; he plays the part of lover no more convincingly than he had earlier played the *esprit fort*. Silvandre's lines reflect the traditional submission of reason to the power of love, but Alidor, far from being submissive, is seen once more to claim complete mastery over himself. The criterion of *raison* which he had used earlier in the unconvincing defence of his inconstancy is now employed to justify his reaffirmed love for the heroine; his final and inevitable capitulation is hidden behind renewed protestations of self-domination, no more appropriate now than before:

> *Je ne m'obstine plus à meriter sa haine,*
> *Je me sens trop heureux d'une si belle chaisne,*
> *Ce sont traits d'esprit fort que d'en vouloir sortir,*
> *Et c'est où ma raison ne peut plus consentir.* (1374–7)

In this monologue, Corneille suggests again the particular complexity of his hero. At the start of the scene, his language had been that of the traditional lover, but by the end a curious metamorphosis has taken place. Instead of appearing as the reformed hero, looking forward with joy to a reconciliation with his beloved, he now speaks the language of the villain, quite aware of the deception he has committed.[19] He remembers the written promise of marriage, signed by Cleandre, but which he had given to Angelique in his own name, and he resolves to take it back:

> *Sur ma foy toutefois elle le prist sans lire,*
> *Et si le Ciel vangeur comme moy ne conspire,*
> *Elle s'y fie assez pour n'en avoir rien leu.*
> *Entrons à tous hazards d'un esprit resolu,*
> *Desrobons à ses yeux le tesmoing de mon crime.* (1390–4)

When he pleads with the heroine in Act V Scene 7 in a last attempt to persuade her of the authenticity of his love, the ambiguity of his character is underlined. He casts himself firmly in the role of lover, claiming that his very name denotes and captures the extent of his affection: '*Suis je plus Alidor? vos feux sont-ils esteints / Et quand mon amour croist produit-il vos desdains?*'

(1508–9). When finally Hylas had fallen in love in Act V Scene 1 of
Mareschal's *L'Inconstance d'Hylas*, he too had alluded to his name,
now seemingly changed:

> *Ne suis-je plus Hylas? & ne sçaurois-je apprendre*
> *Si je serois passé de moy-mesme en Sylvandre?*
> *Cet envieux Demon de constance & d'ennuy*
> *Voudroit-il me punir & me changer en luy?* (p. 115)

In these lines there is a simple and clearly delineated juxtaposition of two characters: Hylas who embodies inconstancy, and
Sylvandre who embodies fidelity in love. The speaker complains
that he has lost one personality and gained another; by the end of
the play, Hylas is fixed in a new role of faithful lover. For Alidor,
however, there is no such unity. His question is a telling
reminder of the earlier monologue of Act IV Scene 4, in which
Alidor the *esprit fort* had protested his strength of will with a
similar reference to his own name. His claims of self-control were
quite unconvincing, less a manifestation of power as an attempt
to persuade himself of a doubtful truth. For Alidor the lover, the
same suggestions of self-deception are apparent.

The complexity of his character is most evident in the final
monologue of the comedy, as the hero, now isolated, prides
himself on his 'victory' over love. It is not uncommon indeed for a
comedy to end with the monologue of an *esprit fort*. At the end of
Coste's *Lizimène*, Nisbé dissociates himself completely from the
ties of love, and seeks solace elsewhere, happy in his isolation.
Defeat in love leaves him with no regrets, and the audience with
no feelings of sympathy:

> *Je dis encore un coup que les Amans sont fous,*
> *Je n'en soupire plus, bien qu'elle soit jolie,*
> *Je n'ay plus dans l'esprit cette étrange folie,*
> *Berenis comme moy la voulut regarder,*
> *Donc je prie le Ciel qu'il la puisse garder.* (p. 66)

Such a character is sufficient unto himself, just like the more
farcical Guillaume, who, at the end of du Ryer's *Amarillis*, Act V
Scene 4, finds total happiness in wine: '*Pour moy qui fuis l'amour, je*
m'en vais sous nos treilles, / Au lieu de ces beautez courtiser des
bouteilles' (p. 141).

On one level, Alidor's isolation is presented in a more
obviously comic light than this; whereas both Nisbé and

Guillaume protest what the audience knows to be true,
Corneille's hero remains to the last a character whose extravagant
notions of strength conceal evident weakness. At the beginning
of the monologue, he is quite open again about the love he had
begun to feel for Angelique:

> J'avois beau la trahir, une secrette amorce
> R'allumoit dans mon coeur l'amour par la pitié,
> Mes feux en recevoient une nouvelle force,
> Et tousjours leur ardeur en croissoit de moitié, (1566–9)

and against this background, his renewed protestations of self-
control are singularly unconvincing: 'Impuissant ennemy de mon
indifference, / Je brave, vain amour, ton debile pouvoir . . .' (1574–5). In
his proud boasts, he resembles the fanfaron who creates in his
own imagination a sequence of triumphs, one who, like
Matamore at the end of Mareschal's Véritable Capitan Matamore,
can transform defeat and his own credulity into a poetic victory:

> Le champ m'est demeuré, je suis victorieux;
> Quels lauriers ne sont dus à mon front glorieux?
> L'ennemy qui s'enfuit m'abandonne la place . . . (p. 147)[20]

The comic discrepancy between words and reality is a
traditional one, but in this context it has suggestive implications.
Behind Alidor's language of joyful self-control, Corneille suggests the hero's consciousness of a love which is now lost forever.
As he sees himself again as the esprit fort, he alludes by
implication to all that has passed in the previous Acts; the
triumph he forsees in the future recalls the failure which he hopes
to bury in the past: 'Beautez, ne pensez point à resveiller ma flame, / Vos
regards ne sçauroient asservir ma raison . . .' (1582–3). For Alidor,
this term 'raison' conveniently conceals the profound ambiguity
of his feelings; in his own usage, it has justified both subservience
to love and control over it.

This confusion within him is sustained as he resorts again to
the kind of litany which had characterised his first appearance in
the play:

> Nous feindrons toutefois pour nous donner carriere,
> Et pour mieux desguiser nous en prendrons un peu,
> Mais nous sçaurons tousjours rebrousser en arriere,
> Et quand il nous plaira nous retirer du jeu. (1586–9)

He fails once more to draw a clear distinction between role and reality, *feinte* and spontaneity. His aim may be to control himself, but even as he contemplates this possibility, he indulges again in attempted self-deception. He tells himself that if he falls in love again, it will merely be '*pour mieux desguiser*', a claim whose very lack of conviction recalls all the complexity of his relationship with Angelique. As he rejoices in this apparent victory over love, there appear in his words the two elements which have suggestively combined in him from the beginning: a fear of love and yet an inability to banish it completely from his mind. The suffering which Angelique has undergone and which drives her ultimately to withdraw underlines this paradox in his character which he simply cannot resolve, even at the last:

> Cependant Angelique enfermant dans un Cloistre
> Ses yeux dont nous craignions la fatale clarté,
> Les murs qui garderont ces tyrans de paroistre
> Serviront de remparts à nostre liberté. (1590–3)

6

Les premiers Acteurs y achevent bizarrement, & tout ce qui les regarde fait languir le cinquiéme Acte, où ils ne paroissent plus à le bien prendre que comme seconds Acteurs.[21]

La Place Royale stands out as a daring and sophisticated experiment. Its elements are traditional – the *esprit fort*, the forgiving heroine, the *fille gaie*, the plot which separates lovers, – but out of these Corneille makes something quite unique.

The sensitivity in his presentation of character is clear. In Alidor, he creates a figure of fascinating originality, a hero who hovers suggestively between two distinct roles: the one who rejects love and the one who rejoices in it. It is a juxtaposition which gives an additional dimension to the traditionally comic type of the *esprit fort*, but which suggests also the complexity of a character who fears to play his own role as the lover. The same originality is evident also in Angelique, who is not simply a tragic heroine who has stepped into the wrong play, but one whose character has its own particular comic depth. Her absolute commitment to love is exploited to throw into relief Alidor's constant hesitation before it, but through this she is seen gradually to become aware of her own vulnerability and of what it may imply.

The play is also quite remarkable, however, for its dramatic boldness. The process of expectations built up and disappointed, evident already in Corneille's earlier works, is taken here to a point beyond which no development is possible. Comedy frequently depends on the audience's confidence in the dramatist, an implied certainty that all will be well in the end. Corneille himself encourages this confidence in his presentation of the protagonists – a heroine clearly prone to forgiveness, a hero whose claims to have control over love are constantly seen to be groundless, a *fille gaie* who makes sure that all despair is kept in perspective. And yet, this tradition of comedy which sees all characters happy at the end is deliberately and boldly rejected. Tensions apparent already in the *dénouements* of the last two comedies are here brought finally to the surface, and Corneille presents characters who are simply unable to bend to the exigencies of convention. A carefully prepared aesthetic shock points in retrospect to the logic of characters which remains intractable to the end. Alidor's fear of love prevents him from ever convincing in that role, and Angelique's fear of Alidor, and of herself, causes her finally to reject him. Psychological insight and theatrical originality are brought together here in a way which was quite unique in plays of the time.

VII

L'Illusion Comique
The actor triumphant

1

Voicy un éstrange monstre que je vous dédie.[1]

Of all Corneille's comedies, *L'Illusion Comique* has aroused the most widespread reactions. Its echoes of many scenes traditional in contemporary tragi-comedy have been pointed out,[2] and the play is often criticised for its apparent lack of coherence and unity, its inconsistency of characterisation and tone.[3] It is a work which for some commentators is little more than a dramatic *pot-pourri*, suggesting a stage of temporary uncommitment, a prelude to the tragedies which Corneille is about to write.[4] Other critics concentrate on the play's underlying theme of theatrical illusion, suggested by the presence of Alcandre, the magician who raises spirits to enact the adventures of Clindor for the benefit of Pridamant, the hero's father in search of his son. This particular structure has given rise to a vast range of interpretations. The comedy has been seen as an exposure of the emptiness of heroism, an examination and anticipation of work to come,[5] or a covert acknowledgement of the vanity and profitability of the theatre as a profession.[6] Others find it a more searching statement about the nature of illusion and reality in the broadest philosophical terms,[7] while others again see in the presentation of Alcandre's grotto a symbol of the theatre itself.[8]

It is a work most often interpreted in isolation, so different does it appear from other plays of the time, so vividly and uniquely does it seem to reflect the peculiar spirit of the age. However, seen in the context of *comédies* being performed in the 1630s, *L'Illusion Comique* suggests a fascinating response to certain

dramatic conventions, and, in the more particular context of
Corneille's own output in the comic genre it holds a central and
critical position. It is in these terms that I propose to analyse the
play.

2

Il y en a mesme un qui n'a d'estre que dans l'imagination, inventé exprés pour faire rire, et dont il ne se trouve point d'original parmy les hommes.[9]

Of the traditional characters taken over by Corneille in this play,
Matamore is perhaps the most fascinating, the braggart who
vainly courts Isabelle and who is constantly thwarted by Geronte,
her father, and Clindor, his own servant and rival. The *soldat
fanfaron* was a clearly established comic type before *L'Illusion
Comique*, featuring often in largely episodic roles. As Garapon has
pointed out,[10] it was in this figure that particular kinds of
linguistic exuberance were preserved at a time when this form of
comedy was out of fashion. The braggart constantly evokes
pictures of that martial prowess which exists only in his
imagination, from Don Quichotte in Pichou's *Folies de Cardenio*,
Act III Scene 5: '*L'honneur suit mes desseins, la victoire mes pas, / Et
l'un de mes regards peut causer cent trespas* . . .' (p. 56) to Le Vaillant
in Rayssiguier's *La Bourgeoise*, Act I, Scene 6: *C'est parmy les
dangers que je prens mes esbats; / Le poisson vit dans l'eau, je vis dans les
combats* (p. 22) and this characteristic hybris is often the pretext for
sustained flights of fancy, where dramatists create their own
forms of comic language. In *La Belle Alphrède*, Act I Scene 3, for
instance, Rotrou gives Ferrande the following speech, as the
braggart calls bravely after those who have just attacked his
master:

> *Toi, monstre renaissant, toi chien achérontide,*
> *Redoutables objets de la fureur d'Alcide,*
> *Dieux, Parques, animaux, hommes, démons, enfers,*
> *Eprouvez aujourd'hui de quel bras je me sers* . . . (II, p. 350)

and in Mareschal's *Le Railleur*, Act I Scene 4, Taillebras is seen to
vent his wrath thus colourfully on the feeble poet Lyzante, as
each tries unsuccessfully to court the fair Clytie:

> *M'interrompre? parler? ah! ventre! quelle audace!*
> *Jette ce Mirmidon jusques dessus Parnasse;*

> *Que là, de ses desirs amoureux & hautains*
> *Il aille entretenir ses neuf vieilles Putains,*
> *Et que ce Farfadet pour guerir sa migraine*
> *Boive tout l'Helycon, puise tout l'Hypocreine.* (p. 18)

In both cases, the ridiculous cowardice of the speaker is clear from the context, and yet they are seen here to retreat into a safely remote mythological universe, where they can happily protest their courage.

Matamore has roots in this tradition, and yet Corneille makes of him a type of particular sophistication. The braggart clearly offers the opportunity for linguistic bravura,[11] but in his use of it Corneille exhibits a fine comic feeling for the character whose strength is purely imaginary. In Act II Scene 2, Matamore outlines his qualities to Clindor, proud of the powers he has to strike terror and arouse affection wherever he wishes:

> *Regarde, j'ay quitté cette effroyable mine*
> *Qui massacre, destruit, brise, brusle, extermine,*
> *Et, pensant au bel oeil qui tient ma liberté,*
> *Je ne suis plus qu'amour, que grace, que beauté . . .* (249–52)

The attributes he gives himself are quite traditional, as, too, is their unreality; the braggart's courage is as rare as his magnificent beauty. And yet, his evocation in words of these imagined qualities has a power which is significant compensation for his inability to put them into deeds. His control over his language is here as absolute as his subsequent lack of control over his actions, and with careful modulations of tone and rhythm he moves from a picture of limitless ferocity with its stabbing enumeration of synonyms to the tranquillity of the final line which suggests the irresistible charm of strength subdued.

Nowhere is Corneille's sophistication more apparent than in the remarkable speech of Act III Scene 4, in which Matamore imagines the conflagration which would ensue were he to draw his sword. Threatened by Geronte, the braggart justifies his reluctance to defend himself in these words:

> *Ouy, mais les feux qu'il jette en sortant de prison*
> *Auroient en un moment embrazé la maison,*
> *Devoré tout à l'heure ardoises et goutieres,*
> *Faites, lattes, chevrons, montants, courbes, fillieres,*
> *Entretoises, sommiers, colomnes, soliveaux,*
> *Parnes, soles, appuis, jambages, traveteaux . . .* (747–52)

In its sheer linguistic virtuosity, the speech reflects the dramatist's positive response to a challenge to his ingenuity, but it is
given also a more specific comic function. The audience is
certain of the motives which inspire the vision, and yet it has a
particular logic which compels attention. Such is the nature of
the language and its breathless piling up of terms, that it takes
on a life of its own and draws the spectator into Matamore's
world; the character transforms reality for himself, but for the
public as well.

However, if Corneille suggests moments of particular conviction in Matamore's *rodomontades*, he is sensitive also to the comic
potential in a character whose control is not always total. On
certain occasions, the braggart's cowardice is carefully implied
in the language itself. As he waits for Isabelle in Act III Scene 7,
for instance, his inordinate fear of Geronte's servants is subtly
suggested through the timeless identity which the *fanfaron* has
created for himself. He retains the mask of an ageless, heroic
warrior, but through this, the extent of his trepidation is
exaggerated:

> *Vieux resveur, malgré toy j'attends icy ma Reine.*
> *Ces diables de valets me mettent bien en peine.*
> *De deux mille ans et plus je ne tremblay si fort.*
> *C'est trop me hazarder: s'ils sortent, je suis mort.* (857–60)

Similarly, in Act IV Scene 4, Corneille delights in the absurd
juxtaposition of the coward's great hunger, the result of his
unheroic retreat into an attic, and his claim that the divine
foodstuffs on which he has been feeding all this time have no
true sustaining power:

> *C'est un mets delicat et de peu de soustien:*
> *A moins que d'estre un Dieu, l'on n'en vivroit pas bien.*
> *Il cause mille maux, et des l'heure qu'il entre,*
> *Il allonge les dents et restressit le ventre.* (1191–4)

The vanity of his protestations is clearly exposed. As hunger
overpowers the braggart, his mask falls visibly, and from the
refined circumlocution of his opening line he is led to the
language of brutal reality.

These comic discrepancies are exploited particularly in Matamore's scenes with other characters. In Act III Scene 3, for
instance, the braggart is completely crushed by Geronte, his

protestations of valour deflated by the cutting and brutally sarcastic retort of the old man:

> *Je ne suis pas d'humeur à rire tant de fois*
> *Du crotesque recit de vos rares exploits.*
> *La sottise ne plaist qu'alors qu'elle est nouvelle . . .* (719–21)

Defeat here is total and unconditional, the *fanfaron* exposed for the coward he is known to be, the validity of his imagined world undermined. The character is reduced to the comic expression of complete disbelief at the severity of this attack:

> *Il a perdu le sens de me parler ainsi!*
> *Pauvre homme, sçais tu bien que mon nom effroyable*
> *Met le grand Turc en fuite et fait trembler le diable?*
> *Que, pour t'aneantir, je ne veux qu'un moment?* (724–7)

He may seem to threaten the father here, but beneath these warnings is clearly sensed the coward's fear; death for the enemy will not be instantaneous, but will take '*un moment*', the time needed for a hasty retreat.

This cowardice is suggested further in the heroic lament into which Matamore launches himself in the following scene. In noble lines he justifies his inaction by transforming his fear of this uncompromising adversary into an imputed respect for the love he bears his assailant's daughter:

> *Respect de ma maistresse, incommode vertu,*
> *Tiran de ma vaillance, à quoy me reduis tu?*
> *Que n'ay-je eu cent rivaux à la place d'un pere*
> *Sur qui, sans t'offencer, laisser choir ma colere?* (735–8)

The tone of the speech certainly does not correspond to the reality of the incident, but this is not just simply comic over-reaction. Through the very arguments which the character uses to imply a courageous self-control, Corneille suggests the further exposure of his cowardice. His language has been seen to anticipate Rodrigue's *stances* in *Le Cid*,[12] but the conclusion he reaches is the opposite one to that of his heroic successor. While for the later hero, respect for his love ultimately forces him to attack the father, for Matamore it is a pleasing pretext for withdrawal; the '*incommode vertu*' is, for the *fanfaron*, very convenient indeed.

In Matamore, Corneille exploits with great skill the comic possibilities of a braggart's language. He goes further than the simple juxtaposition of incongruous tones or gratuitous exhibitions of verbal exuberance, and suggests a wide range of comic effects from the splendid conviction of a character whose language effectively transforms reality to the struggles of a coward whose heroic façade crumbles with ever-increasing fear.

Equally striking, however, is the presentation of Matamore's relationship with other characters. Often, in comedies of the time, the braggart is the object of scathing observations from an onlooker. In Pichou's *Folies de Cardenio*, the role of Sanche Pansa is not so much to follow in the footsteps of his visionary master but to underline his foolishness, opposing prosaic reality to the imaginative flights of Don Quichotte as he responds thus in Act V Scene 5:

> *Que vous me faites rire, ô le plaisant mensonge,*
> *Je meure s'il ne faut que ce soit quelque songe,*
> *L'apparence autrement d'avoir fait tout cecy,*
> *Sans avoir veu personne, & sans bouger d'icy?* (p. 121)

and in Gougenot's *Comédie des comédiens*, Act II Scene 2, the Capitaine is summarily deflated by the penetrating irony of Turlupin and Guillaume: '*Capitaine, parlez en homme de jugement, & non pas en demoniaque; remettez vostre espée au fourreau, de peur que vous assembliez icy les petits enfans*' (607–10). In *L'Illusion Comique*, Geronte partly fulfils this function, but in Clindor's relationship with the coward, Corneille goes further than this traditional juxtaposition of madman and cynical onlooker; this character does not mock from a distance, but encourages the *fanfaron* in his folly by appearing to accept him on his own terms.

From the start of Act II Scene 2, Clindor's ironical flattery is apparent, and on several occasions he actually takes the place of the braggart in the evocation of prestigious exploits:

> *Et ce fut en ce temps que la peur de vos armes*
> *Fit nager le grand Caire en un fleuve de larmes:*
> *Vous veniez d'assommer dix Geans en un jour,*
> *Vous aviez desolé les pays d'alentour,*
> *Razé quinse chasteaux, applani deux montagnes,*
> *Fait passer par le feu villes, bourgs et campagnes,*
> *Et deffait vers Damas cent mille combattans . . .* (449–55)

This reversal of tradition is complemented by Matamore's own reaction to such praise, as he responds with a modesty which is quite uncharacteristic: '*Que tu remarques bien et les lieux et les temps! / Je l'avois oublié*' (456–7).

This particular comic relationship is most clearly exploited in Act III Scene 9. Here, Matamore realises that Isabelle does not love him but Clindor, but in his rival he finds one no less accomplished in the language of aggression. The coward is exposed again, and he transforms signal defeat into a comically inappropriate expression of generosity:

> *Parbieu, tu me ravis de generosité!*
> *Va, pour la conquerir n'use plus d'artifices,*
> *Je te la veux donner pour prix de tes services.*
> *Plains toy doresnavant d'avoir un maistre ingrat!* (944–7)

This scene has a parallel in Rotrou's *Amélie*, Act III Scene 7, where threats from the hero Dionis elicit an unconvincingly heroic response from Emille. However, whereas on this occasion Dionis shows detached amusement at the ridiculous braggart before him:

> *Dieux! quelle extravagance a son âme saisie,*
> *Et qui peut rire assez de cette frénésie?*
> *Il repaist son esprit d'imaginations*
> *Qui lui font estimer toutes ses actions,* (III, p. 317)

Clindor again acts a part, accepting Matamore's image of himself in an expression of noble gratitude:

> *A ce rare present d'aise le coeur me bat.*
> *Protecteur des grands Roys, guerrier trop magnanime,*
> *Puisse tout l'univers bruire de vostre estime!* (948–50)

Matamore, in his role-playing, attracts from Clindor a similar theatrical response which exaggerates and throws into relief his own.

The *fanfaron* presents in its traditions great comic potential, and Corneille certainly provides accomplished variations on the familiar hybris and cowardice of the type. In Matamore, he creates a character whose language moves from evident inconsequentiality to its own irresistible logic, and who inspires in others a corresponding mixture of scornful disbelief and ironical acceptance. Like that of his predecessors, his dramatic function is largely episodic, contributing little to the development of the principal action. In thematic terms, however, he has a much greater significance, highlighting in various ways essential qualities in the other characters. It is to these that I shall turn now.

3

Le premier Acte ne semble qu'un Prologue. Les trois suivans forment une Piece que je ne sçay comment nommer.[13]

The main plot, which depicts the tense and exciting struggles of Clindor and Isabelle against those who threaten their happiness, is firmly rooted in the theatrical traditions of the time. The events themselves are largely conventional, but Corneille's presentation of them has important implications which deserve close attention.

Immediately striking in these central Acts is the way the dramatist deliberately juxtaposes different registers. Act II Scene 5, for instance, portrays the protagonists' mutual declaration of love; Isabelle interrupts Clindor's protestation and affirms the extent of her own feelings thus:

> . . . *Espargnez ces propos superflus.*
> *Je les sçay, je les croy: que voulez vous de plus?*
> *Je neglige à vos yeux l'offre d'un diademe,*
> *Je dedaigne un rival, en un mot je vous ayme.* (487–90)

Following as it does a scene in which Matamore has heroically paid court to her, the heroine's speech may seem to suggest a certain comic exaggeration and irony. The reference here to the braggart as a serious rival certainly does not coincide with the comic presentation of this character, and yet this evident discrepancy of tones has no clear ironical purpose. The earlier scene of comedy is quite forgotten, and Clindor's lines of grateful and sincere affection reflect those of many a tragi-comic hero, whose poverty and uncertain background do not blind the heroine to the value of his love:

> *En ce piteux estat ma fortune si basse*
> *Trouve encor quelque part en vostre bonne grace,*
> *Et d'un rival puissant les biens et la grandeur*
> *Obtiennent moins sur vous que ma sincere ardeur!* (501–4)

In such protestations he echoes the devotion of Aglante in his classic encounter with the heroine at the end of Mairet's *Silvanire*, Act V Scene 10:

> Bien faut-il avouer que l'amour est constante
> Qui vous fait épouser les misères d'Aglante,
> Aglante qui n'a rien que l'on puisse estimer
> Hors qu'il a le coeur bon et qu'il sait bien aimer. (2381–4)[14]

A scene of moving drama follows one of comedy, but in such a way that the two registers are kept quite separate, the one exerting no influence on the other.

This coexistence of two distinct tones is found again in Isabelle's attitude towards Adraste, a rival suitor. In Act II Scene 3, the dramatist writes a scene of disdainful rejection which follows in the tradition of encounters seen frequently in comedy of the time and, indeed, in his own *La Galerie du Palais*, Act II Scene 1 and *La Suivante*, Act III Scene 2. In Isabelle's account of the suffering she endures in Adraste's presence, she demonstrates the charming confidence of a character fully in control of herself and of her language:

> Nous donnons bien souvent de divers noms aux choses:
> Des espines pour moy, vous les nommez des roses;
> Ce que vous appelez service, affection,
> Je l'appelle supplice et persecution. (365–8)

The calmness with which the heroine outlines her argument only serves to accentuate the crushing blow which it delivers; the control she displays throws into relief the pitiful struggles of her suitor. Like many ridiculous lovers Adraste uses traditional arguments quite inappropriately, vainly speaking of divinely ordained attachments, not to account for a reciprocated passion already enjoyed, but to persuade Isabelle that she should thus love him:

> Ouy, le Ciel au moment qu'il me fist respirer
> Ne me donna du coeur que pour vous adorer;
> Mon ame prit naissance avecque vostre idée;
> Avant que de vous voir vous l'avez possedée . . . (375–8)

The suitor's ridiculous lack of conviction is clearly underlined as Isabelle further distorts the traditional argument – if Adraste's feelings are inspired by 'le Ciel', so too then are hers:

> Le Ciel m'eust fait plaisir d'en enrichir un autre.
> Il vous fit pour m'aymer, et moy pour vous haïr:
> Gardons nous bien tous deux de luy desobeir. (382–4)

The relationship is seen here in a purely comic light, in its stylised opposition of scathing irony and pleading ineffectuality. However, later in the play, Corneille depicts the heroine's absence of love in a strikingly different way. In Act III Scene 1, she meets her father in an encounter which has all the dramatic tension traditional in such meetings of parent and daughter. In Geronte, there are suggested none of those struggles which characterise Geraste, the would-be tyrant of *La Suivante*; his words are firm, without being hysterical:

> *Appaisez vos soupirs et tarissez vos larmes;*
> *Contre ma volonté ce sont de foibles armes;*
> *Mon coeur, quoy que sensible à toutes vos douleurs,*
> *Escoute la raison et neglige vos pleurs.* (625–8)

This evident seriousness is sustained in Isabelle. She rejects Adraste again, certainly, but not in a spirit of scorn at the expense of a character whom she has been seen to ridicule. Her lines are fluent, mature, dignified, as she explains, quite simply, how she does not and could not love the partner proposed for her:

> *Mais, si vostre bonté me permet en ma cause*
> *Pour me justifier de dire quelque chose,*
> *Par un secret instint que je ne puis nommer,*
> *J'en fais beaucoup d'estat, et ne le puis aymer.* (637–40)

Isabelle has moved here from the ready wit of the *fille gaie* to the dignified self-awareness of heroines such as Célinde in Baro's play of that name, who, in Act II Scene 3, expresses a similar inability to love on demand, however worthy the suitor: '. . . *ce n'est pas qu'il ne vaille beaucoup, mais un secret destin veut que cela mesme, d'où une autre tireroit de la gloire, me soit une matière de mescontentement*' (p. 80), or of Diane in *L'Astrée*, V 6, who explains to her father that she can do no other than prefer Silvandre to Paris: '*Ce n'est pas j'aye de la haine pour luy, ny que je manque de jugement pour cognoistre l'honneur que ce me seroit; mais pour le confesser ingenûment, j'ayme mieux Silvandre*' (p. 261). If there is inconsistency here, it is a fault apparent in many plays of the time which, in their juxtaposition of different registers, suggest a total lack of concern for a unity of tone. It was a quality vigorously defended by Ogier in his important preface to Schelandre's *Tyr et Sidon*, who saw in it a true reflection of the vagaries of human fortune:

Car de dire qu'il est mal séant de faire paroistre en une mesme piece les mesmes personnes traittant tantost d'affaires serieuses, importantes et Tragiques, et incontinent apres de choses communes, vaines, et Comiques, c'est ignorer la condition de la vie des hommes, de qui les jours et les heures sont bien souvent entrecoupées de ris et de larmes, de contentement et d'affliction . . . (p. 159)

This same facility in moving from register to register is particularly clear in the presentation of Lise, Isabelle's servant. In her first monologue of Act II Scene 8, she speaks with a colloquial verve as she contemplates Clindor's pursuit of Isabelle and imagines a suitable punishment for one she believes to have ideas above his station:

> *L'arrogant croyt desja tenir ville gaignée,*
> *Mais il sera puny de m'avoir desdaignée.*
> *Par-ce qu'il est aymable, il fait le petit Dieu,*
> *Et ne veut s'adresser qu'aux filles de bon lieu . . . (609–12)*

Her villainous intentions have none of that suggestive complexity implied in Amarante's remarks. Instead of personal hurt, her lines express the character's comic delight at the thought of Clindor's demise, a vision which is one of the most distinctly farcical in Corneille's entire *oeuvre*:

> *Il se dit riche et noble, et cela me fait rire:*
> *Si loin de son pays, qui n'en peut autant dire?*
> *Qu'il le soit, nous verrons ce soir, si je le tiens,*
> *Dancer sous le cotret sa noblesse et ses biens. (617–20)*

But then, in Act III Scene 6, after Clindor has quite unexpectedly suggested to her that she become his mistress, she is given a speech of fury and outraged dignity, in which she defends her offended honour with heroic pride:

> *L'ingrat! il trouve enfin mon visage charmant,*
> *Et pour me suborner il contrefait l'amant!*
> *Qui hait ma saincte ardeur m'ayme dans l'infamie,*
> *Me desdaigne pour femme et me veut pour amie! (815–18)*

The lowly status of the speaker is forgotten in this expression of noble offence, which develops into an eloquent internal debate, enjoyable on its own terms:

> *Que de pensers divers en mon coeur amoureux,*
> *Et que je sens dans l'ame un combat rigoureux!*
> *Perdre qui me cherit! espargner qui m'affronte!*
> *Ruyner ce que j'ayme! aymer qui veut ma honte! (843–6)*

Corneille is again firmly set in that tradition of tragi-comedy which happily sacrifices all psychological coherence for the sake of *beaux effets*, pleasurable to dramatist, actor and audience alike. In Scudéry's *Le Prince déguisé*,[15] Act III Scene 6, Melanire, the wife of a gardener, is similarly given language of furious outrage at the prince's disdain of her passion for him. Although quite inconsistent with her status, this language has no comic intention; in Act III Scene 6, her words have a validity of their own, and the speaker is forgotten:

> *Prince, ou non, il n'importe à ma juste allegeance:*
> *J'aurois plus de douceur d'une illustre vengeance:*
> *Je le verrois périr d'un sourire mocqueur,*
> *Fust-il Roy du Levant, comme il l'est de mon coeur . . .* (p. 61)

In his earlier comedies, Corneille had reacted against such obvious theatrical *tableaux*, eager to suggest a close relationship between speaker and language. Here, however, true to his evident desire to write traditionally tragi-comic scenes, he shows no concern for such consistency.

It is against this background that the particular presentation of Clindor should be seen. Similar shifts of tone here have inspired many interpretations of this character as an adventurer and cynical lover, who moves from role to role in the interests of his own fortune.[16] From the humble, yet dignified suitor of Isabelle, he is transformed in Act III Scene 5 into a flattering seducer, redolent of Hylas in his evident sensitivity to the female charms of Lise:

> *Si l'on brusle pour toy, ce n'est pas sans sujet;*
> *Je ne cognus jamais un si gentil objet:*
> *L'esprit beau, prompt, accord, l'humeur un peu railleuse,*
> *L'embonpoint ravissant, la taille avantageuse,*
> *Les yeux doux, le teint vif et les traits delicats,*
> *Qui seroit le brutal qui ne t'aymeroit pas?* (775–80)

The metamorphosis is total, as he now seems to regard his relationship with Isabelle as one of convenience, undertaken out of purely materialistic motives and with no respect for the individual concerned:

> *Les plaisirs sont plus grands à se voir moins souvent;*
> *La femme les achepte, et l'amante les vend;*
> *Un amour par devoir bien aisement s'altere;*
> *Les noeuds en sont plus forts quand il est volontaire;*

> *Il hait toute contrainte, et son plus doux appas*
> *Se gouste quand on ayme et qu'on peut n'aymer pas.* (795–800)

Clindor appears as a particularly scheming lover, and yet what is significant here is not so much the cynical ideas of the hero as the fact that, once again, they are quite traditional. In Mairet's *Les Galanteries du Duc d'Ossonne*, Act III Scene 4, Camille is similarly unscrupulous as he contemplates his simultaneous pursuit of two girls:

> *Un amant à mon gré serait bien ridicule,*
> *Qui s'embarrasserait de semblable scrupule.*
> *On n'est pas criminel envers une beauté,*
> *Quand sans rompre avec elle on suit la nouveauté . . .* (1074–7)

and in Rotrou's *Bague de l'oubly*, Act I Scene 6, the king makes a similar suggestion to his sister, encouraging her to take both a husband and a lover: '*Ce mignon qui vous plaît est bon pour favori; / Mais le duc de Calabre est meilleur pour mari*' (I, 229–30). In his scene, Corneille is not so much making a particular point about Clindor as reproducing an attitude to love with which his audience would be already quite familiar. In the scenes which follow, this aspect of the hero's character is given no further emphasis; when the meeting is over, it ceases to have dramatic importance.

That Clindor is not to be reduced to the status of calculating deceiver is apparent from two scenes later in these central Acts. In Act III Scene 8 Isabelle declares again her love for the hero, but in this protestation of total devotion, Corneille is not interested to suggest the potential suffering of a heroine deceived; the avowal has a positive and unequivocal comic function. The lovers are seen to express their mutual affection, unaware that Matamore is listening in; the *fanfaron*'s belief that Isabelle loves him is totally deflated as the heroine stresses again and again that she loves Clindor, and Clindor alone:

> *Un rival par mon pere attaque en vain ma foy,*
> *Vostre amour seul a droit de triompher de moy.*
> *Des discours de tous deux je suis persecutée;*
> *Mais pour vous je me plais à estre mal traictée;*
> *Il n'est point de tourments qui ne me semblent doux,*
> *Si ma fidelité les endure pour vous.* (887–92)

The impact of the scene is not complicated, nor the comedy darkened by the audience's awareness of the earlier scene. Here again, this meeting is to be taken and enjoyed on its own terms, and the declaration serves no other purpose, either explicit or implicit, than that of discountenancing the ridiculous Matamore.

Clindor's prison monologue of Act IV Scene 7 has a similarly prescribed dramatic function; the speech, traditional in tragi-comedy of the time, is intended to underline the pathos of the ideal hero in captivity.[17] When he refers to Isabelle, there are no suggestions of either hypocrisy or forgetfulness with regard to his affection for Lise; that earlier scene is forgotten, and the character's heroic status is unalloyed:

> Quel bon heur m'accompagne à la fin de ma vie!
> Isabelle, je meurs pour vous avoir servie,
> Et, de quelque tranchant que je souffre les coups,
> Je meurs trop glorieux, puisque je meurs pour vous! (1253–6)

These are not the lines of a cynical fortune-seeker, but of a hero totally committed to a noble love.

Nor indeed, is Clindor cast in an ironical light. By this stage of the Act, it is certainly clear that his fears are unfounded, and that he is to be released from prison, yet his heroic resolve to die loses for all that none of its dignity:

> Aimables souvenirs de mes cheres delices
> Qu'on va bien tost changer en d'infames supplices,
> Que, malgré les horreurs de ce mortel effroy,
> Vous avez de douceurs et de charmes pour moy! (1237–40)

In this speech, Corneille clearly delights in the sensitive evocation of his character's thoughts before apparently imminent death. Context is forgotten, and the audience is invited to enjoy the speech for its own sake, its attention fixed by the force and logic of the hero's visions:

> Je sors les fers aux pieds, j'entends desja le bruit
> De l'amas insolent d'un peuple qui me suit;
> Je voy le lieu fatal où ma mort se prepare;
> Là, mon esprit se trouble et ma raison s'egare;
> Je ne decouvre rien propre à me secourir,
> Et la peur de la mort me fait desja mourir! (1283–8)

Just as Matamore was seen to have moments both of heroic grandeur and ridiculous cowardice, so too the protagonists of these central Acts are presented in a variety of different ways: Isabelle is both the witty *fille gaie* and the eloquent defender of her love, Clindor is both the noble suitor and the pleasure-seeking seducer, Lise both the pert servant and the honour-conscious heroine. These evident metamorphoses have been seen to reflect that mixture of genres which was typical of much tragi-comedy of the time. For Ogier, such aesthetic flexibility was defensible in the interests of *vraisemblance*; for Corneille, however, it has quite different implications which he explores and analyses in the final Act.

4

> Mais, puisqu'il faut passer à des effets plus beaux,
> Rentrons pour evoquer des fantosmes nouveaux:
> Ceux que vous avez veus representer de suite
> A vos yeux estonnez leurs amours et leur fuite,
> N'estant pas destinez aux hautes fonctions,
> N'ont point assez d'esclat pour leurs conditions.[18]

The tragic scenes of Act V constitute a fascinating appendix to the events of the earlier Acts, presenting the faithlessness of a hero recognised to be Clindor, and his re-conversion to his first love which is followed at once by his death.

The depiction of adultery is, like many other events in the play, a commonplace in the theatre of the time. In Act V Scene 3, the hero speaks of the uncontrollable nature of his new passion for Rosine:

> Je t'ayme, et si l'amour qui m'a surpris le coeur
> Avoit peu s'estouffer au point de sa naissance,
> Celuy que je te porte eust eû cette puissance.
> Mais en vain contre luy l'on tasche à resister:
> Toy mesme as esprouvé qu'on ne le peut dompter, (1492–6)

lines which echo those of many heroes who justify their infidelity in such terms. In Rayssiguier's *Les Thuilleries*, Act II Scene 2, Alcidon explains his faithlessness with these words:

> Mais un puissant Demon mes volontez emporte,
> Cette nouvelle ardeur dans mon sein est plus forte,
> Et tout ce que j'ay fait n'estoit que tesmoigner,
> Qu'il falloit de Daphnide en un mot m'esloigner, (p. 29)

and in Rotrou's *L'Innocente Infidelité*,[19] Act II Scene 4, Felismond is quite open about the treachery which he is powerless not to commit:

> *Je connois leur naissance et leur vie inégale,*
> *J'abhorre comme toi ma passion brutale;*
> *Mais un trop fort instinct me bâtit ma prison,*
> *Et mon âme charmée est sourde à la raison,* (III, p. 120)

an argument which is voiced by other heroes in Rotrou's plays.[20]

What is true of Clindor is indeed true also of Rosine, one of several heroines of the time tempted to abandon their husbands, and swept along by an unbrookable passion. As she enters in Act V Scene 4, ready to satisfy her love:

> *Desbarrassée en fin d'une importune suite,*
> *Je remets à l'amour le soin de ma conduite,*
> *Et, pour trouver l'autheur de ma felicité,*
> *Je prends un guide aveugle en cette obscurité,* (1589–92)

she recalls the determination of Roseline in Mareschal's *La Généreuse Allemande*, Act IV Scene 1, as she gives herself over to her passion for Aristandre:

> *Pardon, ô chasteté! Si mon coeur te refuse,*
> *Mon Amant dans ses yeux te montre mon excuse.*
> *Je ne fay qu'obeir, sousmise à son pouvoir,*
> *Il a forcé mes sens, il fausse mon devoir.* (p. 78)

In the face of a now repentant hero, however, this passion shades into uncomprehending frustration, and Corneille's scene hovers on the brink of comedy as the eager heroine urges Clindor to forget that honour about which he has suddenly become so scrupulous:

> *Perfide, est-ce de moy que tu le dois apprendre?*
> *Dieux! jusques où l'amour ne me fait point descendre!*
> *Je luy tiens des discours qu'il me devroit tenir,*
> *Et toute mon ardeur ne peut rien obtenir!* (1681–4)

The confrontation recalls the meeting of Angelique and Alidor in *La Place Royale*, Act II Scene 2, but also several other comic encounters in contemporary tragi-comedy. In Rotrou's *Cléagenor et Doristée*, Act IV Scene 3, Diane experiences the same exasperation as she tries to force her attentions on the disguised Doristée:

> *Quelle crainte, cruel, et quel soupçon te reste?*
> *Crains d'être cru stupide, en paroissant modeste;*
> *Crois que tu fais brûler ce coeur qui t'est suspect,*
> *Et ne me parle plus avec tant de respect . . .* (I, p. 233)

and in a similar scene in Scudéry's *Le Prince déguisé*, Act III Scene 6, the gardener's wife, Melanire, is almost driven to distraction by the prince's persistent reticence:

> *Es-tu si peu sçavant en l'art de deviner?*
> *Remarque mes souspirs, & sans que je le die,*
> *Afin de me guarir, connois ma maladie.* (p. 40)

Equally traditional are the laments of Isabelle in the presence of the faithless hero. In her resolution to accept the passing of her husband's love, she sees the inevitable transcience of her own beauty as the ultimate cause and justification of his change: '*Puisque mon teint se fane et ma beauté se passe,* / *Il est bien juste aussi que ton amour se lasse*' (1521–2). In Hardy's *Alcméon*, Act II Scene 2, Alphésibée makes a similar response to a husband who avows himself unfaithful:

> *L'offence tolerable est quasi legitime,*
> *Veu que de mes defauts tu derives ton crime,*
> *Manque d'attraits, de grace, & de qui ja le teint*
> *Apparoît de l'hyver d'une vieillesse atteint,*
> *Ma laideur à bon droit merite ce dommage,* (595–9)

and these lines are echoed by several other heroines of the time. In Scudéry's *Le Trompeur puny*, Act III Scene 5, Nerée attributes the apparent faithlessness of her lover to her own lack of beauty:

> *Quand je me plains de luy seule dans la maison,*
> *Je trouve qu'un miroir me dit qu'il a raison,*
> *Veu que je n'ay plus rien dans les traicts de la face,*
> *Qu'un reste de beauté que la tristesse efface,* (p. 57)

and in Rotrou's *La Belle Alphrède*, Act I Scene 4, Alphrède uses this same argument as she accuses Rodolphe of deceiving her: '*Ton coeur dément ta voix, et mon peu de beauté* / *Paroit, hélas! paroit en ta déloyauté*' (II, p. 351).

The Isabelle of Act V is indeed like many heroines who have abandoned everything to follow their beloved. As she upbraids her husband in Act V Scene 3:

> *Quelle tendre amitié je recevois d'un pere:*
> *Je l'ay quitté pourtant, pour suivre ta misere,*
> *Et je tendis les bras à mon enlevement,*
> *Ne pouvant estre à toy de son consentement . . .* (1421–4)

her words are typical of many in the same predicament. In Schelandre's *Tyr et Sidon*, Part II, Act IV Scene 3, Meliane laments in similar terms at the thought that Belcar has abandoned her:

> *Ingrat, tu fais mourir celle qui t'a faict vivre,*
> *Tu deslaisses, cruel, celle qui pour te suivre*
> *Deslaissoit librement sa natale maison,*
> *Ses grandeurs, ses amis, et son pere grison,* (1731–4)

and in Beys' *Céline*, Act I Scene 3, the heroine argues thus as she accuses Lisanor of being indifferent to her:

> *J'ay quitté pour toy nos bois & nos campagnes,*
> *J'ay perdu l'amitié de mes cheres compagnes.*
> *J'ay mesprisé pour toy tant de biens apparens,*
> *Et ceux que me rendoient les devoirs de parens . . .* (pp. 10–11)[21]

The fate of the heroine in these final scenes is then quite traditional, but what is particularly significant is the way Corneille is at pains to suggest that it follows on logically from the events of the previous Acts, and that the characters seen here are indeed the same Clindor and Isabelle known already to the audience. On one level, this suggestion of continuity might be seen to imply a curious glimpse behind the traditionally happy ending of comedy;[22] apparently ideal lovers are suddenly subjected to considerable tension and conflict as their affection dwindles with the passage of time. And yet, as has been seen, this situation, however suggestive its implications, was commonplace in tragi-comedy of the time, and certainly not particular to Corneille.

This careful sewing together of Acts, however, has a more important and original function. By implying that the protagonists of these final scenes are still Clindor and Isabelle, Corneille seeks to convince both Pridamant and the audience that the events they witness are as real as all the others they have seen. This intention is suggested in Alcandre's own reaction to the final tragedy. In earlier Acts, he had comforted the timorous Pridamant, who constantly believed that his son was in danger. At the end of Act III, for instance, he looked forward with confident insight into the happy events of the following Act: '*Un peu de patience, et, sans un tel secours, / Vous le verrez bien tost heureux en ses amours*' (979–80). In Act V Scene 6, however, this is no longer the case, as he confirms now the evidence of the spectators' eyes, suggesting that the protagonists have indeed ultimately met their downfall:

> Ainsi de nostre espoir la fortune se jouë;
> Tout s'esleve ou s'abaisse au branle de sa rouë,
> Et son ordre inegal qui regit l'univers
> Au milieu du bon heur a ses plus grands revers . . . (1725–8)

It is a speech which, like that of the chorus in Mairet's *Silvanire*, Act IV Scene 5, for example, is clearly intended to articulate the audience's fears that happiness is irretrievable:

> Nos plus beaux jours s'en vont pour ne revenir pas,
> Mille et mille chemins conduisent au trépas,
> Et pas un toutefois ne ramène à la vie. (1768–70)

Corneille carefully follows a traditional path to this, the lowest point of the drama, when all hope seems lost; from here, the revelation that all is in fact well, will be all the more unexpected and satisfying.

5

> Quel charme en un moment estouffe leurs discords
> Pour assembler ainsi les vivants et les morts?[23]

The final revelation that Clindor and Isabelle have joined a troupe of actors, and that their 'tragedy' was nothing more than a theatrical performance, gives Corneille the opportunity to proclaim his faith in the value of the acting profession. At Pridamant's dismay at the thought of his son's career, Alcandre replies at once with this defence:

> Cessez de vous en plaindre: à present le Theatre
> Est en un point si haut qu'un chacun l'idolastre,
> Et ce que vostre temps voyoit avec mespris
> Est aujourd'huy l'amour de tous les bons esprits. (1781–4)

At the time of *L'Illusion Comique*, such glorification of the theatre was not uncommon in dramatic works. Isolated remarks at the end of certain plays looked forward to the immortalisation of the adventures in a theatrical performance. Mention was made in the first chapter of Baro's exhortation at the end of *Célinde*, and in Auvray's *Dorinde*, Act V Scene 7, Gondebaut alludes again to the pleasure which an exciting plot may provide: '*Les beaux Esprits du temps de l'honneur idolatres, / Feront voir à l'envi votre histoire aux theatres'* (p. 162). In certain earlier works, too, dramatists use the technique of the play within the play, making the theatre itself an explicit theme of their work. In Baro's *Célinde*, for instance, the four main characters act out a tragedy, *Holoferne*, a performance which is prefaced by this speech of praise by Amintor in Act III Scene 1: *'Autrefois elles ont esté le divertissement des plus grands Monarques, & les Republiques mesmes en ont usé pour donner quelque horreur du vice & de l'amour pour la vertu; que si j'en avois le temps, je ferois cognoistre qu'il n'est rien de plus honneste, de plus plaisant, ny de plus utile . . .'* (p. 109).

This subject is yet more fully discussed in two other plays of the time: the *Comédie(s) des comédiens* of both Gougenot and Scudéry. In Gougenot's play, the opening Acts depict the difficulties in bringing together a theatrical troupe in time for a performance before the king, and in so doing, the dramatist presents not only the farcical quarrels of aspiring actors, Turlupin, Guillaume and Gaultier, but also gives more serious and theoretical consideration to the function and value of the theatre. In Act I Scene 3, Beauchasteau gives an extended justification of the profession on moral grounds, and in Act III Scene 2, the entire company assert the respectability of their art throughout the ages. Even Turlupin is endowed with uncharacteristic erudition for these purposes, referring to the time of Cicero as he makes his contribution to the discussion: *'De son temps, les Senateurs alloient souvent voir la Comedie comme des exercices honorables & profitables, tenans ces representations comme une eschole pour apprendre l'art de se bien exprimer au rapport du mesme Valere le grand'* (1065–9). Similar protestations are to be found in Scudéry's play, where, in Act I Scene 3, la Beau Soleil speaks out in defence of the dignity of actresses, and in Act II Scene 1, Blandimare outlines to the troupe his admiration for a profession which he would like to join: *'Car il faudroit estre privé de raison, pour mespriser une chose tant estimable'* (345–6). Such scenes have thematic importance, certainly, but they are rather loosely integrated into the rudimentary bipartite structure of the texts: a preliminary *pièce à thèse* which pleads the virtue of the theatre is followed in both cases by a second play, in which the actors simply give an exhibition of their talents.

L'Illusion Comique clearly has its roots in this tradition, but in his adaptation of it Corneille demonstrates great originality and acute dramatic sense. Here, the value of the theatre is proclaimed not simply through the mouth of individuals, but is given a far more specific and central role. In the *dénouement*, Corneille has the theatre perform a role just as unifying and harmonising as 'Love' or 'the gods' do in *comédie*. Traditionally, when all seems lost and the chaos total, an omnipotent *deus ex machina* appears to resolve all conflicts; new identities are revealed, characters miraculously raised from the dead and harmony exposed beneath apparent discord. The eulogy of *Amour* at the end of Rayssiguier's adaptation of *Aminta*, Act V Scene 6, reflects this particular dramatic function:

> *Amour que tes secrets ont d'estranges ressorts,*
> *Tu redonnes la vie à ceux que l'on croit morts,*
> *Et d'un mal evident, ta puissance supreme,*
> *Lors qu'on y pensoit moins, a faict un bien extreme . . .* (pp. 124–5)

Frequently, such power is associated with the arrival of a stranger who seems possessed of the requisite knowledge to restore everything to order. In du Ryer's *Cléomédon*, Act V Scene 6, Clorimante is announced thus as the bearer of vital secrets: '*Nous avons un vieillard, dont la science obscure / Vous pourra contenter dessus cette avanture . . .* (p. 100), and the same ability is shared by the *mire* who comes at the end of Scudéry's *Ligdamon et Lidias*, Act V Scene 2, to bring the 'dead' main characters back to life:

> *Illustres Senateurs, vous Pere venerable,*
> *Je viens vous faire voir une chose admirable,*
> *Car je veux retirer ces amans du trepas.* (p. 127)[24]

In *L'Illusion Comique*, this resurrection is achieved by Alcandre, whose power is that of creating theatrical illusion. Heroes miraculously returned to life are replaced here by actors who emerge safely from the ashes of the tragic characters they have embodied, and the final glorification of 'Love', which was seen so often to conceal the self-portrait of the dramatist in his omnipotence, becomes a more explicit and literal eulogy of the theatre.

It is through this parallel that Corneille gives particular force to a theme treated before him in Scudéry's *Comédie des comédiens*: the conversion of the outsider to the value of the acting profession. In this earlier play, Blandimare appears in search of his nephew, and, on discovering that he has joined a theatrical troupe in Act I Scene 5, he has scathing remarks to make: '*En un mot, le titre de*

voleur est une qualité annexe à celle de Portier de Comedie . . .' (182–3).
By Act II Scene 1, however, it is apparent that these criticisms have
only been feigned, and the character is resolved to join the actors:
*'bien loing de soubçonner vostre Profession d'ignominie, je la tiens fort
glorieuse; je la veux embrasser moy-mesme, si vous me voulez recevoir'*
(355–8). Pridamant's conversion, however, is more carefully
integrated into the structure of the play. He is shown the events of
his son's life in a special theatrical performance, and, throughout,
his reactions are seen to be those of an ideal spectator in a *comédie*;
totally engrossed in the *péripéties* depicted on stage, he fears that all
is lost and that his son is dead. When he learns of his mistake, his
surprise is expressed in traditional terms. His words of
astonishment which head this section echo those of many
characters taken aback by an unexpected reversal of fortune:
Clitophon's surprise at the news that his beloved Lucipe is not
dead, announced in du Ryer's *Clitophon*, Act III Scene 2, is no less
absolute: *'Mais dis moy mon souci quel remede assez fort / Te delivre
aujourd'huy d'une tragique mort* (p. 99). Similarly in Pridamant's
amazement at his own credulity: *'J'ay pris sa mort pour vraye, et ce
n'estoit que feinte'* (1777), there is echoed that traditional transition
from illusion to truth, as characters thought dead are revealed to be
alive. Elpin's announcement of order in d'Alibray's adaptation of
Aminta, Act V Scene 1, expresses the survival of the hero in just
these terms: *'Amis soyez joyeux, C'estoit un faux rapport / Tout ce que
vous avez entendu de sa mort'* (p. 141). As has been seen, however,
this is no ordinary reversal of fortune, created arbitrarily by a *deus
ex machina*; Clindor is resurrected because his death has simply
been a theatrical performance. Pridamant's joy, therefore, at the
news that his son is not dead is ultimately linked with this
revelation of the theatrical art which lies behind such a reversal and
makes it possible. Clindor, revealed as an actor, has come back to
life to the delight of his father, but equally, as an actor, he has
provided an aesthetic pleasure for his audience. The transition
from despair to joy is thus made simultaneously on two levels, and
through the experience of this personal surprise and relief,
Pridamant is made to understand the equivalent pleasure aroused
in the public by the theatre:

> *Il est vray que d'abord mon ame s'est esmeuë:*
> *J'ay creu la Comedie au point où je l'ay veuë;*
> *J'en ignorois l'esclat, l'utilité, l'appas,*

> *Et la blasmois ainsi, ne la cognoissant pas.*
> *Mais depuis vos discours, mon coeur plain d'allegresse*
> *A banny cette erreur avecque la tristesse.* (1809–14)

The conversion of Pridamant by practical demonstration rather than theoretical argument underlines what is a constant in Corneille's dramatic principles: the belief that the theatre has value principally for the entertainment it provides and not for the moral lessons it may impart. It is a point which he makes quite clearly in his *Epître* to *La Suivante*: '*Cependant mon advis est celuy de Terence. Puisque nous faisons des Poëmes pour estre representez, nostre premier but doit estre de plaire à la Cour et au Peuple, et d'attirer un grand nombre à leurs representations*' (*ed. cit.*, pp. 5–6), and which is echoed, of course, in the final words of Alcandre at the end of this play:

> *Servir les gents d'honneur est mon plus grand desir.*
> *J'ay pris ma rescompence en vous faisant plaisir.*
> *Adieu, je suis content, puisque je vous voy l'estre.* (1819–21)

It is through this perspective that *L'Illusion Comique* ultimately finds its unity. The diverse elements constantly juxtaposed in it, the apparent incoherence of characterisation, the shifting of registers, are features which so often in plays of the time indicate the sacrifice of dramatic tautness for the sake of indulging popular taste. Here, however, they are brought together in what is a unique and explicit demonstration of the pleasure generated by the happy union of dramatist and actor in a theatrical performance.

6

. . . tout cela cousu ensemble faict une Comedie[25]

L'Illusion Comique holds a curious place in Corneille's comic *oeuvre*, so different in many respects from all the preceding works. Like the other plays, it is designated a *comédie* and yet in its conception of the term it suggests a marked difference from them. Here, Corneille visibly reverts to those elements of the tragi-comedy which he had quite strikingly rejected before: violent stage action, excitement and suspense, the thrill of a surprising *dénouement*. He seems less concerned now with sophisticated ways of making an audience laugh or with examining the complexities of love and the human heart, but concentrates more on the art of the theatre, its value and power.

A link between this play and its predecessors is suggested, however, in the character of Matamore. As a traditional braggart, he constantly tries to persuade himself and those around him that he is other than he is. Like several other such characters in Corneille's comedies – Philandre and Alcidon, Célidée and Alidor – Matamore has an image of himself which is seen by the audience not to correspond to his true identity. For the dramatist, this quality has a certain comic potential which he is careful to exploit. In the context of the play, however, the sustained role-playing of the *fanfaron* suggests a distortion of another figure whose function it also is to adopt a personality more prestigious than his own: the actor.[26]

In the course of *L'Illusion Comique*, the principal characters are seen to play a variety of roles, and yet, however striking the metamorphosis, each individual performance is convincing on its own terms; this quality is revealed particularly in Act V, where the events, although acted, are accepted as real by the audience as well as by Pridamant. The actor has an ability to deceive which is suggested in Alcandre's description of Clindor's rise to fame in Act I Scene 2:

> Sous un meilleur destin sa fortune rangée,
> Et sa condition avec le temps changée,
> Personne maintenant n'a de quoy murmurer
> Qu'en public de la sorte il ose se parer. (141–4)

The lines deliberately juxtapose two levels of meaning, referring equally to the character whose fortune may change abruptly in the course of the *comédie* and the actor who knows similar transformations on stage. For the enlightened spectator, the remark may suggest a hint as to the final outcome of the drama. More significantly, however, the ambiguity it carries points to an essential confusion of role and reality, to the audience's willing suspension of disbelief which is the basis of theatrical illusion. What Corneille demonstrates so perfectly in his play, d'Aubignac was later to express on a theoretical level in his *Pratique du théâtre*, III 4:

Je sçay bien que le Theatre est une espece d'illusion, mais il faut tromper les Spectateurs en telle sorte, qu'ils ne s'imaginent pas l'être, encore qu'ils le sçachent; il ne faut pas tandis qu'on les trompe, que leur esprit le connoisse; mais seulement quand il y fait reflexion. (p. 210)

This emergence of the actor in the *dénouement*, significant on its own terms, suggests also a fascinating development from the endings of Corneille's earlier plays. In his first comedies, the dramatist was seen to avoid the artificiality of convention, insisting on the logic of his characters which would not so easily bend to the demands of comic tradition. In this play again, he refuses to distort the reactions of his protagonists for the sake of harmony, and creates once more a *dénouement* which derives logically from their nature, as it is known already to the audience. In this case, however, the result is not that suggestive strain issuing from the complexity of the human heart but a triumphant revelation of order as the player emerges from his role. Forgiveness traditional at the end of comedy can indeed be effortless and automatic, suffering easily forgotten, because characters are simply actors who play parts; the happy ending of *comédie* is here inevitable and natural, because it is only a *comédie*, a play:

> *L'un tue et l'autre meurt, l'autre vous faict pitié,*
> *Mais la Scene preside à leur inimitié;*
> *Leurs vers font leur combat, leur mort suit leurs paroles,*
> *Et sans prendre interest en pas un de leurs roolles,*
> *Le traistre et le trahy, le mort et le vivant*
> *Se trouvent à la fin amis comme devant.* (1755–60)

Instead of depicting lovers trying to come to terms with their feelings, Corneille moves now to the actor, confident in himself and in his role. It is this figure who will feature again when the dramatist returns to comedy so successfully some years later and creates *Le Menteur*.

VIII

Le Menteur
Reminiscence and development

1

J'ai fait le Menteur pour contenter les souhaits de beaucoup d'autres qui, suivant l'humeur des François, aiment le changement, et après tant de poëmes graves dont nos meilleures plumes ont enrichi la scène, m'ont demandé quelque chose de plus enjoué qui ne servît qu'à les divertir.[1]

Le Menteur was written some years after Corneille's previous comedies, at a time when the *comédie d'intrigue* in its various forms was particularly popular. Certain playwrights looked to Plautus for inspiration in these years – Rotrou in *Les Sosies*, Mareschal in *Le Véritable Capitan Matamore*, and the anonymous author of *Le Capitan* – plots whose pleasure derived from the elaborate scheming of servants or gods to deceive the protagonists. The dominant influence, however, was that of Spain, which provided dramatists with many an intrigue so designed as to create the maximum confusion for the characters involved in the action, and the maximum pleasure for the audience whose detachment from it was assured. The very titles of many such plays suggest their essential comic force: *Les Fausses Véritez,*[2] *L'Absent chez soy,*[3] *Les Innocens coupables,*[4] *Les Songes des hommes esveillez.*[5] Dramatists such as Brosse, Boisrobert or d'Ouville delighted in the careful construction of plots, rich in incidents of mistaken identity and unlikely coincidence. In the *Avis au Lecteur* to *Les Innocens coupables*, for instance, Brosse prides himself on the pleasing effects which derive from the intricate structuring of his play: '*Je te prie seulement de considérer l'invention de mon sujet, la nouveauté des incidents qui l'intriguent, la ressemblance de deux filles en corsage & en habits qui ne cause pas de pites [sic] méprises, le rapport de deux jardins qui ne fait pas un equivoque désagreable*', and the same qualities are highlighted by d'Ouville in the *Dédicace* to his *La Dame suivante*[6] where he speaks of the plot: '*que l'on a trouvé surprenant, extrêmement intrigué, & raisonnablement debrouïllé*'.

In these comedies is lost the charm found in certain plays of the previous decade, which offered suggestive insights into the human heart. This is replaced by a certain sentimentality and a return to idealised, if at times rather unsubtle presentations of human emotion. Heroines fall in love at once with strangers, heroes risk everything to come to their assistance. Characters undergo no changes in the course of the action but are led from elementary confusion to final elucidation. Neither the writer nor the spectator is concerned with the nature of the protagonists' love or the implications of their suffering. Dramatists' insistence in prefatory remarks on the ingenuity of their plots rather than on the plights of their characters is echoed in the comedies themselves, where feelings have no role to play and suffering is always subordinated, explicitly or implicitly, to a sense of bewilderment. Cesar's lines in *Les Innocens coupables* are classic in this respect: '*Bien que mes maux soient tels que rien n'est au dessus, / Je suis moins affligé que je ne suis confus*' (IV 1, p. 67).

In certain other plays, dramatists also draw comic effects from the relationship of master and witty valet, the latter often looking on with cynical disbelief at the impetuosity of the hero. In d'Ouville's *L'Esprit folet*,[7] Act I Scene 2, Camille tries to warn the hero of his apparent folly, unconvinced by his gallant motives: '*Mais pourquoy voulez-vous prendre son interest, / Sans l'avoir jamais veue, & sans sçavoir qui c'est?*' (p. 4), and in *La Dame suivante*, Act I Scene 4, another servant, Carlin, fears the worst, as his master happily puts complete trust in a mysterious, but attractive heroine: '*Ne nous fions, Monsieur, nullement aux visages, / Chacun joue à Paris d'estranges personnages . . .*' (p. 8). This form of servant comedy is found also in the more burlesque plays which were growing in popularity at this time. In such works, heroic roles are frequently played by those most unsuited to them, and comic effects derive from this juxtaposition of the noble and the banal. In *Le Gouvernement de Sanche Pansa*,[8] Guérin de Bouscal imagines the discomfiture of a cowardly servant suddenly given a kingdom to rule and defend, and in the first comedy of Scarron, *Jodelet, ou le Maître valet*,[9] Jodelet and his master exchange roles, and the servant blunders with nonchalant

awkwardness through the romantic courtship of an astonished
heroine in Act II Scene 7:

> *Je vous vois donc enfin, ô beauté que j'espère,*
> *Vous me voyez aussi, mais pourray-je sçavoir*
> *Si vous prenez grand goust en l'honneur de me voir.* (p. 51)

Certain of these qualities – the influence of Spain, the delight in
misunderstanding, the greater emphasis given to confusion than
to suffering, the comic relationship of valet and master – recur in
Le Menteur, and situate the play clearly in this particular tradition
of comedy in the early years of the 1640s. As a play, it seems thus
totally divorced in spirit from Corneille's earlier works, depicting
as it does the amorous adventures of an impetuous hero, whose
delight in the telling of tall stories and whose mistake about the
name of his beloved combine to create great confusion both for
others and for himself. Only rarely do critics attempt to set it in
the context of the dramatist's personal comic *oeuvre*, and where a
link is hinted at in their commentaries, it is seen to lie rather
vaguely in its realistic setting,[10] or in its presentation of a love
imbroglio which has that particular charm frequently ascribed to
the other works.[11] In its adaptation of a Spanish source, however,
Le Menteur suggests a much more complex and significant
relationship with these earlier comedies which I propose to study
in more detail now.

2

> . . . *J'appelle rêveries*
> *Ce qu'en d'autres qu'un maître on nomme menteries;*
> *Je parle avec respect.*[12]

That a particular source for *Le Menteur* is known, *La Verdad
sospechosa* of Alarcón,[13] provides a precious opportunity to
analyse closely the nature of Corneille's comic imagination. The
play has been compared before with its source, but not
specifically from this point of view. Martinenche praises the
French flavour of the text;[14] Viguier makes a detailed comparison, examining Corneille's re-structuring of Alarcón's plot, but
without looking closely at the implications of this;[15] and Staves
deals with adaptations of *La Verdad sospechosa*, by both Corneille
and Steele, highlighting the general preoccupations of each

dramatist in his play, but with little analysis of detail.[16] In his *Épitre*, Corneille speaks of *Le Menteur* simply as a copy of his source, whom at that time he believed to be Lope de Vega, and to whom he thus pays homage: '*En un mot, ce n'est ici qu'une copie d'un excellent original qu'il a mis au jour sous le titre de* la Verdad sospechosa' (p. 131). A study of the two works, however, reveals a rich and significant adaptation.

Immediately apparent from a comparison of the texts is the way Corneille frequently extracts comedy from characters or incidents which, in Alarcón, do not have such a force. Figures such as the servant, rival or father serve variously in the Spanish play to highlight elements of an essentially tense and suggestive drama; in *Le Menteur*, Corneille makes of them sophisticated comic characters. In *La Verdad sospechosa*, for instance, the hero's servant, Tristan, serves as a moral guide, correcting and reproving his master for his untruths. When don Beltran offers Tristan to his son in the opening scene of the play, this role is made quite clear. '*Non es criado el que te doy, / Mas consejero y amigo*' (17–18).[17] In *Le Menteur*, however, Cliton has a much more important comic presence, his remarks being not so much the expression of an accepted ethical code against which the hero's behaviour is judged but rather those of a witty servant, characterised by his shrewd observations and penetrating advice.

In Act I Scene 1, he is ready to counsel Dorante as he embarks on a gallant courtship, sensitive to the delicacy needed in the offering of presents:

> *Tel donne à pleines mains qui n'oblige personne:*
> *La façon de donner vaut mieux que ce qu'on donne.*
> *L'un perd exprès au jeu son présent déguisé;*
> *L'autre oublie un bijou qu'on auroit refusé.*
> *Un lourdaud libéral auprès d'une maîtresse*
> *Semble donner l'aumône alors qu'il fait largesse,* (89–94)

and in Act I Scene 4, he has more trenchant remarks to make about the natural garrulity of women:

> *Ah! depuis qu'une femme a le don de se taire,*
> *Elle a des qualités au-dessus du vulgaire;*
> *Cette perfection est rare, et nous pouvons*
> *L'appeler un miracle, au siècle où nous vivons.* (209–12)

Cliton's attitude to his master's lies is also quite different, revealing considerably less moral outrage than that of Tristan.

After hearing Dorante tell Clarice and Lucrèce, girls he has just met, quite fictitious tales of his courage in war, he forbears to judge him directly, not because he condones the flight into untruth but because he fears a beating. For this valet, absolute moral standards apply only when there is no danger to those who defend them. In Alarcón, Tristan reveals Garcia to himself and to the audience; in Corneille, Cliton has a personality of his own, as compelling on the spectators' attention as Dorante's.

A similar increase in the play's comic force is apparent in Corneille's presentation of Alcippe and his relationship with the hero. Both Dorante and Alcippe love Clarice, but this rivalry is complicated by the fact that Dorante believes his beloved to be called Lucrèce; when Alcippe thus professes his affection for Clarice, it leaves Dorante unmoved. This situation is found also in the Spanish source, but Corneille makes some significant changes. In Alarcón's play, Juan (the model for Alcippe) is a characteristically noble hero; he loves Jacinta (Clarice) and tells Garcia of his concern at the rumour that she has been lavishly fêted at night by a mysterious suitor. He has seen Garcia follow Jacinta with his gaze as she left the stage in Act I Scene 7, and when this hero then flippantly pretends to be the gallant lover, giving a colourful account of a nocturnal tryst, Juan is convinced that they are rivals. Garcia's longing look and Juan's awareness of it create an atmosphere of tension and bring momentarily to the surface a real and significant source of conflict. In *Le Menteur*, Act I Scene 5, however, Dorante gives Clarice no such glance; the presentation of Alcippe and his rivalry with the hero is thus quite transformed. Without this proof of the eye, the cause of jealousy becomes simply the extravagant tale of the hero. His ragings to Philiste are hence cast in a more obviously ridiculous light, inspired as they are by evidence whose improbability is clearly pointed out:

Alcippe: . . . *Je meurs de jalousie.*
Philiste: *Sans raison toutefois votre âme en est saisie:*
           Les signes du festin ne s'accordent pas bien.
Alcippe: *Le lieu s'accorde, et l'heure; et le reste n'est rien.* (305–8)

Alcippe, like many of Corneille's earlier comic characters, is seen here resolved to act out a particular role, not because he has substantial proof to justify it but because he is blinded by his own folly.

When Alcippe confronts Clarice in Act II Scene 3, therefore, he is already more comic a character than his Spanish counterpart. In *La Verdad sospechosa*, Act I Scene 9, Juan accuses Jacinta as much with the evidence of his eyes as with that of his ears, and the heroine takes this accusation of dishonour seriously. For her, Juan's anger is not comically incomprehensible; his lines insult her, and she takes offence. In Corneille, the presentation of the scene is quite different. Not only does Clarice not take Alcippe's ravings seriously, but also her calm refusal to take offence both punctuates and punctures the lover's rage, isolating him as a ridiculous dupe and throwing into relief the inappropriateness of his role:

Alcippe: *T'en ai-je dit assez? Rougis, et meurs de honte.*
Clarice: *Je ne rougirai point pour le récit d'un conte.*
Alcippe: *Quoi! je suis donc un fourbe, un bizarre, un jaloux?*
Clarice: *Quelqu'un a pris plaisir à se jouer de vous.* (517–20)

The lack of dramatic seriousness in this rage is further underlined by Corneille at the end of the scene, as Alcippe claims the hand of his mistress. For Alarcón, the demand is made in the name of honour, as a measure to safeguard the reputation of both characters, but in Corneille it indicates rather Alcippe's comic petulance. The anger with which he approaches Clarice now would be quickly forgotten, were he granted a kiss of reconciliation:

Je ne t'écoute point, à moins que m'épouser,
A moins qu'en attendant le jour du mariage,
M'en donner ta parole et deux baisers en gage. (528–30)

The particular function of this addition to the source is suggested by the fact that it remains in all the subsequent editions of the text, during a period when Corneille systematically removes from his other comedies all such references to kissing.

This transformation of the rival from the honour-conscious hero to the more ridiculous dupe is certainly characteristic of the dramatist's earlier presentation of villain figures. However, the incident is further significant for the way Corneille extracts comic ironies which lie dormant in the Spanish original. By stressing the fundamental artificiality and ridiculousness of Alcippe's role, the dramatist is able to make more obviously comic in this scene the essential irony of the encounter: the fact that Juan and Garcia,

Alcippe and Dorante *are* actually in love with the same girl, and that the rival's jealousy is dramatically appropriate. Juan is seen to express a jealousy which is inspired in part by dramatic 'truth', the hero's longing glance; his words thus remain on the level of the *drame*, corresponding to reality which he suspects and which the audience knows. Alcippe's jealousy, however, is founded purely on illusion, the fruit of his own folly, and yet it has a truth of which he cannot be aware, but which the audience sees:

> *Je connois tes détours, et devine tes ruses.*
> *Adieu! Suis ton Dorante, et l'aime désormais;*
> *Laisse en repos Alcippe, et n'y pense jamais.* (522–4)

In Alarcón, the hint that the rival's jealousy is appropriate suggests the reality of the drama at work in the play, and increases the tension of the conflict. In Corneille, however, it suggests again that sophisticated form of comic irony developed throughout his *oeuvre*, which juxtaposes truth and falsehood, reality and fantasy.

Corneille's careful exploitation of this irony is further apparent as the play develops. Géronte, Dorante's father, proposes Clarice as a partner in marriage for his son, a suggestion which the hero, not realising that Clarice is the name of the girl he loves, strongly resists by claiming that he is already secretly married. Immediately afterwards, he is challenged to a duel by Alcippe, and, still quite ignorant of his rivalry with him, Dorante creates his own imaginary explanation of events. In Act IV Scene 1, he tells Cliton how he has killed in a duel this enemy who for several months has been his bitter rival. The story is told with a characteristic blend of dramatic commitment and an ironical love of the understated:

> *Hier nous nous rencontrons; cette ardeur se réveille,*
> *Fait de notre embrassade un appel à l'oreille;*
> *Je me défais de toi, j'y cours, je le rejoins,*
> *Nous vidons sur le pré l'affaire sans témoins;*
> *Et le perçant à jour de deux coups d'estocade*
> *Je le mets hors d'état d'être jamais malade.* (1137–42)

This tale, although considerably shorter, corresponds largely to that of Garcia in *La Verdad sospechosa*,[18] and it is followed, as is Garcia's, by the immediate entry of the seemingly dead rival.

The obvious deflation of the lie which this suggests is registered by both Tristan and Cliton.

Corneille, however, creates a comic dimension not present in Alarcón. When Juan enters, he is in the company of don Beltran, Garcia's father. The rival does not address Garcia directly, but tells don Beltran that his son's story of a secret marriage was, in fact, untrue. The lie which Garcia has just told Tristan is thus situated in the wider moral context of the lie to his father; its comic force is minimised. The tension here built up leads to a climax in the following scene, Act III Scene 9, in which the hero is once more given a serious upbraiding.

Tension becomes comedy in Corneille as the dramatist changes the rival's role, and has Alcippe announce instead to Dorante that he is betrothed to Clarice. This alteration not only removes the atmosphere of tense moral conflict deliberately created by Alarcón, but it has its own positive comic purpose. By thus drawing attention to his own successful courtship of Clarice, Alcippe underlines quite unawares the fact that he is Dorante's rival, and the hero's tale of a bloody rivalry has its own ironical appropriateness. In his imagination, Dorante has played the part of Alcippe's rival in love, which he is known to be; in his comic ignorance of this truth, he is led to wish his interlocutor every happiness: '*Le ciel te donne un hymen sans souci*' (1167). The conflict which, in Alarcón, will lead to a dramatic climax is transformed by Corneille into sophisticated comedy. The rivalry between characters in the real world is metamorphosed and rendered comic by the superimposition of a rivalry between two actors who, through ignorance, folly or stubbornness play their parts of jealousy and violence in a world of their own imagining. It is indicative of Corneille's particular originality here that in Boisrobert's *Jalouse d'elle-mesme*,[19] a play which, in its presentation of an equally unconscious rivalry between two heroes, shows clearly the influence of *Le Menteur*, there is little exploitation of this refined comic irony.

The tendency implied in these details of adaptation suggests not only Corneille's ability to perceive and exploit the comic potential of his source, but points also to a significant shift of emphasis from the lie, which in Alarcón is at the core of the play's tension. This is evident particularly in the changes Corneille brings to two central scenes of *La Verdad sospechosa*, the scenes in which Juan and then don Beltran discover that they have been taken in by Garcia's tales.

When, in Act II Scene 13, Felix tells Juan that the hero's tale of the nocturnal feast is untrue, he first remarks on the essential unlikelihood of the story, but then emphasis moves to and remains on the moral flaw in Garcia's character which this lie implies. Juan is left to ponder for a moment on the mixture of valour and dishonour mysteriously embodied in the hero, and the scene ends with his resolution never again to trust a man who can thus lie: '*Y sus verdades serán / Ya consejos para mi*' (1918–19).[20] He leaves to tell Jacinta of the nature of this deception.

In *Le Menteur*, Act III Scene 2, however, Corneille reverses this emphasis. Alcippe's initial disbelief that Dorante could be capable of such untruth is followed at once by Philiste's observation that they have been very gullible. Alcippe's doubts, therefore, are not used to underline Dorante's seemingly enigmatic character but rather, and more significantly, to suggest his unwillingness to admit that he has been fooled, a hesitation noticed at once by Philiste:

> *Ayez sur ce sujet moins d'incrédulité,*
> *Et vous-même admirez notre simplicité:*
> *A nous laisser duper nous sommes bien novices!* (819–21)

Similarly, the emphasis at the end of the scene is not on the liar, who will be able no longer to make himself believed, but on the dupe who has made himself ridiculous. Alcippe does not leave the stage to enlighten Clarice about the flaw in Dorante's character, as Juan had done. He sees the heroine arrive, and decides to flee her mockery:

> *Si du jour qui s'enfuit la lumière est fidèle,*
> *Je pense l'entrevoir avec son Isabelle.*
> *Je suivrai tes conseils, et fuirai son courroux*
> *Jusqu'à ce qu'elle ait ri de m'avoir vu jaloux.* (841–4)

A parallel change of stress is reflected in Géronte's lamenting monologue of Act V Scene 2, and in the scene with Dorante which immediately follows. In *La Verdad Sospechosa*, don Beltran is aware from the beginning of his son's weakness for lies, and when he laments in Act II Scene 6, it is the moral implications of this fault which are the prime and only cause. Corneille, however, sets this speech of parental displeasure in a quite

different context. In his scene with Argante of Act V Scene 1,
Géronte learns not only that his son tells lies but also, in
consequence, that he has been taken in by one such: Dorante's
tale of his marriage in Poitiers. Thus at the end of his monologue,
his indignation at his son's apparent moral deviation is exceeded
by his frustration at having been so gullible:

> Comme si c'étoit peu pour mon reste de vie
> De n'avoir à rougir que de son infamie,
> L'infâme, se jouant de mon trop de bonté,
> Me fait encor rougir de ma crédulité! (1497–500)

When don Beltran laments in his turn that he has been
deceived by his son, it will be again in purely moral terms. In his
speech of Act III Scene 9, ll. 2892 ff., he expresses concern at the
loss of honour which this implies and at the fact that he may be
thought to be his son's accomplice. In Géronte's anger of Act V
Scene 3, which corresponds to that of don Beltran, he visibly
upbraids his son:

> Est-il vice plus lâche, est-il tache plus noire,
> Plus indigne d'un homme élevé pour la gloire?
> Est-il quelque foiblesse, est-il quelque action
> Dont un coeur vraiment noble ait plus d'aversion? . . . (1521–4)

Such anger is fluently expressed, and on the strength of such
moments the character has often been taken in earnest by
critics.[21] However, behind this moral indignation, Corneille is
careful to suggest Géronte's more comic self-criticism at his
having been so naïve: 'Tu me fais donc servir de fable et de risée, /
Passer pour esprit foible, et pour cervelle usée!' (1541–2), an attitude
which then shades into the expression of paternal affection as he
protests that he never wished to impose his will on Dorante in the
choice of a wife:

> Si quelque aversion t'éloignoit de Clarice,
> Quel besoin avois-tu d'un si lâche artifice?
> Et pouvois-tu douter que mon consentement
> Ne dût tout accorder à ton contentement,
> Puisque mon indulgence, au dernier point venue,
> Consentoit à tes yeux l'hymen d'une inconnue? (1545–50)

The father who, in Alarcón, is the embodiment of an absolute
principle becomes, in Le Menteur, a more obviously comic figure;
the scene of direct reproach throws light less on the moral

complexity of a hero prone to lying, than on the gullibility of an old man who realises that he has been fooled.

3

> *Vous seriez un grand maître à faire des romans;*
> *Ayant si bien en main le festin et la guerre,*
> *Vos gens en moins de rien courroient toute la terre.*[22]

Corneille's deliberate transformation of drama into comedy in such scenes as those just analysed is most significant, however, in his reconception of the hero and of the nature of his lies. Several critics have pointed out the essentially artistic emphasis given to Dorante's fantasies, defending the character against an implied moral criticism. Morçay notes the absence of moralising in the play (p. 331), and the protagonist is variously seen as an *'artiste'*,[23] *'hâbleur'*,[24] *'amateur de canulars'*,[25] as *'a particularly effective entertainer'*[26] and as one for whom lies are simply *'jokes'*.[27] The comic implications of Corneille's conception of his protagonist become fully apparent through a comparison with the source.

In Alarcón, Garcia is of noble stock, living in a clearly defined social context. Stress is constantly laid on the importance of his moral education, undermined by his mysterious tendency to tell lies. For Garcia himself, such untruths are simply the way to make himself noticed in society; it is this that he seeks above all else, as he tells his valet in Act I Scene 8: *'Ser famosos es gran cosa / El medio qual fuere sea'* (861–2).[28] In Corneille, there is no talk of the hero's education or social ambition. Instead, stress is placed on the fertility of Dorante's imagination and his delight in the creation of fantasies which are more than just the means to an end:

> *J'aime à braver ainsi les conteurs de nouvelles;*
> *Et sitôt que j'en vois quelqu'un s'imaginer*
> *Que ce qu'il veut m'apprendre a de quoi m'étonner,*
> *Je le sers aussitôt d'un conte imaginaire,*
> *Qui l'étonne lui-même, et le force à se taire.* (I 6, 362–6)

Whereas Tristan will reprove his master after his tall story of martial prowess told to Jacinta and Lucrecia, stressing in Act I Scene 8 the destructive and dishonourable nature of the hero's deed, Cliton is given the lines which head this section, lines which stress a more positive, artistic conception of Dorante's inventiveness.

This fundamental difference is clear from the very beginning of the play. Garcia's first tale to the ladies in Act I Scene 5 is set already in a moral context, prefaced, as was remarked above, by scenes in which the father learns of and laments his son's weakness for untruth. The hero's story of his great exploits in war is thus seen as the first manifestation of this perplexing deficiency, for which the audience has been prepared. The first impression of Dorante, however, is not that of a flawed nobleman but of a charming if colourless courtier, of a law student who wishes to pass himself off as a gallant lover as soon as he arrives in Paris:

> *Mais puisque nous voici dedans les Tuileries,*
> *Le pays du beau monde et des galanteries,*
> *Dis-moi, me trouves-tu bien fait en cavalier?* (5–7)

When he meets Clarice, he is quick to lament his suffering in love, his legal mind constructing an intricate argument in defence of this sudden passion, but whose fragility is pointed out in a calm, undramatic way by the voice of common sense: '*Cette flamme, Monsieur, est pour moi fort nouvelle, / Puisque j'en viens de voir la première étincelle*' (145–6).

Against this background of discreet *badinage*, Dorante's tale of his courage in battle strikes the audience not so much as a morally ambiguous lie but as the hero's desperate attempt to impress. He presents himself as a valiant warrior, undefeated in battle but vanquished now by the lady's beauty:

> *Vaincre dans les combats, commander dans l'armée,*
> *De mille exploits fameux enfler ma renommée,*
> *Et tous ces nobles soins qui m'avoient su ravir,*
> *Cédèrent aussitôt à ceux de vous servir.* (181–4)

Trying now to convince Clarice that he is other than he is, Dorante falls into the mould of the braggart, a type where, clearly, any discrepancy between role and reality has a comic, not a moral force. It is in this light that he is later seen by Isabelle, Clarice's servant, in Act III Scene 3, who is quite sensitive to this natural instinct in young lovers:

> *Dorante est-il le seul qui, de jeune écolier,*
> *Pour être mieux reçu s'érige en cavalier? . . .*

> *Il aura cru sans doute, ou je suis fort trompée,*
> *Que les filles de coeur aiment les gens d'épée,*
> *Et vous prenant pour telle, il a jugé soudain*
> *Qu'une plume au chapeau vous plaît mieux qu'à la main.*
>   (859–60; 869–72)

Similarly, for the valet, such fantasies are not so much outrageous as quite incomprehensible, not a fault but an illness akin to madness. It is not by coincidence, perhaps, that the astonished spectator of these outbursts should be called Cliton, as was the servant of Eraste, and it is a significant indication of Dorante's role here that the bewildered question of this onlooker, '*Votre ordinaire est-il de rêver en parlant?*' (312), should echo the surprise of Artabaze at the sudden poetic flights of Amidor, the deranged poet in *Les Visionnaires*, Act III Scene 2: '*Dittes, vostre fureur vous prend-elle souvent?*' (785).

This visionary quality of Dorante's tales is suggested also in the changes which Corneille brings to the context of his tale of marriage. In *La Verdad sospechosa*, Act II Scene 9, Garcia's lie that he is already married follows a speech of reproof by his father, aware of his moral flaw. Indeed, it is because of Garcia's tendency to lie that don Beltran is so eager to see him married. The lie which follows is thus set in a tense and ambiguous dramatic context. This is not the case in Corneille. The prelude to the hero's tale in Act II Scene 5, is not a speech on the dishonour of falsehood but one of *rêverie*, as father and son marvel together at the magic of a growing city:

> *Paris semble à mes yeux un pays de romans.*
> *Je croyois ce matin voir une île enchantée:*
> *Je la laissai déserte, et la trouve habitée;*
> *Quelque Amphion nouveau, sans l'aide des maçons,*
> *En superbes palais a changé ses buissons.* (552–6)

Such poetic visions may reflect Corneille's care to give his play local colour, his attempt to re-set the Spanish play in a recognisable context, as he explains in his *Avis au Lecteur*.[29] Similar evocations of the new Paris were not unusual in plays of the period,[30] and yet it is quite significant that what is most often found in the opening scene of such plays should here be delayed. Dorante's wide-eyed admiration in these lines not only brings to life the contemporary city in a general way, but it has a precise and important dramatic function, setting a tone of fantasy in a scene which is to be so characterised. Modern Paris suggests to the admiring hero a magical transformation of reality which he himself will emulate in the tale which follows. In Alarcón, it is the liar and his moral flaw which concerns the audience throughout the scene; in Corneille, it is the artist and his ability to dream.

The changes which Corneille makes here suggest important differences in the way he conceives not only the nature of the lies themselves but also his hero's attitude to them. With Garcia, such tales are oddly dishonourable flights into falsehood, stories devoid of factual truth and divorced from the reality with which, otherwise, the hero associates and defines himself. With Dorante, however, the fantasies reflect an essential trait in his personality, a constant process of total self-transformation which is not curiously distinct from his ordinary life but is an integral part of it.

This difference of emphasis is quite clear in the reaction of each hero to the lie told of a former marriage. In Alarcón's play, there is nothing comic or fantastical about Garcia's feelings for Jacinta. By the time don Beltran announces his desire for his son to be married in Act II Scene 9, Garcia has already received details of 'her' family and a signed note which invites him to a nocturnal tryst. The lie which he tells, imaginative as it may be, is seen clearly as the sincere defence of a particular passion, about which he seems to know so much. In Act II Scene 14, Garcia, alone, reflects on this love which he holds so dear and which he has now safeguarded with such apparent success.

In *Le Menteur*, Act II Scene 6, however, the emphasis is quite different. Here Dorante also expresses satisfaction with his lie, but in this case it does not so much reflect the depth of his passion, now happily protected, but rather his delight at a brilliantly found invention, a victorious response to a challenge:

> Que dis-tu de l'histoire, et de mon artifice?
> Le bonhomme en tient-il? m'en suis-je bien tiré?
> Quelque sot en ma place y seroit demeuré;
> Il eût perdu le temps à gémir et se plaindre,
> Et malgré son amour, se fût laissé contraindre.
> Oh! l'utile secret de mentir à propos! (686–91)

Garcia is seen alone, the character examining his feelings. Dorante, on the other hand, does not look inside himself, but outside, and, like an actor, looks for approbation in his audience, Cliton, for the impressive performance he has just given.

Dorante's more obviously theatrical approach to his life is apparent also in Corneille's presentation of his reaction to Alcippe's challenge. In *La Verdad sospechosa*, Act II Scene 3, Garcia is silent and puzzled when he receives Juan's letter, anxious at this seemingly inexplicable threat to his honour. At the equivalent moment, however, Dorante responds with unalloyed enthusiasm, seeing in the *cartel* a challenge not so much to his reputation as to his quick-wittedness and ability to adapt to circumstances:

> D'aujourd'hui seulement je produis mon visage,
> Et j'ai déjà querelle, amour et mariage . . .
> Se charge qui voudra d'affaires plus pressantes,
> Plus en nombre à la fois et plus embarrassantes:
> Je pardonne à qui mieux s'en pourra démêler.
> Mais allons voir celui qui m'ose quereller. (II 8, 721–2, 725–8)

In Alarcón, Garcia has the reactions of a hero, and the audience's awareness of his earlier lies merely serves to throw into relief the peculiar complexity of his character, noble yet flawed. In Corneille, though, truth and falsehood do not stand opposed in the hero, but coalesce. Dorante's heroic response to Alcippe's challenge is expressed with the same enthusiasm and commitment as his earlier fantasies. Just as he creates for himself in his imagination a series of heroic identities, he reacts now to the demands of reality with no less dramatic a conception of his life. For Dorante, experiences either imagined or lived elicit the same response; truth merges with fantasy, the character with the actor.

This particular response to life is most significant in the last Act when, finally cornered by his father, the hero is obliged to tell the truth. In *La Verdad sospechosa*, Act III Scene 9, Garcia defends his love for 'Lucrecia' with an undistorted ardour. Sincerity of intention contrasts with the hero's unwitting mistake, and creates an atmosphere of tension as he is seen to force himself further and further into an *impasse*. The equivalent scene in *Le Menteur*, Act V Scene 3, opens in a mood of classical comedy, with suggestions of the familiar juxtaposition of old age and youth, gullibility and guile. Géronte is seen not so much as the voice of moral reproof, but as another challenge to Dorante's ingenuity. For Cliton, the onlooker, this suggests the ultimate test of his master's skill: '*Voici pour votre adresse une assez rude touche*' (1558). Like Garcia, Dorante here tells the truth, but it is expressed in a particular way. Apparent is not so much the sincerity of his feelings, but the enthusiasm with which his tale of love is told, and it is significant indeed that the opening lines of this avowal, of this *'vérité pure'* (v. 1557) which evoke the typically romanesque *coup de foudre*:

> Épris d'une beauté qu'à peine ai-je pu voir
> Qu'elle a pris sur mon âme un absolu pouvoir,
> De Lucrèce, en un mot, vous la pouvez connoître, (1559–61)

should echo in their style and theme the earlier tale of his marriage at Poitiers, told in Act II Scene 5:

> Je la vis presque à mon arrivée.
> Une âme de rocher ne s'en fût pas sauvée,
> Tant elle avoit d'appas, et tant son oeil vainqueur
> Par une douce force assujettit mon coeur! (605–8)

The parallel of these two evocations of love, the one imagined, the other real, does not simply suggest that Dorante's lived adventure is as romanesque as his invented one, or indeed that his love for 'Lucrèce' is as false as his love for a fictitious spouse. More importantly, it implies again that the hero approaches the worlds of fiction and of fact in the same way, bringing to each that blend of commitment and detachment which is that of an actor who enthusiastically plays his role.

What Corneille suggests in this presentation of the hero is underlined in the following scene, for which there is no equivalent in Alarcón. Here, Dorante confesses to Cliton that he now feels himself attracted equally to Lucrèce and Clarice. Such an admission has important consequences for the impact of the *dénouement*, which will be examined later, but it also emphasises the coherence of Dorante's status as the comic hero. His confession of truth in the previous scene, authentic as it is in terms of the facts of the plot, is revealed to be not simply a spontaneous avowal of love, as was the case with Garcia, but just another role, chosen by Dorante as the most appropriate to placate his father:

Cliton: Mais pourquoi donc montrer une flamme si grande,
         Et porter votre père à faire la demande?
Dorante: Il ne m'auroit pas cru, si je ne l'avois fait.
Cliton: Quoi? même en disant vrai, vous mentiez en effet! (1625–8)

At this point, the superimposition of truth on falsehood, which characterised the suggestive presentation of Alcidon and Daphnis, Célidée and Alidor, reaches a high point of refinement. The dramatic tension of Alarcón is rendered comic in a fundamental way, as face shades into mask, and the character who sincerely expresses his feelings is transformed into the actor who plays the part of himself.

It is such a presentation of Dorante which lies behind the complete transformation of the dramatic axis in the Spanish play. In *La Verdad sospechosa*, tension derives from the juxtaposition of lies and truth, of Garcia's morally reprehensible tendency to tell untruths and the dramatic truth of his love for Jacinta, whom he believes to be called Lucrecia. This mistake becomes a source of particular moral ambiguity, as the liar is led with the sincerest of intentions to make statements which do not correspond to the truth. In *Le Menteur*, however, the hero's tales are conceived not as moral flaws but as creative flights of fancy, not as strange aberrations from normal heroic behaviour, but as entirely consonant with his nature, which delights in the transformation of reality, in the excitement and drama of the romanesque. His love for 'Lucrèce' is a role which he plays with the same enthusiasm as that of the courageous soldier or the liberal lover; he is committed to all roles in the same way. Where in Garcia, there is tension, ambiguity and conflict, in Dorante, there is unity and coherence. Such a difference is of great significance on several levels in the *dénouement*.

4

Pour moi, j'ai trouvé cette manière de finir un peu dure, et cru qu'un mariage moins violenté seroit plus au goût de notre auditoire. C'est ce qui m'a obligé à lui donner une pente vers la personne de Lucrèce au cinquième acte, afin qu'après qu'il a reconnu sa méprise aux noms, il fasse de nécessité vertu de meilleure grâce, et que la comédie se termine avec pleine tranquillité de tous côtés.[31]

The love which Dorante has begun to feel for the real Lucrèce certainly reflects Corneille's desire to smooth an ending which, in Alarcón, is characterised by tension and coercion. Whereas in *La Verdad sospechosa*, there is no indication that Garcia has any feeling for Lucrecia at all, in *Le Menteur*, Act V Scene 6, the hero is able to accept the consequences of his mistake with no suggestions of reluctance or suffering: '*Et comme dès tantôt je la trouvois bien faite, / Mon coeur déjà penchoit où mon erreur le jette'* (1725–6). Here is a happy coincidence of mistake and inclination, '*erreur*' and '*coeur*', not found in the Spanish source. And indeed, Corneille's eagerness to suggest no tension at all in the ultimate pairings of his characters is implied equally as far as the heroines are concerned. In an earlier scene between Clarice and Lucrèce, in Act IV Scene 9, the dramatist is quite careful to point out that Clarice suffers in no way at the thought of losing Dorante, whom seemingly she loved. She is able to tease Lucrèce about the love which she herself feels for the hero and which he appears to reciprocate, insisting at the same time, and quite unlike Jacinta in *La Verdad sospechosa*, in Act III Scene 4, that she is perfectly content to accept Alcippe:

> *Il t'en veut tout de bon, et m'en voilà défaite;*
> *Mais je souffre aisément la perte que j'ai faite:*
> *Alcippe la répare, et son père est ici.* (1389–91)

Such an ending would seem to imply a return to the aesthetic principle of *comédie*, in which affections may be transferred at will with little regard for coherence of character. Indeed, the *dénouement* has often been criticised on these very grounds as being facile, improbable and unconvincing.[32] For such critics, Dorante is not to be distinguished from the countless heroes and heroines, whose acquiescence to the inevitable is unproblematical and absolute. The lines of many a character in romanesque comedy are echoed by these of Climante, hero of d'Ouville's *La Dame suivante* in Act V Scene 8: '*Puis que je voy qu'ici la chose est sans remede, / Qui [sic] ferois-je, Madame? il faut bien que je cede*' (p. 165).

Dorante's final gesture, however, suggests more than just peaceful acceptance, '*tranquillité*' in the face of inexorable formal demands. It implies more, too, than a parody of traditional endings in all their artificiality, such as will be found later in the remark of Corbineli at the end of Cyrano de Bergerac's *Pédant joué*,[33] Act V Scene 10: '*Hé-bien! ne sçavez-vous pas que la conclusion d'un Poëme Comique est toujours un Mariage?*' (p. 146), or in the terms of Cliton's final acceptance of a partner in Thomas Corneille's *L'Amour à la mode*,[34] Act V Scene 10: '*J'y consens; il faut bien qu'en fin je me marie: / Pourrions-nous autrement finir la Comédie?*' (1889–90). Corneille no more accepts the simple solution here than he does elsewhere in his comedies. Dorante's role is quite positive, not negative, and it is significant that his acceptance of Lucrèce in Act V Scene 6 is voiced not in terms of a hero, happy in the fulfilment of his love, but once more in terms of the actor who again responds enthusiastically to a challenge:

> *Ne me découvre point; et dans ce nouveau feu*
> *Tu me vas voir, Cliton, jouer un nouveau jeu.*
> *Sans changer de discours, changeons de batterie.* (1727–9)

Seen in this light, his action suggests not so much lack of internal coherence but complete consistency with the logic of his character. Just as the accomplished *'faiseur de romans'* had cast himself in various roles according to the demands of the moment – the valiant warrior, the secretly married man, the lover of 'Lucrèce', roles which brought together the poles of truth and falsehood, reality and fantasy – so too now the hero transforms himself again, both committed to and detached from the part he plays, loving and, at the same time, acting the role of lover.

It is here that the difference in conception of Garcia and Dorante is at its most significant. At the end of Alarcón's play, Garcia is obliged to give up Jacinta, and to marry Lucrecia whom he does not love; the order of comedy is strained. The hero's lies, seen as morally reprehensible throughout the play, are conceived now, in addition, as responsible for the aesthetic tension implied in this coerced marriage. It is on such a warning from Tristan that the play ends:

> *Y aquí verás cuán dañosa*
> *Es la mentira; y verá*
> *El senado que en la boca*
> *Del que mentir acostumbra,*
> *Es la verdad sospechosa.* (3118–22)[35]

In *Le Menteur*, however, the aesthetic force of Dorante's lies is given a new and formal importance. The deliberate and consistent play acting of the hero does not work against the eventual harmony, but actually creates it, transforming an ending of tension and punishment into one of triumph:

> *Comme en sa propre fourbe un menteur s'embarrasse!*
> *Peu sauroient comme lui s'en tirer avec grâce.*
> *Vous autres qui doutiez s'il en pourroit sortir,*
> *Par un si rare exemple apprenez à mentir.* (1801–4)

The eulogy of the hero and his power echoes significantly that praise of the dramatist which traditionally ends much comedy. Dorante's talent is indeed analogous to that of the playwright, both of whom have the supreme ability to transform reality with the strength of their imagination. Not a victim of events but their master, the *menteur* can thus create order out of chaos, for the satisfaction of himself and for the delight of his audience.

5

. . . *et s'il m'est permis de dire mon sentiment touchant une chose où j'ai si peu de part, je vous avouerai en même temps que l'invention de celle-ci me charme tellement, que je ne trouve rien à mon gré qui lui soit comparable en ce genre, ni parmi les anciens, ni parmi les modernes.*[36]

Among the comedies of the 1640s *Le Menteur* stands alone. Corneille's recasting of the Spanish original reveals his eye for comic ambiguities and ironies only potential in Alarcón, and the result is a comedy certainly more refined in its effects than those of his contemporaries. Most significant in the adaptation, however, is the creation, in Dorante, of a positive and wholly comic hero, a type noticeably lacking in the Spanish inspired comedy of this period. Dorante clearly belongs to the tradition of the *visionnaire*, a figure whose colourful, imaginative fantasies have an important role in *comédie* from the time of Pichou's *Folies de Cardenio* and Rotrou's *L'Hypocondriaque*. His purpose is to entertain through the comic extravagance of his visions, a role which Mareschal makes clear in the *Dédicace* to his *Véritable Capitan Matamore*: 'Il *vous entretiendra comiquement de ses imaginaires avantures, & si vous vous hazardez d'ouïr ses debites, il va perdre l'haleine plus de mille fois dans de nouveaux & agreables efforts de memoire, pour vous montrer la gentillesse de son esprit & de son humeur'*, and which is echoed, too, in Guérin de Bouscal's adaptation of *Dom Quixote de la Manche*,[37] Act III Scene 5, where Ferrande has the following reaction to the deranged hero: '*Laissons-le comme il est, & taschons seulement / Qu'il nous puisse donner du divertissement'* (p. 74). Such a type is also the hero of Gillet de la Tessonerie's dramatisation of *La Comédie de Francion*.[38] The conscious fantasies of the protagonist have their own comic force as he ascribes to himself in Act III Scene 1, a visionary omnipotence in order to dupe a gullible fool:

J'arrache d'un seul mot les estoilles des Cieux
Et je suis obey des Demons & des Dieux,
Mais pour vous tesmoigner que je suis veritable
Je vais vous raconter une histoire notable. (p. 64)

In all such plays, however, the exhibition of the hero's fantasy, conscious or unconscious, tends to take place at the expense of the overall dramatic balance. Alarcón's play, therefore, was the ideal opportunity for Corneille to fix the imaginative *envolées* of his hero in a much tighter knit structure, where movement and context have as important a comic function as the language itself.

Le Menteur, however, holds a central place in Corneille's own comic *oeuvre*, and shows clear links with his earlier plays. In the changes which he brings to Alarcón's text, he may reflect the popularity of unproblematical comedies of confusion, but the skill in his adaptation of the Spanish plot recalls the preoccupations of his earliest works. Once again, the dramatist's careful focus on the character as well as on the language he speaks leads to a significant shift from tense drama to comedy. This process lies behind the metamorphosis of Tristan, Juan and don Beltran into Cliton, Alcippe and Géronte, comic characters who are constantly detached from their roles. Their language of honour, jealousy or moral reproof no longer has a direct impact on its own terms, but is seen to imply instead the speaker's folly, stubbornness or ridiculous credulity. And this process is most important, indeed, in the reconception of the hero. The levels of comic ambiguity which had been suggested in the language of earlier characters are here taken to their most refined limits. All heroic stances are conceived quite literally as roles by Dorante the actor who fuses fact and fiction, seeing reality in terms of a play in which he is the protagonist.

Particularly fascinating, though, is that Corneille should have been inspired in this way by *La Verdad sospechosa*. Alarcón's is a play which falls into the tradition of so many comedies of confusion, with their chance meetings, mysterious ladies, duels and mistaken identities, but which extracts from such elements suggestions of suffering and tension. The order of comedy is established at the end, but beneath this is sensed a peculiar strain and moral ambiguity. The four principal characters are married, but Garcia is unable to commit himself with conviction to his partner, to forget so easily the love which has motivated him in

the course of the play. In this sense, the play bears a strange
affinity with Corneille's own earlier comedies, and it does not
seem surprising that he should express such admiration for it,
both at the time of his own play and in the *Examen*. His process of
adaptation implies then, to this extent, not only a comment on
Alarcón's comedy, but also an important development from his
own.

In Dorante, Corneille offers the ultimate solution to that
tension apparent in his first comedies, where characters were
unable to adapt with ease to the demands made of them. For the
menteur, actions are not so much inspired by personal feelings as
by a desire to react positively to a challenge; unlike either Garcia
or Corneille's own earlier protagonists, Dorante does not have
one inflexible identity which he seeks to protect in all circumstances, but he constantly creates new identities for himself which
suit the demands of the moment. This hero may lack that
suggestive complexity which characterised Célidée, Hippolyte or
Alidor, but instead he is given a compelling commitment to the
world of his imagination, a unique ability to blend fact and
fiction, experience and performance which makes of this actor
the supreme comic hero and which lies behind the logic and
conviction of the order he creates.

IX

La Suite du Menteur
The play as
entertainment

Elle n'a pas été si heureuse au théâtre que l'autre, quoique plus remplie de beaux sentiments et de beaux vers.[1]

La Suite du Menteur is the adaptation of Lope de Vega's *Amar sin saber a quién*,[2] a work which depicts the adventures of Juan who nobly has himself imprisoned in order to save the life of don Ferrando, awakens the love of Leonarda, Ferrando's sister, and eventually marries her. In many ways, the play reflects the less impressive, less dynamic tendencies of comedy at this time, where the energy generated by an intricate mechanism of confusion is lost, and where the traditional separation of serious and comic episodes is little more than the awkward juxtaposition of the sentimental and the burlesque. In *Le Menteur*, Corneille was seen to transform Alarcón's tense drama into a particularly sophisticated comedy; in his adaptation of Lope's play, he has quite different purposes.

A comparison with the source reveals, for instance, Corneille's frequent expansion of its lyrical elements, the dramatist clearly seizing every opportunity to write '*beaux vers*'. When, in Act IV Scene 6, Mélisse realises that she has declared her love to the wrong man, having in the darkness of night mistaken Philiste for Dorante, Corneille takes the simple remark of Lope's heroine in Act II Scene 12: '*Ay, mi senor, que engañada / le hablé por ti!*' (p. 303)[3] and amplifies it into a romantic evocation of love, which thus accounts for her mistake:

> *L'erreur n'est pas un crime; et votre chère idée,*
> *Régnant sur mon esprit, m'a si bien possédée,*
> *Que dedans votre objet le sien s'est confondu,*
> *Et lorsqu'il m'a parlé je vous ai répondu.* (1469–72)

Significantly, the most famous passage in the play, the heroine's discourse on love in Act IV Scene 1 which was so popular at the time of its creation and much later too,[4] is also purely of Corneille's invention. Here, the dramatist reverts quite explicitly to the ideal world of *L'Astrée* where the matching of couples is held to correspond to a faultless, divine plan and which lends to lovers an instinctive confidence in their feelings:

> *On s'estime, on se cherche, on s'aime en un moment:*
> *Tout ce qu'on s'entre-dit persuade aisément;*
> *Et sans s'inquiéter de mille peurs frivoles,*
> *La foi semble courir au-devant des paroles.* (1227–30)

In a similar way, Corneille gives to his hero an increased dosage of fine poetic displays. In Lope's text, Juan is seen prepared to forgo his love of the heroine in favour of his rival, don Louis, actually leaving the stage, only to be recalled later by Louis, a hero as magnanimous as he. In *La Suite du Menteur*, however, this piece of dramatic action is sacrificed as Corneille amplifies instead the lovers' scene of separation, giving Dorante lines of majestic nobility and self-control:

> *Ce grand excès d'amour que font voir vos douleurs*
> *Triomphe de mon coeur sans vaincre mes malheurs.*
> *On ne m'arrête pas pour redoubler mes chaînes,*
> *On redouble ma flamme, on redouble mes peines;*
> *Mais tous ces nouveaux feux qui viennent m'embraser*
> *Me donnent seulement plus de fers à briser.* (1683–8)

However, if such passages suggest the dramatist's love of noble verse and his desire to expand and exploit the poetic potential of his source, he is no less keen to increase the dosage of burlesque elements, which are its inevitable complement. The Cliton of this play falls firmly into the tradition of valets, whose concrete language and ideas provide comic interludes in plots of more abstract romanticising. Lope's valet, Limon, has a ready tongue, indeed, but Corneille amplifies his role. In Act III Scene 2, Dorante's evocation of the spiritual qualities of Mélisse, who has anonymously sent gifts to him in prison, is followed at once by verses from the servant who stresses instead her more material attributes:

> *Adorable et riche beauté,*
> *Qui joins les effets aux paroles,*

> *Merveille qui m'as enchanté*
> *Par tes douceurs et tes pistoles . . .* (939–42)

Similarly, in Act V Scene 1, Corneille adds an entire scene, in
which Cliton and Lyse, the servant of Mélisse, court each other in
a manner parallel to that of their master and mistress, Cliton
being given lines of quite farcical directness:

> *J'ai le goût fort grossier en matière de flamme:*
> *Je sais que c'est beaucoup qu'avoir le coeur et l'âme;*
> *Mais je ne sais pas moins qu'on a fort peu de fruit*
> *Et de l'âme et du coeur, si le reste ne suit.* (1621–4)

Furthermore, Cliton is not just another witty valet, but is linked
more specifically to the growing tradition of French comic roles
written for Jodelet. In Act I Scene 2, for instance, Corneille does
not hesitate to make reference to the personality of this popular
actor and to his particularly nasal manner of speech, enriching in
a not very subtle way, the atmosphere of farce:

> Cliton: *Touche, je veux t'aimer, tu seras mon souci:*
> *Nos maîtres font l'amour, nous le ferons aussi.*
> *J'aurai mille beaux mots tous les jours à te dire;*
> *Je coucherai de feux, de sanglots, de martyre;*
> *Je te dirai: 'Je meurs, je suis dans les abois,*
> *Je brûle . . .*
> Lyse: *Et tout cela de ce beau ton de voix?* (221–6)

The separation of these two registers leads to very little
dramatic tautness in Lope's play, and yet, curiously, in his
adaptation, Corneille moves even further away from creating
tension and excitement, underplaying or cutting out any such
elements present even in his Spanish source. In Lope, for
instance, there is the hint of potential conflict between brother
and sister over the sister's love. Indeed, in plays of this time, the
brother is often a real, if ultimately unconvincing threat to the
happy accomplishment of the heroine's passion. In Corneille,
however, this threat is explicitly rejected as a dramatic possibility:
it is made quite clear, in Act IV Scene 2, that Cléandre wishes his
sister to marry Dorante:

> *Loin d'éteindre ce feu, je voudrois l'allumer,*
> *Qu'il eût de quoi vous plaire, et voulût vous aimer;*
> *Je tiendrois à bonheur de l'avoir pour beau-frère:*
> *J'en cherche les moyens, j'y fais ce qu'on peut faire.* (1311–14)

Corneille's careful avoidance of dramatic tension is crystallised, however, in his particular conception of Lope's play as a *Suite du Menteur*. The audience is invited not so much to see here the drama of a romantic hero and heroine, but the new adventures of characters with whom they are already familiar. His protagonists do not inhabit a distant land, but are seen as contemporaries of the audience, living quite clearly in the same world. The opening line of the comedy:

Cliton: *Ah! Monsieur, c'est donc vous?*
Dorante: *Cliton, je te revoi.* (1)

reflects the spirit of recognition and reminiscence which fills the text. Allusions to *Le Menteur* are frequent and are manifestly more important to Corneille and more interesting to the audience than any thrills or excitement generated by Lope's plot. Thus, for instance, in Act I Scene 3, when Dorante, like the traditional Spanish hero, discloses his name in a letter to the mysterious lady of mercy, he is criticised by Cliton, not because he mistrusts the heroine's motives, as is Limon's argument in Lope's play, but rather because the name Dorante can only suggest one thing:

> . . . *Oui, dans Paris, en langage commun,*
> *Dorante et le Menteur à present ce n'est qu'un,*
> *Et vous y possédez ce haut degré de gloire*
> *Qu'en une comédie on a mis votre histoire.* (269–72)

On one level, this fusion of the audience's world and the characters' leads to interludes of quite suggestive self-advertisement, as actors simultaneously enhance and undermine their credibility in the parts they perform by drawing attention to themselves as actors. In Act I Scene 3, for instance, Cliton describes a performance of *Le Menteur*, and in his description of Jodelet, role and reality merge:

> *Le héros de la farce, un certain Jodelet,*
> *Fait marcher après vous votre digne valet;*
> *Il a jusqu'à mon nez et jusqu'à ma parole,*
> *Et nous avons tous deux appris en même école:*
> *C'est l'original même, il vaut ce que je vaux;*
> *Si quelque autre s'en mêle, on peut s'inscrire en faux . . .* (281–6)

However, Corneille's attempt to set his second play in terms of its successful predecessor, to create the effect of having familiar actors involved in a further and totally distinct adventure is ultimately unsuccessful. The principal link between the two texts is the tendency of the hero to 'lie', but this connection is only tenuous in the extreme. In *Le Menteur*, the hero's untruths had been part of his essentially theatrical approach to life, manifestations of his constant dramatisation of reality. In the *Suite*, however, Dorante, like Juan his model, is presented as a quite honourable and selfless hero, who lies out of purely noble motives and who is prepared to save the life of another in a spirit of generosity. In Act II Scene 2, Cléandre expresses the utmost admiration for these qualities: '*C'est le plus généreux qui ait jamais vécu; / C'est le coeur le plus noble, et l'âme la plus haute*' (494–5), and in Act III Scene 1, the hero himself explains the natural instinct which compelled him to act as he did:

> *N'appelez point faveur ce qui fut un devoir:*
> *Entre les gens de coeur il suffit de se voir.*
> *Par un effort secret de quelque sympathie*
> *L'un à l'autre aussitôt un certain noeud les lie.* (805–8)

The Dorante of this play could not be more different from his namesake.

The reputation of immorality which *Le Menteur* acquired at the time of its creation clearly forced Corneille however to insist on links between the generous Spanish hero and the seemingly dishonourable protagonist of the earlier comedy, to point out that it is the same Dorante who acts out this noble role. From the start of the play, the hero presents himself as a reformed character, more mature than that other Dorante held to be of such doubtful principles: '. . . *Le temps m'a fait connoître / Quelle indignité c'est, et quel mal en peut naître*' (143–4), a confession which is repeated to Philiste in Act II Scene 4:

> *Formez en ma faveur de plus saines pensées:*
> *Ces petites humeurs sont aussitôt passées;*
> *Et l'air du monde change en bonnes qualités*
> *Ces teintures qu'on prend aux universités.* (619–22)

This particular intention is made quite explicit by Philiste at the end of the play, in Act V Scene 5:

> *S'il vous en faut encor des motifs plus puissants,*
> *Vous pouvez effacer avec cette seconde*
> *Les bruits que la première a laissés dans le monde,*
> *Et ce coeur généreux n'a que trop d'intérêt*
> *Qu'elle fasse partout connoître ce qu'il est.* (p. 388, var. 1)

The result, however, is a failure in aesthetic terms, making the comedy something of a laboured *pièce à thèse* which is made even more leaden by Cliton. The servant's ironical refusal to see noble motives behind his master's lies in Act I Scene 6, for instance, is not so much a traditional comic interlude, designed to throw into relief the hero's qualities, but a rather burdensome reminder that the gallant nobleman before the audience is none other than the *menteur*, so often reviled:

> Et c'est ainsi, Monsieur, que l'on s'amende à Rome?
> Je me tiens au proverbe: oui, courez, voyagez;
> Je veux être guenon si jamais vous changez:
> Vous mentirez toujours, Monsieur, sur ma parole . . . (364–7)

In consequence, Dorante is left with neither the coherence or verve of his predecessor, nor the full heroic impact of his Spanish model.

As early as the *Épître* to the comedy, Corneille shows himself aware of the faults to which this enforced attempt to exonerate his *Menteur* had given rise. He is unable to argue that the new found honour of the hero makes this comedy superior to its predecessor:

> Pour moi, qui tiens avec Aristote et Horace que notre art n'a pour but que le divertissement, j'avoue qu'il est ici bien moins à estimer qu'en la première comédie, puisque, avec ses mauvaises habitudes, il a perdu presque toutes ses grâces, et qu'il semble avoir quitté la meilleure part de ses agréments lorsqu'il a voulu se corriger de ses défauts. (p. 280)

Corneille did not believe that a play could successfully bear the strain of an explicit moral lesson, and he saw the risk he was taking. For him, the dramatist's aim and duty was primarily to entertain, and he clearly tried to correct the balance of his play by simultaneously implying its value as an enjoyable spectacle. It is this concern above all which is clear in those aspects of his adaptation analysed at the beginning of this chapter: the amplified scenes of poetic outburst or burlesque humour, the deliberate relaxation of tension and the insistent topical references. The protagonists are less important for their feelings than for their words, less striking as characters than as actors.

It is this perspective which Corneille is eager to underline at the end of his comedy where, unlike in Lope's play, stress does not lie on the triumphant union of hero and heroine. The glorious future so often evoked at the end of comedy is not that of love, the communal harmony implied not that of marriage: the final emphasis of *La Suite du Menteur* rests, instead, on the theatre. In Act V Scene 6, the assembled company contemplate the dramatisation of their adventures, in which marriages will simply be the fruit of a dramatist's imagination, and the shared joy that of a theatrical troupe, delighting in the performance of its own drama: '*Fais-en ample mémoire, et va le lui porter; / Nous prendrons du plaisir à la représenter*' (p. 388, var. 1). It is entirely consistent with this perspective that in Cliton's final monologue the traditional hailing of joy which ends all suffering should refer not to the trials of hero and heroine who have found happiness in their romantic world, but to the suffering of the spectator, uncomfortable in the theatre during the performance and now blessedly released:

> *Tout change, et de la joie on passe à la tristesse;*
> *Aux plus grands déplaisirs succède l'allégresse,*
> *Ceux qui sont las debout se peuvent aller seoir,*
> *Je vous donne en passant cet avis, et bonsoir.* (p. 389, var. 1)

For all this, however, *La Suite du Menteur* remains a fragmented and unsatisfactory play. The heroic verse has a certain value when taken on its own terms, but it gains no force, either dramatic or comic, from the constant insistence on the identity of the speaker. Dorante, the lively *menteur*, for whom theatre and reality merge so suggestively, is no longer to be found beneath the mask of an essentially conventional Spanish hero. The fundamental concept of the theatre, of the comic act, which knits together the diverse elements of *Le Menteur*, just as it had earlier given unity to *L'Illusion Comique*, is here reduced to obtrusive set pieces, and superficial references to a particular actor or to a particular play, in short to a rather banal notion of the play as entertainment. Too trivial and vague, it is not enough to compensate for the leaden moral message which Corneille had reluctantly adopted, and ultimately fails to give that general coherence and order which, in their different ways, lies behind the greatness and originality of these two earlier comedies.

Conclusion
Experiments
in the comic

Que'on en nomme l'invention bijarre & extravagante tant qu'on voudra, elle est nouvelle, & souvent la grace de la nouveauté parmy nos François n'est pas un petit degré de bonté.[1]

Corneille's comedies were written at a particularly fruitful period of French literature, at a time when the genre, with its few theoretical requirements, could accommodate plays which strove either to excite or amuse, to give poetic entertainment or offer a charming investigation into the human heart. Like many of his contemporaries, Corneille reflects this diversity of interest in his own work, as he ranges from the refined comic effects of *La Veuve* to the spirit of *divertissement* in *Le Menteur*, from the delicacy and suggestiveness of *La Galerie du Palais* to the bold theatricality of *L'Illusion comique*. It has become evident that to see the originality of Corneille's comedy merely in terms of a particular tone or preoccupation does full justice neither to the variety of his *oeuvre* nor to the achievements of his contemporaries.

Nevertheless, Corneille's plays do stand out in different ways against this rich and varied background. Immediately apparent is the dramatist's sustained development and refinement of comic techniques. Popular scenes, such as the meeting of rivals, the abduction of heroines, the ravings of madmen, the rejection of importunate lovers are the starting point for ever more sophisticated comic incidents. From the abduction of Clarice to that of Angelique, from the ridiculing of Philandre to that of Theante, from the ravings of Eraste to those of Dorante, and from the confrontation of Tirsis and Philandre or of Lysandre and Dorimant to that of Dorante and Alcippe, the increased refinement is clear. Evident from the start of Corneille's career is his refusal to accept the easy solution of farce in the creation of comic effects, and it has been seen how he refines the stylisation of language and character which in dramatists such as Mareschal, Claveret or du Ryer remains largely on the level of literary pastiche. Most significant of all is his development of a particular form of linguistic ambiguity peculiarly his own, which brings together truth and falsehood, spontaneity and pretence. It is this focus which characterises and distinguishes the comic force of such characters as Alcidon, Alidor and Dorante, setting them apart from the simpler creations of villain, *esprit fort* or madman. This, the feature least often recognised in his work, is not the least important of them.

It is through his unique adaptation of these techniques that Corneille acquires particular acuteness in his analysis of human feelings. The counterpointing of belief and disbelief, ignorance and suspicion which characterises the comic encounter of Mélite and Cloris offers, in the meetings of Hippolyte and Célidée, Amarante and Daphnis a more sensitive evocation of doubts and self-deception, bitterness and scorn. Discrepancies between what characters are and what they claim to be which, in the early comedies, have a simple comic function, become in these central · plays far more suggestive, implying now the fascinating pretence of lovers hesitating about their feelings, uncertain in their relationships with others and themselves. Corneille's originality is most striking in the *dénouements* of such plays, where, more obviously than any of his contemporaries, he investigates the inadequacies and inconsistencies of convention. Going beyond that ironical presentation of harmony which is found in certain comedies of the period, and which he himself uses in his earliest plays, he moves from discreet suggestions of tension in *La Galerie du Palais* and the ambiguous distortions of *La Suivante* to the final collapse of order in *La Place Royale*. Most significant is that such strains grow out of plots which are, by tradition, comic – a lovers' quarrel, a simple misunderstanding, the antics of a ridiculous lover who claims to be in control of his passion. Such plots presuppose certain endings, but these Corneille rejects as unsatisfactory. With a boldness which is quite without parallel at this time, he manipulates the expectations of his audience, and, by so doing, throws into relief the complexity and intractable logic of the characters he creates.

Corneille's particular experiments take many forms, and yet running throughout the *oeuvre* may be uncovered a particular angle of vision which, in certain respects, unifies and defines the comedies: his presentation of the character as an actor, and of his language as a role. In these plays protagonists are not so much directly involved in the *péripéties* and eventual harmony of the traditional plot, but are seen to act or see themselves as acting parts in them; language is not so much the direct means of expression for their feelings, but a mask which conceals or distorts. It is through this perspective that Corneille turns the excitement potential in the plots of *Mélite* and *La Veuve* into more sophisticated comedy; it underlies the suggestive analysis of characters in the central plays, who act their parts as lovers with a blend of conviction and hesitation; it forms the basis of that highly original investigation into the literal relationship of actor and role which is *L'Illusion comique*, and in *Le Menteur* it is this focus which characterises his transformation of the liar into one who acts out with great virtuosity the dramatic events of his life, both imagined and real. This sustained highlighting of the actor's performance takes Corneille to the essential principle of comedy which is the theatrical act, to the archetypal comic hero, the *comédien*.

Corneille's comedies suggest the fascinating union of mind and material, the work of a particularly original dramatist eager to explore the possibilities of a genre which was at a critical stage in its development. In the context of his complete output, however, they offer a suggestive insight into the nature of his art. The link between the early work and the later tragedies has often been discussed, but, as was seen in the Introduction, the influence of the two genres is frequently reversed, and it is with the tragedies in mind that the comedies are interpreted; themes are highlight-ed in the early plays which critics see brought to fruition in the later ones – the hero's increasing awareness of and power over his will and reason, the problems of enforced marriage, the morality of might.

The conclusions of the foregoing analysis, however, suggest development on a quite different level, as he adapts comic techniques for an investigation of tragic dilemmas. In his early plays, the conception of the character as performer had been used as an instrument to create sophisticated comedy, to suggest the charms of self-deception or the accomplishment of the professional actor. In his succeeding tragedies, however, it is used to analyse a far tenser drama as heroes seek to come to terms with the demands now made of them by political or moral codes, or by the equally inexorable call of their own self-regard. Reactions to such demands may be positive, but beneath the seemingly unequivocal acts and expressions of heroism – Chimène's relentless quest for justice or Cinna's commitment to a political cause, Attila's protestations of power or Bérénice's defence of her love – Corneille suggests complexities of motive, mixtures of strength and weariness, conviction and doubt.

More than this, however, the comedies are the first expression of that desire to experiment which may be seen to be an underlying element in Corneille's dramaturgy as a whole. If these plays reveal great diversity among themselves, they, in turn, form part of a complete *oeuvre* which brings together tragedies as different from each other as *Cinna* and *Théodore*, *Rodogune* and *Suréna*, and which ranges from spectacular *pièces à machines* to the creation of that curious hybrid, the *comédie héroïque*. As early as his preface to *Clitandre*, the dramatist prides himself on his versatility, and there is a perceptible delight in theatrical challenge as he composes *Le Menteur* concurrently with *La Mort de Pompée*, noting in his preface to the former: '*Je vous présente une pièce de théâtre d'un style si éloigné de ma dernière, qu'on aura de la peine à croire qu'elles soient parties toutes deux de la même main, dans le même hiver*' (Marty-Laveaux, IV, p. 130). There is a boldness which accompanies Corneille throughout his career, and in the dramatist who can say in the *avis* to *Nicomède*: '*Il est bon de hasarder un peu . . .*' is easily recognisable the creator of such original plays as *La Suivante* and *La Place Royale*. This constant willingness to take risks leads, of necessity, to mixed fortunes, in the eyes of his contemporaries and of posterity: the adulation accorded *Le Cid* brings with it, almost inevitably, the rejection of *Pertharite*, just as the cool reception given to *La Suivante* and *La Suite du Menteur* goes hand in hand with the triumph of *La Veuve* and *La Galerie du Palais*. In all cases, however, Corneille's fascination with the possibilities of the theatre remains clear, and the same spirit of delight which informs his *Dédicace* to *L'Illusion comique*, a success, is felt in his later preface to *Agésilas*, a failure: '*On court, à la vérité, quelque risque de s'égarer, et même on s'égare assez souvent, quand on s'écarte du chemin battu; mais on ne s'égare pas toutes les fois qu'on s'en écarte: quelques-uns en arrivent plus tôt où ils prétendent, et chacun peut hasarder à ses périls*' (Marty-Laveaux, VII, 5–6).

Notes

Introduction

1   Jean de La Bruyère, *Les Caractères*, Des Ouvrages de l'esprit, 54; ed. R. Garapon (Paris: Garnier, 1962), p. 87.
2   Jacques Scherer, 'Activités cornéliennes 1939–49', *Revue d'Histoire du Théâtre*, 2 (1950), 59–70.
3   Georges May, 'Sept Années d'études cornéliennes', *Romanic Review*, 43 (1952), 282–92.
4   Georges Couton, 'État présent des études cornéliennes', *Information Littéraire*, 8 (1956), 43–8.
5   L. W. Tancock, 'Work on Corneille since 1945', *Modern Languages*, 40 (1959), 109–14.
6   Robert Brasillach, *Pierre Corneille* (Paris: Arthème Fayard, 1938) p. 77.
7   Auguste Dorchain, *Pierre Corneille* (Paris: Garnier, 1918), p. 58.
8   Adolphe Hatzfeld, *Les Commencements de P. Corneille* (Grenoble: Prudhomme, 1857), p. 19.
9   Ferdinand Brunetière, *Les Epoques du théâtre français, 1636–1850* (Paris: Hachette, 1896), p. 38.
10 Geoffrey Brereton, *French Comic Drama from the Sixteenth to the Eighteenth Century* (London: Methuen, 1977), p. 15.
11 Jules Marsan, *La Pastorale dramatique en France à la fin du XVIe et au commencement du XVIIe siècle* (Paris: Hachette, 1905), p. 350.
12 Felix Gaiffe, *Le Rire et la scène française* (Paris: Boivin, 1931), p. 93.
13 Octave Nadal, *Le Sentiment de l'amour dans l'oeuvre de Pierre Corneille*, Bibliothèque des Idées (Paris: Gallimard, 1948), p. 22.
14 Pierre Voltz, *La Comédie*, Collection U, Série 'Lettres Françaises' (Paris: A. Colin, 1964), p. 53.
15 Roger Guichemerre, *La Comédie avant Molière, 1640–1660* (Paris: A. Colin, 1972), p. 12.
16 Louis Rivaille, *Les Débuts de P. Corneille* (Paris: Boivin, 1936), p. 190.
17 Gustave Lanson, *Corneille*, Les Grands Ecrivains Français (Paris: Hachette, 1946), pp. 50–1.

18   Jean Schlumberger, *Plaisir à Corneille, promenade anthologique* (Paris: Gallimard, 1936), p. 32.

19   Léon Lemonnier, *Corneille* (Paris: Tallandier, 1945), p. 46.

20   H. C. Lancaster, *A History of French Dramatic Literature in the Seventeenth Century*, 9 vols. (Baltimore: Johns Hopkins Press, 1929–42), Pt. I vol. 2 (1929), 568.

21   Antoine Adam, *Histoire de la littérature française au XVIIe siècle*, 5 vols. (Paris: Domat, 1948–56), I, 490.

22   Walter Küchler, 'Pierre Corneille's *Mélite*', *Germanisch-Romanische Monatsschrift*, 5 (1913), 677–89 (p. 688).

23   P. J. Yarrow, *Corneille* (London: Macmillan, 1963), p. 83.

24   Jacques Maurens, *Préface* in: Pierre Corneille, *Théâtre complet* (Paris: Garnier-Flammarion, 1968), I, 15.

25   Giovanni Dotoli *Introduction* in: Antoine Mareschal, *Le Railleur* (Bologna: Patrón Editore, 1973), p. 79.

26   Lawrence E. Harvey, 'The Noble and the Comic in Corneille's *La Veuve*', *Symposium*, 10 (1956), 291–5 (p. 291).

27   Jacques Scherer, *La Dramaturgie classique en France* (Paris: Nizet, (1950)), p. 321.

28   Peter Bürger, *Die frühen Komödien Pierre Corneilles und das französische Theater um 1630: eine wirkungsästhetische Analyse* (Frankfurt: Athenäum, 1971), p. 273.

29   Cynthia B. Kerr, 'Violence et obstacle dans *La Place Royale*', *French Review*, 49 (1975–6), 496–504.

30   Christine Moisan-Morteyrol, 'Les Premières Comédies de Corneille: prélude à *La Place Royale*', *Europe*, 540–1 (April–May 1974), 91–9 (p. 97).

31   Serge Doubrovsky, *Corneille et la dialectique du héros*, Bibliothèque des Idées (Paris: Gallimard, 1963), p. 81.

32   Georges Couton, *Réalisme de Corneille* (Paris: Les Belles Lettres, 1953), p. 35.

33   André Stegmann, *L'Héroïsme cornélien: Genèse et Signification*, 2 vols. (Paris: A. Colin, 1968), I, 56.

34   Robert J. Nelson, *Corneille: His Heroes and their Worlds* (Philadelphia: University of Pennsylvania Press, 1963).

35   Philip Koch, 'The Hero in Corneille's Early Comedies', *PMLA*, 78 (1963), 196–200.

36   R. J. Fournier, 'Corneille's Early Comedies: A Study in Dramatic Development' (unpublished Ph.D. dissertation, University of Western Ontario, 1973).

37   Bernard Dort, *Pierre Corneille, dramaturge*, Les Grands Dramaturges, 16 (Paris: L'Arche, 1957), p. 31.

38   Colette Cosnier, *Introduction* in: T. Corneille, *L'Amour à la mode* (Paris: Nizet, 1973), p. 66.

39   Jean Rousset, *La Littérature de l'âge baroque en France: Circé et le Paon* (Paris: Corti, 1953), pp. 205–6.

40   Serge Gaubert, 'De la Comédie des signes aux signes de la comédie', *Europe*, 540–1 (April–May 1974), 76–86.

41 John Pedersen, 'Le Joueur de rôles: un personnage typique des comédies de Corneille', *Revue Romane*, 2 (1967), 136–48.

42 David Lee Rubin, 'On Theatricality in Pierre Corneille's Later Comedies', *Papers on French Seventeenth Century Literature*, 7 (1977), 81–101.

43 Jean Emelina, *Les Valets et les servantes dans le théâtre comique en France de 1610 à 1700* (Grenoble: Presses Universitaires de Grenoble, 1975), p. 29.

44 A. Gill, *Introduction* in: *Les Ramonneurs*, comédie anonyme en prose, STFM (Paris: Didier, 1957), p. 99.

Chapter I

1 Jean de Mairet, *La Silvanire, ou la Morte-vive*, tragi-comédie pastorale (Paris: F. Targa, 1631); ed. J. Scherer in: *Théâtre du XVIIe Siècle*, Bibliothèque de la Pléiade (Paris: Gallimard, 1975), pp. 475–593, *Préface* (p. 482).

2 Georges de Scudéry, *La Comédie des comédiens*, poème de nouvelle invention (Paris: A. Courbé, 1635); ed. J. Crow, Textes Littéraires, 19 (University of Exeter, 1975), p. 27.

3 Jean de Schelandre, *Tyr et Sidon*, tragi-comédie divisée en deux journées (Paris: R. Estienne, 1628); ed. J. W. Barker (Paris: Nizet, 1974).

4 De Rayssiguier, *L'Aminte du Tasse*, tragi-comédie pastoralle (Paris: A. Courbé, 1632).

5 Pierre du Ryer, *Clitophon*, tragi-comédie (unpub. MS. Bib. Nat. FR 25496).

6 du Ryer, *Argenis et Poliarque, ou Theocrine*, tragi-comédie (Paris: N. Bessin, 1630).

7 Scudéry, *Le Fils supposé*, comédie (Paris: A. Courbé, 1636).

8 Honorat de Bueil, marquis de Racan, *Les Bergeries*, pastorale, Cinquiesme Edition, reveuë & corrigée (Paris: T. du Bray, 1632); ed. J. Scherer, *op. cit.*, pp. 287–391.

9 Mairet, *Sylvie*, tragi-comédie pastorale (Paris: F. Targa, 1628); ed. J. Scherer, *op. cit.*, pp. 393–473.

10 Balthasar Baro, *Célinde*, poème héroïque (Paris: F. Pomeray, 1629).

11 Baro, *Clorise*, pastoralle (Paris: A. de Sommaville, 1634).

12 Rayssiguier, *La Célidée sous le nom de Calirie, ou de la Générosité d'amour*, tragi-comédie (Paris: T. Quinet, 1635).

13 Rayssiguier, *Tragi-comédie pastorale, où les Amours d'Astrée et de Celadon sont meslées à celles de Diane, de Silvandre et de Paris, avec les inconstances d'Hilas* (Paris: N. Bessin, 1630).

14 Jean Desmarets de Saint-Sorlin, *Aspasie*, comédie (Paris: J. Camusat, 1636).

15 cf. also: Mairet, *Silvanire*, II 1; Scudéry, *Le Fils supposé*, I 2.

16 Charles de Vion, Seigneur d'Alibray, *L'Aminte du Tasse*, pastorale (Paris: P. Rocolet, 1632).

17 C. S. de La Croix, *L'Inconstance punie*, tragi-comédie (Paris: J. Corrozet, 1630).

18 cf. also: Jean Chapelain, '*Discours de la poésie représentative*' in: *Opuscules critiques*, ed. A. C. Hunter, STFM (Paris: Droz, 1936), p. 128.

19 François Hédelin, abbé d'Aubignac, *La Pratique du théâtre* (Paris: A. de Sommaville, 1657).

20 The Five were: Boisrobert, Colletet, Corneille, l'Estoile and Rotrou. The group, brought together by Richelieu, produced three plays of which two were subsequently published: *La Comédie des Tuilleries*, comédie (Paris: A. Courbé, 1638); *L'Aveugle de Smyrne*, tragi-comédie (Paris: A. Courbé, 1638); the third work, *La Grande Pastorale*, is lost. Each dramatist contributed one Act to each play, and it is generally agreed that Corneille wrote Act III of the *comédie* and Act I of the *tragi-comédie*. (See: Marty-Laveaux, II, 305–9; Lancaster, II 1, 97–103, 204–8; Adam, I, 504–7.)

21 Quoted in: *Marty-Laveaux*, II, 307.

22 du Ryer, *Lisandre et Caliste*, tragi-comédie (Paris: P. David, 1632).

23 cf. also: François le Métel, Seigneur de Boisrobert, *Pyrandre et Lisimène, ou l'Heureuse Tromperie*, tragi-comédie (Paris: T. Quinet, 1633), II 4.

24 Scudéry, *Le Trompeur puny, ou l'Histoire septentrionale*, tragi-comédie (Paris: A. de Sommaville, 1634).

25 Jean de Rotrou, *Les Captifs, ou les Esclaves*, comédie (Paris: A. de Sommaville, 1640).

26 cf. also: Scudéry, *Le Trompeur puny*, V 6; Boisrobert, *Pyrandre et Lisimène*, V 4; Rotrou, *La Belle Alphrède*, comédie (Paris: A. de Sommaville et T. Quinet, 1639), II 2.

27 '*Discours à Cliton sur les Observations du Cid*' in: *La Querelle du Cid*, ed. A. Gasté (Paris: Weller, 1898), pp. 241–82 (p. 265).

28 Rotrou, *L'Heureuse Constance*, tragi-comédie (Paris: T. Quinet, 1636).

29 De Monléon, *L'Amphytrite* (Paris: Vve. M. Guillemot, 1630).

30 Scudéry, *L'Apologie du théâtre* (Paris: A. Courbé, 1639).

31 Guillaume de Coste, *Lizimène*, comédie pastoralle (Paris: T. de la Ruelle, 1632), *Prologue*, p. 4.

32 Charles de Beys, *Le Jaloux sans sujet*, tragi-comédie (Paris: T. Quinet, 1636).

33 Rayssiguier, *Les Thuilleries*, tragi-comédie (Paris: A. de Sommaville, 1636).

34 Rotrou, *Diane*, comédie (Paris: F. Targa, 1635).

35 cf. also: Racan, *Les Bergeries*, IV 3; Scudéry, *Ligdamon et Lidias, ou la Ressemblance*, tragi-comédie (Paris: F. Targa, 1631), I 1; Jean-Oger de Gombauld, *Amaranthe*, pastorale (Paris: F. Pomeray, A. de Sommaville et A. Soubron, 1631), II 3.

36 Rotrou, *Florimonde*, comédie (Paris: A. de Sommaville, 1655).

37 cf. also: Gombauld, *Amaranthe*, II 3; Mairet, *Silvanire*, V 1.

38 Mairet, *Chryséide et Arimand*, tragi-comédie (Paris; jouxte la copie imprimée à Rouen chez J. Besongne, 1630); ed. H. C. Lancaster,

Johns Hopkins Studies in Romance Literatures and Languages, 5
(Baltimore: Johns Hopkins Press, 1925).

39   cf. also: Pichou, *Les Folies de Cardenio*, tragi-comédie (Paris: F.
     Targa, 1630).
40   Rotrou, *Filandre*, comédie (Paris: A. de Sommaville, 1637).
41   Rotrou, *Céliane*, tragi-comédie (Paris: T. Quinet, 1637).
42   cf. also: Scudéry, *Le Fils supposé*, IV 1; Rotrou, *Clorinde*, comédie
     (Paris: A. de Sommaville, 1637), I 2.
43   Rotrou, *Célimène*, comédie (Paris: A. de Sommaville, 1636).
44   cf. also: Beys, *Le Jaloux sans sujet*, III 3.
45   L.-C. Discret, *Alizon*, comédie desdiée aux jeunes veufves et aux
     jeunes filles (Paris: J. Guignard, 1637); ed. J.-D. Biard, Textes
     Littéraires, 7 (University of Exeter, 1972), *Advertissement*.
46   Rotrou, *La Bague de l'oubly*, comédie (Paris: F. Targa, 1635).
47   Mairet, *Les Galanteries du duc d'Ossonne*, comédie (Paris: P. Ro-
     colet, 1636); ed. J. Scherer, *op. cit.*, pp. 595–668.
48   Rotrou, *Les Ménèchmes*, comédie (Paris: A. de Sommaville, 1636).
49   Rotrou, *Les Sosies*, comédie (Paris: A. de Sommaville, 1638).
50   Rotrou, *Clarice, ou l'Amour constant*, comédie (Paris: T. Quinet,
     1643).
51   Antoine Mareschal, *Le Railleur, ou la Satyre du temps*, comédie
     (Paris: T. Quinet, 1638). For a more detailed study of this play,
     see my article: 'Mareschal's *Le Railleur*: Topicality and the Search
     for the Comic'. *Newsletter of the Society for Seventeenth-Century
     French Studies*, 4 (1982), 40–7.
52   Mareschal, *Le Véritable Capitan Matamore, ou le Fanfaron*, comédie
     (Paris: T. Quinet, 1640).
53   Discret, *Les Nopces de Vaugirard, ou les Naifvetéz champestres*, pastor-
     alle dédiée à ceux qui veulent rire (Paris: J. Guignard, 1638).
54   Le Vert, *Le Docteur amoureux*, comédie (Paris: A. Courbé, 1638).
55   Anon., *La Comédie de chansons* (Paris: T. Quinet, 1640).
56   Adrien de Montluc, prince de Chabannais, *La Comédie de proverbes*,
     pièce comique (Paris: F. Targa, 1634).
57   N. du Peschier, *La Comédie des comédies*, tragi-comédie (Paris: N.
     La Coste, 1629).
58   Mareschal, *L'Inconstance d'Hylas*, tragi-comédie pastorale (Paris: F.
     Targa, 1635).
59   du Ryer, *Amarillis*, pastorale (Paris: T. Quinet, 1650).
60   Jean de Claveret, *L'Esprit fort*, comédie (Paris: F. Targa, 1637).
61   cf. also: Rotrou, *Clorinde*, I 3; Rayssiguier, *Palinice, Circeine et
     Florice*, tragi-comédie (Paris: A. de Sommaville, 1634), II 2; du
     Ryer, *Les Vendanges de Suresne*, comédie (Paris: A. de Sommaville,
     1636), I 4.
62   Urbain Chevreau, *L'Advocat duppé*, comédie (Paris: T. Quinet,
     1637).
63   Desmarets de Saint-Sorlin, *Les Visionnaires*, comédie (Paris: J.
     Camusat, 1637); ed. H. G. Hall, STFM (Paris: Didier, 1963).
64   Mairet, *Silvanire*, *Préface* (Scherer, p. 483).

65   d'Aubignac, however, disputed that the happy ending was proper
     to comedy alone. See: *La Pratique du théâtre*, II 10, p. 189.
66   cf. Racan, *Les Bergeries*, Gombauld, *Amaranthe*.
67   cf. Mairet, *Sylvie*, La Croix, *L'Inconstance punie*.
68   cf. Baro, *Célinde*, Scudéry, *Ligdamon et Lidias*.
69   Antoine Gaillard, *La Carline*, comédie pastorale (Paris: J. Corrozet,
     1626).
70   Alexandre Hardy, *Corine, ou le Silence* in: *Théâtre*, ed. E. Stengel, 5
     vols. (Marburg: Elwert, 1883–4), III, 227–64.
71   Honoré d'Urfé, *L'Astrée*, ed. H. Vaganay, 5 vols. (Lyon: Masson,
     1925–28).
72   du Ryer, *Cléomédon*, tragi-comédie (Paris: A. de Sommaville, 1637).
73   Mairet, *Les Galanteries du duc d'Ossonne*, Epître (Scherer, pp. 597–8).
74   Chevreau, *L'Advocat duppé*, Au Lecteur.
75   R.-M. du Rocher, *La Mélize*, pastorale comique (Paris: J. Corrozet,
     1634).
76   Gaultier Garguille, *Chansons*, précédées d'une approbation
     facétieuse de 1641 (s.l.n.d.); ed. E. Fournier (Paris: Jannet, 1858).
77   Rotrou, *Cléagenor et Doristée*, tragi-comédie (Paris: A. de Sommavil-
     le, 1634).
78   Pichou, *La Filis de Scire*, comédie pastorale (Paris: F. Targa, 1631).
79   Mareschal, *La Généreuse Allemande, ou le Triomphe d'amour*, tragi-
     comédie mise en deux journées (Paris: P. Rocolet, 1631).
80   Beys, *Céline, ou les Frères rivaux*, tragi-comédie (Paris: T. Quinet,
     1637).

Chapter II

1   *Mélite, Examen*, ed. cit., p. 136.
2   *Mélite ou les Fausses Lettres*, pièce comique (Paris: F. Targa, 1633); ed.
    M. Roques and M. Lièvre, TLF (Genève: Droz, 1950).
3   cf. Racan, *Les Bergeries*; Gaillard, *La Carline*; Mairet, *Sylvie*; La Croix,
    Climène; Auvray, *Madonte*.
4   cf. Gombauld, *Amaranthe*.
5   cf. Racan, *Les Bergeries*; La Croix, *Climène*; Pichou, *Les Folies de
    Cardenio*; Rotrou, *L'Hypocondriaque, ou le Mort amoureux*, tragi-
    comédie (Paris: T. du Bray, 1631).
6   cf. d'Urfé, *La Sylvanire, ou la Morte-vive*, fable bocagère (Paris: R.
    Fouet, 1627); La Croix, *L'Inconstance punie*; du Ryer, *Clitophon*; Baro,
    Célinde.
7   Jean Starobinski, 'Sur Corneille', *Temps Modernes*, 10 (1954–5), 713–
    29.
8   H. Francq, 'Corneille: premières amours et première comédie',
    Revue de l'Université d'Ottawa, 38 (1968), 177–209 (p. 189).
9   Couton, *Corneille*, Connaissance des Lettres, 52 (Paris: Hatier, 1969),
    p. 17.
10 Jacques Maurens, *La Tragédie sans tragique: le neo-stoïcisme dans
    l'oeuvre de Pierre Corneille* (Paris: A. Colin, 1966), pp. 185–7.

11 M. S. Poole, 'A Re-reading of Corneille's *Mélite*, *The Classical Tradition in French Literature: Essays presented to R. C. Knight* ed. H. T. Barnwell *et al*. (London: Grant & Cutler, 1977), pp. 49–60.
12 cf. Racan, *Les Bergeries*, II 4; Mairet, *Sylvie*, III 3.
13 Jean Auvray, *Madonte*, tragi-comédie (Paris: A. Courbé, 1631).
14 *Dorinde*, tragi-comédie (Paris: A. de Sommaville & A. Soubron, 1631).
15 cf. Raoul Morçay (and Pierre Sage), *Le Préclassicisme* (Paris: del Duca, 1962), p. 299; Imbrie Buffum, *Studies in the Baroque from Montaigne to Rotrou* (New Haven: Yale University Press, 1957), p. 205.
16 cf. Rivaille, p. 195; van Roosbroeck, 'A Commonplace . . .', p. 143; Francq, p. 197; Armand Helmreich-Marsilien, 'Un Inspirateur paradoxal du tragique racinien: Corneille comique', *Australian Journal of French Studies*, 2 (1965), 291–312 (p. 305).
17 *Climène*, tragi-comédie pastorale (Paris: J. Corrozet, 1629).
18 cf. also the madness of Adraste in *L'Astrée*, III 9, p. 379.
19 *La Folie de Silène*, pastorale in: *Le Théâtre français* (Paris: P. Mansan & C. Colet, 1624), pp. 255–338.
20 *Mélite*, II 6, 611.
21 *L'Infidèle Confidente*, tragi-comédie (Paris: F. Targa, 1631).
22 For a fuller discussion of Corneille's later attitude to his comedies, see my article: 'The Variants of Corneille's Early Plays', *Modern Language Review*, 77 (1982), 547–57.
23 cf. Baro, *Célinde*, II 1; Mairet, *Silvanire*, I 1; La Croix, *Climène*, I 1; *L'Inconstance punie*, I 1; Mareschal, *La Généreuse Allemande*, I 2.
24 Jean Auvray, *Le Banquet des Muses* (Rouen: D. Ferrand, 1628), p. 50. cf. also *Dorinde*, II 1.
25 Hardy, *Gésippe, ou les Deux Amis*, tragi-comédie, in: *Théâtre*, ed. cit., IV, 165–207.
26 cf. also *L'Astrée*, I 6, 208 f.
27 *Mélite*, *Examen*, ed. cit., p. 138.
28 Mairet, *Silvanire*, V 15, vv. 2632–4.
29 cf. Bürger, p. 123.
30 *Mélite*, *Examen*, ed. cit., p.137.
31 cf. Hardy, *Corine*, V 4; Rotrou, *La Bague de l'oubly*, V 8.
32 Bürger, p. 123; Doubrovsky, pp. 43–4; Francq, p. 201; Moisan-Morteyrol, p. 93.
33 Lawrence E. Harvey, 'The Dénouement of *Mélite* and the Role of the Nourrice', *Modern Language Notes*, 71 (1956), 200–3.
34 *Mélite*, 'Au Lecteur', ed. cit., p. 4.

Chapter III

1 *La Vefve, ou le Traistre trahy*, comédie (Paris: F. Targa, 1634); ed. M. Roques and M. Lièvre, TLF (Genève: Droz, 1954), '*Au Lecteur*', p. 5.
2 cf. Brasillach, p. 119; Couton, p. 43; Doubrovsky, pp. 45–6.
3 cf. Couton, p. 43; Doubrovsky, p. 47; Maurens, *La Tragédie* . . ., p. 190; Roques, ed. cit., p. 27.

4   La Croix, *L'Inconstance punie*, tragi-comédie (Paris: J. Corrozet, 1630).

5   cf. also: Mairet, *Silvanire*, II 1; Baro, *Clorise*, IV 3; Rayssiguier, *Tragi-comédie pastorale*, IV 1; Racan, *Les Bergeries*, V 2; Pichou, *Les Folies de Cardenio*, II 4; Scudéry, *Le Trompeur puny*, IV 2.

6   *La Veuve*, *'Au Lecteur'*, ed. cit., p. 5.

7   *La Veuve*, IV 7, v. 1507.

8   *La Veuve*, *'Au Lecteur'*, ed. cit., p. 5.

9   *Le Mercier inventif*, pastorale (Troyes: N. Oudot, 1632).

Chapter IV

1   *La Galerie du Palais, ou L'Amie Rivalle*, comédie (Paris: A. Courbé, 1637) ed. M. R. Margitić, TLF (Genève: Droz, 1981) (I 9, 276–8).

2   *Examen*, ed. cit., pp. 151–2.

3   cf. Brasillach, pp. 121–2; Gaiffe, p. 94; Lancaster, I 2, 605.

4   *La Bourgeoise, ou la Promenade de S. Cloud*, tragi-comédie (Paris: P. Billaine, 1633).

5   *La Pèlerine amoureuse*, tragi-comédie (Paris: A. de Sommaville, 1637).

6   *La Galerie du Palais*, *Examen*, ed. cit., p. 151.

7   *La Galerie du Palais*, II 5, 547–52.

8   Rotrou, *Amélie*, tragi-comédie (Paris: A. de Sommaville, 1638).

9   Antoine Furetière, *Dictionnaire universel . . .*, 3 vols. (La Haye: Arnout et Reinier Leer, 1690).

10 cf. also Racan, *Les Bergeries*, II 3; du Ryer, *Alcimédon*, tragi-comédie (Paris: A. de Sommaville, 1635), V 4.

11 *La Galerie du Palais*, II, 4 (497–500)

12 *L'Astrée*, I 4, p. 132.

13 *La Climène*, tragi-comédie pastorale (Paris: J. Corrozet, 1629).

14 cf. Bürger, p. 145; Scherer, p. 140.

15 *La Galerie du Palais*, *Epître*, ed. cit., p. 3.

Chapter V

1   *La Suivante*, *Epistre*, ed. cit., p. 5.

2   *La Suivante*, comédie (Paris: F. Targa, 1637); ed. M. R. Margitić, TLF (Genève: Droz, 1978).

3   cf. Adam, I, 495; Brasillach, p. 123; Dorchain, p. 111.

4   cf. Schlumberger, p. 37.

5   cf. Bürger, p. 208; Nelson, p. 61; Judd D. Hubert, 'Le Jeu de l'amour et de l'honnêteté', *Esprit Créateur*, 15 (1975), 49–58.

6   cf. Couton, p. 41; Emelina, p. 124; Lemonnier, p. 50; Nadal, p. 84; Scherer, p. 64.

7   cf. Doubrovsky, p. 57.

8   cf. also d'Urfé, *L'Astrée*, III 2, p. 53; Scudéry, *Ligdamon et Lidias*, I 1; Rotrou, *Céliane*, II 3.

9   *La Suivante*, IV 4, 1093–4.

10   cf. also Hardy, *Le Triomphe d'Amour*, I 4; Baro, *Clorise*, IV 2; Mairet, *Sylvie*, II 3; *Silvanire*, III 3; du Ryer, *Amarillis*, IV 1; *Les Vendanges de Suresne*, II 6.
11   *La Suivante*, III 6, 835–6.
12   cf. Bürger, p. 208; Doubrovsky, p. 56; Lancaster, I 2, 606; Nadal, p. 84; Nelson, p. 55; Schlumberger, p. 37.
13   Gougenot, *La Comédie des comédiens*, tragi-comédie (Paris: P. David, 1633); ed. D. C. Shaw, Textes Littéraires, 15 (University of Exeter, 1974).
14   *La Suivante*, IV 4, 1101.
15   cf. Brereton, p. 35; Dorchain, p. 114; Schlumberger, p. 38.
16   cf. Bürger, p. 147; Couton, p. 41; Hubert, p. 51; Moisan-Morteyrol, p. 94; Nadal, p. 106; Scherer, p. 64.
17   cf. Lawrence E. Harvey, 'Intellectualism in Corneille: The Symbolism of Proper Names in *La Suivante*', *Symposium*, 13 (1959), 290–3 (p. 292). Margitić, *ed. cit.*, p. 38; Maurens, *Préface*, p. 22; Marie-Odile Sweetser, *La Dramaturgie de Corneille* (Genève: Droz, 1977), p. 96.
18   *La Suivante*, Epistre, *ed. cit.*, p. 3.

Chapter VI

1   *La Place Royalle, ou L'Amoureux extravagant*, comédie (Paris: A. Courbé, 1637); ed. J.-C. Brunon, STFM (Paris: Didier, 1962), I 1, 84.
2   cf. also Clorimene in Rayssiguier's *Les Thuilleries*; Lisante in Rotrou's *Clorinde* and Clytie in Mareschal's *Le Railleur*.
3   *La Place Royale*, I 4, 257.
4   cf. Kerr, p. 498; Rousset, p. 208.
5   cf. Adam, I, 497; Guillaume Huszar, *Pierre Corneille et le théâtre espagnol* (Paris: Bouillon, 1903), p. 239; Lancaster, I 2, 611; Koch, p. 199; M. Larroutis, 'Corneille et Montaigne: l'égotisme dans *La Place Royale*', *RHLF*, 62 (1962), 321–8 (p. 327); Philippe Sénart, '*La Place Royale* au Théâtre de l'Est parisien', *Nouvelle Revue des Deux Mondes* (Dec. 1973), 691–3 (p. 692); Raymonde Temkine, 'A Propos d'une représentation de *La Place Royale*', *Europe*, 540–1 (April–May 1974), 99–102 (p. 99).
6   cf. Dort, p. 37; Doubrovsky, p. 67.
7   Jacques Morel, 'Le jeune Corneille et le théâtre de son temps', *Information Littéraire*, 12 (1960), 185–92 (p. 191).
8   Maurens, *La Tragédie*, p. 194; cf. also Sweetser, pp. 99 ff.
9   *La Place Royale*, III 4, 757–60.
10   *Le Capitan, ou le Miles Gloriosus*, comédie de Plaute (Paris: T. Quinet, 1640).
11   *Les Deux Pucelles*, tragi-comédie (Paris: A. de Sommaville, 1637).
12   cf. also du Ryer, *Arétaphile*, III 2; Boisrobert, *Pyrandre et Lisimène*, II 5.
13   cf. also du Ryer, *Argenis et Poliarque*, IV 1.
14   *La Place Royale*, Examen, *ed. cit.*, p. 114.

15 cf. Doubrovsky, p. 74; T. J. Reiss, 'The Dialectic of Language in the Theatre: Corneille from *Mélite* to *Le Cid'*, *Yale French Studies*, 45 (1970), 87–101 (pp. 93–4); Sweetser, p. 98.

16 *L'Astrée*, V 1, 46.

17 cf. also Alphée in Hardy's *Alphée*, III 1; Angelique in Rotrou's *La Pèlerine amoureuse*, V 4; Amarillis in du Ryer's *Amarillis*, IV 1.

18 cf. also Phillidor in du Ryer, *Amarillis*, I 1; Rodolphe in Rotrou's *La Belle Alphrède*, V 1; Cleante in Rotrou's *Florimonde*, IV 1.

19 cf. Cleonte in Scudéry's *Le Trompeur puny*, III 4; the heroine in Rayssiguier's *La Bourgeoise*, V 6.

20 cf. Rosaran in Rotrou's *Agésilan de Colchos*, II 2; Don Quixote at the end of Pichou, *Les Folies de Cardenio*, V 5.

21 *La Place Royale*, *Examen*, *ed. cit.*, p. 113.

Chapter VII

1 *L'Illusion Comique*, comédie (Paris: F. Targa, 1639), *Dédicace*; ed. R. Garapon STFM (Paris: Didier, 1970), p. 3.

2 cf. Garapon, *ed. cit.*, pp. xxi ff.

3 cf. Lancaster, II 1, 107; Raymond Lebègue, 'Cet étrange monstre que Corneille a donné au théâtre' in: *Mélanges de littérature comparée et de philologie offerts à Mieczyslaw Brahmer* (Warszawa: P.W.N., 1967), pp. 281–94 (p. 288); Maurens, *La Tragédie*, p. 227.

4 cf. Fournier, p. 335; Maurens, *Préface*, p. 25.

5 cf. Dort, p. 43.

6 cf. Colette Cosnier, 'Un Étrange Monstre–*L'Illusion Comique'*, *Europe*, 540–1 (April–May 1974), 103–13 (p. 113).

7 cf. François Xavier Cuche, 'Les Trois Illusions de *L'Illusion Comique'*, *Travaux de Linguistique et de Littérature*, IX, 2 (1971), 65–84; T. J. Reiss, *Toward Dramatic Illusion: Theatrical Technique and Meaning from Hardy to 'Horace'* (New Haven: Yale University Press, 1971), p. 133; Rousset, p. 205; David Lee Rubin, 'The Hierarchy of Illusions and the Structure of *L'Illusion Comique'*, *La Cohérence Intérieure: Etudes sur la Littérature française du XVIIe siècle présentées en hommage à Judd D. Hubert* (Paris: J.- M. Place, 1977), pp. 75–93.

8 cf. Clifton Cherpack, 'The Captive Audience in *L'Illusion Comique'*, *Modern Language Notes*, 81 (1966), 342–4; Robert J. Nelson, 'Pierre Corneille's *L'Illusion Comique*: the Play as Magic', *PMLA*, 71 (1956), 1127–40; A. Donald Sellstrom, '*L'Illusion Comique* of Corneille: The Tragic Scenes of Act V', *Modern Language Notes*, 73 (1958), 421–7; *idem*, 'Addenda to the Sources of Corneille's *L'Illusion Comique'*, *Modern Language Notes*, 76 (1961), 533–6; Carlo François, 'Illusion et Mensonge', *Esprit Créateur*, 4 (1964), 169–74.

9 *L'Illusion comique*, *Examen*, *ed. cit.*, p. 123.

10 Garapon, *La Fantaisie verbale*, p. 156.

11 A close stylistic analysis of Matamore's language is made in Garapon, *La Fantaisie verbale*, pp. 159–73.

12   cf. Dort, p. 43; Ernest Martinenche, *La Comedia espagnole en France de Hardy à Racine* (Paris: Hachette, 1900), p. 199; Nadal, p. 119.
13   *L'Illusion comique, Examen, ed. cit.*, p. 123.
14   cf. also Democle in Hardy, *Alcée, ou L'Infidelité*, pastorale, in: *Théâtre, ed. cit.*, II, 230–87, Act IV Scene 2.
15   Scudéry, *Le Prince déguisé*, tragi-comédie (Paris: A. Courbé, 1636).
16   cf. Cosnier, pp. 104–5; Lebègue, pp. 282–3; Nadal, p. 84; Gordon B. Walters, jnr., 'Society and the Theatre in Corneille's *L'Illusion Comique*', *Romance Notes*, 10 (1968–9), 324–31 (p. 326).
17   cf. similar heroic speeches in Auvray's *Dorinde*, IV 2; Baro's *Celinde*, IV 3; du Ryer's *Clitophon*, II 6; Mairet's *Chryséide et Arimand*, I 2; Schelandre's *Tyr et Sidon*, Pt. II, III 3; Scudéry's *Ligdamon et Lidias*, III 4 and *Le Fils supposé*, II 5; and Rotrou's *La Belle Alphrède*, III 1.
18   *L'Illusion Comique*, IV 10, 1339–44.
19   *L'Innocente Infidelité*, tragi-comédie (Paris: A. de Sommaville, 1637).
20   cf. also Rodolphe in *La Belle Alphrède*, I 4; Filandre in *Célimène*, I 3.
21   cf. also Rotrou, *Diane*, I 1.
22   cf. Bürger, p. 234.
23   *L'Illusion Comique*, V 6, 1751–2.
24   cf. also Veronneau, *L'Impuissance*, IV 1.
25   *L'Illusion Comique, Epître dédicatoire, ed. cit.*, p. 3.
26   For a fuller discussion of this parallel in another play of the period, see my article: '*L'Hospital des Fous* of Charles Beys: the Madman and the Actor', *French Studies*, 36 (1982), 12–25.

Chapter VIII

1   *Le Menteur*, comédie (Paris: A. de Sommaville & A. Courbé, 1644), *Epître*; ed. Ch. Marty-Laveaux, *ed. cit.*, IV, 117–239 (p. 130).
2   Antoine le Métel, sieur d'Ouville, *Les Fausses Véritez*, comédie (Paris: T. Quinet, 1643).
3   *idem, L'Absent chez soy*, comédie (Paris: T. Quinet, 1643).
4   De Brosse, *Les Innocens coupables*, comédie (Paris: A. de Sommaville, A. Courbé, T. Quinet & N. de Sercy, 1645).
5   *idem, Les Songes des hommes esveillez*, comédie (Paris: Vve N. de Sercy, 1646).
6   *La Dame suivante*, comédie (Paris: T. Quinet, 1645).
7   *L'Esprit folet*, comédie (Paris: T. Quinet, 1642).
8   Guyon Guérin de Bouscal, *Le Gouvernement de Sanche Pansa*, comédie (Paris: A. de Sommaville & A. Courbé, 1642).
9   Paul Scarron, *Jodelet, ou le Maître valet*, comédie (Paris: T. Quinet, 1645).
10   cf. Adam, II, 386; Voltz, p. 61; Couton, p. 108.
11   Nelson, p. 138.
12   *Le Menteur*, I 6, 313–15.
13   Juan Ruiz de Alarcón y Mendoza, *La Verdad sospechosa*, ed. E. Barry, fourth edition (Paris: Garnier, n.d.). Translations are taken from *Théâtre*, trans. Alphonse Royer (Paris: M. Levy, 1865).

14   Ernest Martinenche, *La Comedia espagnole en France de Hardy à Racine* (Paris: Hachette, 1900), p. 249.
15   Viguier, 'Parallèle de *La Verdad sospechosa* d'Alarcón et du *Menteur* de Corneille', Marty-Laveaux, IV, 241–73.
16   Susan Staves, 'Liars and Lying in Alarcón, Corneille and Steele', *Revue de Littérature Comparée*, 46 (1972), 514–27.
17   *'Ce n'est pas un valet que je te donne, mais un conseiller et un ami'* (p. 26).
18   *La Verdad sospechosa*, III 7, 2714–73.
19   Boisrobert, *La Jalouse d'elle-mesme*, comédie (Paris: A. Courbé, 1650).
20   *'Ses vérités mêmes seront à l'avenir des fables pour moi'* (p. 68).
21   cf. Couton, *Corneille*, p. 109; Lemonnier, p. 142; Martinenche, pp. 247–48; Paquot-Pierret, p. 74.
22   *Le Menteur*, I 6, 356–8.
23   Dorchain, p. 260.
24   Lanson, p. 55.
25   Maurens, *Préface*, p. 26.
26   Staves, p. 519.
27   Nelson, p. 133.
28   *'La grande affaire c'est d'être remarqué, peu importe le moyen'* (p. 44).
29   *'j'ai entièrement dépaysé les sujets pour les habiller à la française (ed. cit.*, p. 132).
30   cf. Rayssiguier, *Palinice, Circeine et Florice*, I 1, p. 2; d'Ouville, *L'Esprit folet*, I 1, p. 1; Boisrobert, *La Jalouse d'elle-mesme*, I 1, pp. 2–3.
31   *Le Menteur*, Examen, *ed. cit.*, p. 138.
32   cf. *The Complete Works of Voltaire*, vols. 53–5, 'Commentaires sur Corneille', ed. D. Williams (Banbury: The Voltaire Foundation, 1974–5), CIV, 376; Guichemerre, pp. 214–15; Lemonnier, p. 143; Martinenche, p. 249; Paquot-Pierret, p. 78.
33   Savinien de Cyrano de Bergerac, *Le Pédant joué*, comédie (Paris, 1661).
34   Thomas Corneille, *L'Amour à la mode*, comédie (Paris: de Luyne, 1653); ed. C. Cosnier (Paris: Nizet, 1973).
35   *'Vous comprenez maintenant combien le mensonge est nuisible, et l'assemblée comprendra que dans la bouche du menteur la vérité est suspecte'* (p. 99).
36   *Le Menteur*, 'Au Lecteur', *ed. cit.*, pp. 132–3.
37   *Don Quixote de la Manche*, comédie (Paris: T. Quinet, 1639).
38   Gillet de la Tessonerie, *La Comédie de Francion*, comédie (Paris: T. Quinet, 1642).

Chapter IX

1   *La Suite du Menteur*, comédie (Paris: A. de Sommaville & A. Courbé, 1645), Epître; ed. Ch. Marty-Laveaux, *ed. cit.*, IV, 275–389 (p. 279).
2   Lope de Vega Carpio, *Obras*, ninth edition, 13 vols. (Madrid: Galo Saez, 1916–30), XI (1929), *Amar sin saber a quién*, pp. 283–319. Translations are taken from the following edition: *Théâtre*, trans. Damas Hinard, 2 vols. (Paris: G. Charpentier, 1881).

3 '*Helas!, Monseigneur, je croyais parler à vous*' (I, 320).
4 cf. Corneille, '*Discours de l'utilité et des parties du poème dramatique*',
   Marty-Laveaux, I, 19; Voltaire, CIV, 385.

Conclusion

1 *L'Illusion Comique, Dédicace, ed. cit.*, p. 3.

Bibliography

Alphabetical order is followed when more than one work by an author is listed. The date of the first edition is given in brackets where this is not the text cited.

I Primary sources

1 Works of Corneille: texts and editions consulted

Oeuvres de P. Corneille, ed. Ch. Marty-Laveaux, Les Grands Ecrivains de la France, 12 vols. (Paris: Hachette, 1862–8).

Théâtre complet, Volume 1, *Les Comédies*, ed. J. Maurens (Paris: Garnier Flammarion, 1968).

Mélite, ou Les Fausses Lettres, pièce comique (Paris: F. Targa, 1633); ed. M. Roques and M. Lièvre, TLF (Genève: Droz, 1950).

La Vefve, ou Le Traistre trahy, comédie (Paris: F. Targa, 1634); ed. M. Roques and M. Lièvre, TLF (Genève: Droz, 1954).

La Galerie du Palais, ou L'Amie Rivalle, comédie (Paris: A. Courbé, 1637); ed. M. R. Margitić, TLF (Genève: Droz, 1981).

La Suivante, comédie (Paris: F. Targa, 1637); ed. M. R. Margitić, TLF (Genève: Droz, 1978).

La Place Royalle, ou L'Amoureux extravagant, comédie (Paris: A. Courbé, 1637); ed. J.-C. Brunon, STFM (Paris: Didier, 1962).

L'Illusion Comique, comédie (Paris: F. Targa, 1639); ed. R. Garapon, STFM, troisième tirage revu et corrigé (Paris: Didier, 1970).

Le Menteur, comédie (Paris: A. de Sommaville & A. Courbé, 1644).

La Suite du Menteur, comédie (Paris: A. de Sommaville & A. Courbé, 1645).

2 Works of Corneille's contemporaries

Théâtre du XVIIe siècle, ed. J. Scherer, Bibliothèque de la Pléiade (Paris: Gallimard, 1975).

Anon. *Le Capitan, ou le Miles Gloriosus*, comédie de Plaute (Paris: A. Courbé, 1639).

Anon. *La Comédie de chansons* (Paris: T. Quinet, 1640).

Anon. *La Folie de Silène*, pastorale in: *Le Théâtre françois* (Paris: P. Mansan & C. Colet, 1624), pp. 255–338.

Anon.   *Le Mercier inventif*, pastorale (Troyes: N. Oudot, 1632).

Anon.   *Les Ramonneurs*, ed. A. Gill, STFM (Paris: Didier, 1957).

Aubignac, François Hédelin, abbé d'   *La Pratique du théâtre* (Paris: A. de Sommaville, 1657).

Auvray, Jean   *Le Banquet des Muses*, suivi de *L'Innocence descouverte*, tragi-comédie (Rouen: D. Ferrand, 1628) (1623).

— *Dorinde*, tragi-comédie (Paris: A. de Sommaville & A. Soubron, 1631).

— *Madonte*, tragi-comédie (Paris: A. Courbé, 1631).

Baro, Balthasar   *Célinde*, poème héroïque (Paris: F. Pomeray, 1629).

— *Clorise*, pastoralle (Paris: A. de Sommaville, 1634) (1631).

Benserade, Isaac de   *Iphis et Iante*, comédie (Paris: A. de Sommaville, 1637) (1636).

Beys, Charles de   *Céline, ou les Freres rivaux*, tragi-comédie (Paris: T. Quinet, 1637).

— *Le Jaloux sans sujet*, tragi-comédie (Paris: T. Quinet, 1636) (1635).

— *L'Ospital des Fous*, tragi-comédie (Paris: T. Quinet, 1639) (1635).

Boisrobert, François Le Métel de   *La Jalouse d'elle-mesme*, comédie (Paris: A. Courbé, 1650).

— *Pyrandre et Lisimène, ou l'Heureuse Tromperie*, tragi-comédie (Paris: T. Quinet, 1633).

Brosse, de   *Les Innocens coupables*, comédie (Paris: A. de Sommaville, A. Courbé, T. Quinet, & N. de Sercy, 1645).

— *Les Songes des hommes esveillez*, comédie (Paris: Vve. N. de Sercy, 1646).

Brosse, Le jeune   *Le Curieux impertinent, ou Le Jaloux*, comédie (Paris: N. de Sercy, 1645).

Chapelain, Jean   *Opuscules Critiques*, ed. A. C. Hunter, STFM (Paris: Droz, 1936).

Chevreau, Urbain   *L'Advocat duppé*, comédie (Paris: T. Quinet, 1637).

Les Cinq Auteurs   *L'Aveugle de Smyrne*, tragi-comédie (Paris: A. Courbé, 1638)

— *La Comédie des Tuilleries*, comédie (Paris: A. Courbé, 1638).

Claveret, Jean de   *L'Esprit fort*, comédie (Paris: F. Targa, 1637).

Corneille, Thomas   *L'Amour à la mode*, comédie (Paris: de Luyne, 1653); ed. C. Cosnier (Paris: Nizet, 1973).

Coste, Guillaume de   *Lizimène*, comédie pastoralle (Paris: T. de la Ruelle, 1632).

Cyrano de Bergerac, Savinien de   *Le Pédant joué*, comédie (Paris, 1661).

D'Alibray, Charles de Vion, Seigneur   *L'Aminte du Tasse*, pastorale (Paris: P. Rocolet, 1632).

Desmarets de Saint-Sorlin, Jean   *Aspasie*, comédie (Paris: J. Camusat, 1636).

— *Les Visionnaires*, comédie (Paris: J. Camusat, 1637); ed. H. G. Hall, STFM (Paris: Didier, 1963).

Discret, L-C.   *Alizon*, comédie (Paris: J. Guignard, 1637); ed. J.-D. Biard, Textes Littéraires, 7 (University of Exeter, 1972).

— *Les Nopces de Vaugirard, ou Les Naifvetéz champestres*, pastoralle (Paris: J. Guignard, 1638).

Du Peschier, N. *La Comédie des comédies*, tragi-comédie (Paris: N. La Coste, 1629).

Du Rocher, R-M. *La Mélize*, pastorale comique (Paris: J. Corrozet, 1634).

Du Ryer, Pierre *Alcimédon*, tragi-comédie (Paris: A. de Sommaville, 1635) (1634).

— *Amarillis*, pastorale (Paris: T. Quinet, 1650).

— *Arétaphile*, tragi-comédie (unpublished MS., Bibliothèque Nationale, FR 25496).

— *Argenis et Poliarque, ou Théocrine*, tragi-comédie (Paris: N. Bessin, 1630).

— *Cléomédon*, tragi-comédie (Paris: A. de Sommaville, 1637) (1636).

— *Clitophon*, tragi-comédie (unpublished MS., Bibliothèque Nationale, FR 25496).

— *Lisandre et Caliste*, tragi-comédie (Paris: P. David, 1632).

— *Les Vendanges de Suresne*, comédie (Paris: A. de Sommaville, 1636) (1635).

Furetière, Antoine *Dictionnaire universel . . .*, 3 vols. (La Haye: Arnout & Reinier Leers, 1690).

Gaillard, Antoine *La Carline*, comédie pastorale (Paris: J. Corrozet, 1626).

Gasté, Armand (ed.) *La Querelle du Cid* (Paris: Welter, 1898).

Gaultier Garguille *Chansons*, précédées d'une approbation facétieuse de 1641 (s.l.n.d.); ed. E. Fournier (Paris: Jannet, 1858).

Gillet de la Tessonerie *La Comédie de Francion*, comédie (Paris: T. Quinet, 1642).

Gombauld, Jean-Oger de *Amaranthe*, pastorale (Paris: F. Pomeray, A. de Sommaville, et A. Soubron, 1631).

Gougenot *La Comédie des Comédiens*, tragi-comédie (Paris: P. David, 1633); ed. D. C. Shaw, Textes Littéraires, 15 (University of Exeter, 1974).

Guérin de Bouscal, Guyon *Dom Quixote de la Manche*, comédie (Paris: T. Quinet, 1639).

— *Le Gouvernement de Sanche Pansa*, comédie (Paris: A. de Sommaville & A. Courbé, 1642).

Hardy, Alexandre *Théâtre*, ed. E. Stengel, 5 vols (Marburg: Elwert, 1883–84).

La Croix, C.-S. de *La Climène*, tragi-comédie pastorale (Paris: J. Corrozet, 1629).

— *L'Inconstance punie*, tragi-comédie (Paris: J. Corrozet, 1630).

Le Vert *Le Docteur amoureux*, comédie (Paris: A. Courbé, 1638).

Mairet, Jean de *Chryséide et Arimand*, tragi-comédie (Paris, jouxte la copie imprimée à Rouen, chez J. Besongne, 1630).

— *Les Galanteries du duc d'Ossonne*, comédie (Paris: P. Rocolet, 1636).

— *La Silvanire, ou La Morte-vive*, tragi-comédie pastorale (Paris: F. Targa, 1631).

— *La Sylvie*, tragi-comédie pastorale (Paris: F. Targa, 1628).

Mareschal, Antoine *La Généreuse Allemande, ou le Triomphe d'amour*, tragi-comédie mise en deux journées (Paris: P. Rocolet, 1631).

— *L'Inconstance d'Hylas*, tragi-comédie pastorale (Paris: F. Targa, 1635).

— *Le Railleur, ou La Satyre du temps*, comédie (Paris: T. Quinet, 1638) (1637); ed. G. Dotoli (Bologna: Patrón Editore, 1973).

— *Le Véritable Capitan Matamore, ou Le Fanfaron* (Paris: T. Quinet, 1640).

Monléon, de *L'Amphytrite* (Paris: Vve. M. Guillemot, 1630).

Montluc, Adrien de, prince de Chabannais *La Comédie de proverbes*, pièce comique (Paris: F. Targa, 1634) (1633).

D'Ouville, Antoine Le Métel, sieur *L'Absent chez soy*, comédie (Paris: T. Quinet, 1643).

— *La Dame suivante*, comédie (Paris: T. Quinet, 1645).

— *L'Esprit folet*, comédie (Paris: T. Quinet, 1642).

— *Les Fausses Véritez*, comédie (Paris: T. Quinet, 1643).

Pichou *La Filis de Scire*, comédie pastorale (Paris: F. Targa, 1631).

— *Les Folies de Cardenio*, tragi-comédie (Paris: F. Targa, 1630) (1629).

— *L'Infidèle Confidente*, tragi-comédie (Paris: F. Targa, 1631).

Quinault, Philippe *La Comédie sans comédie* (Paris: G. de Luyne, 1657); ed. J.-D. Biard, Textes Littéraires, 13 (University of Exeter, 1974).

Racan, Honorat de Bueil, marquis de *Les Bergeries*, pastorale, Cinquiesme Edition, revuë & corrigée (Paris: T. du Bray, 1632).

Rayssiguier, de *L'Aminte du Tasse*, tragi-comédie pastoralle (Paris: A. Courbé, 1630).

— *La Bourgeoise, ou la Promenade de S. Cloud*, tragi-comédie (Paris: P. Billaine, 1633).

— *La Célidée sous le nom de Calirie, ou de la Générosité d'amour*, tragi-comédie (Paris: T. Quinet, 1635).

— *Palinice, Circeine et Florice*, tragi-comédie (Paris: A. de Sommaville, 1634).

— *Les Thuilleries*, tragi-comédie (Paris: A. de Sommaville, 1636).

— *Tragi-comédie pastorale, où les Amours d'Astrée et de Celadon sont meslées à celles de Diane, de Silvandre et de Paris, avec les inconstances d'Hilas* (Paris: N. Bessin, 1630).

Rotrou, Jean de *Oeuvres* (ed. Viollet-le-Duc), 5 vols (Paris: Th. Desoer, 1820).

— *Amélie*, tragi-comédie (Paris: A. de Sommaville, 1638) (1637).

— *La Bague de l'oubly*, comédie (Paris: F. Targa, 1635).

— *La Belle Alphrède*, comédie (Paris: A. de Sommaville & T. Quinet, 1639).

— *Les Captifs, ou les Esclaves*, comédie (Paris: A. de Sommaville, 1640).

— *Céliane*, tragi-comédie (Paris: T. Quinet, 1637).

— *Célimène*, comédie (Paris: A. de Sommaville, 1636).

— *Clarice, ou l'Amour constant*, comédie (Paris: T. Quinet, 1643) (1642).

— *Cléagenor et Doristée*, tragi-comédie (Paris: A. de Sommaville, 1634).

— *Clorinde*, comédie (Paris: A. de Sommaville, 1637).

— *Les Deux Pucelles*, tragi-comédie (Paris: A. de Sommaville, 1639).

— *Diane*, comédie (Paris: F. Targa, 1635).

— *Filandre*, comédie (Paris: A. de Sommaville, 1637).
— *Florimonde*, comédie (Paris: A. de Sommaville, 1655).
— *L'Heureuse Constance*, tragi-comédie (Paris: T. Quinet, 1636).
— *L'Hypocondriaque, ou le Mort amoureux*, tragi-comédie (Paris: T. du Bray, 1631).
— *L'Innocente Infidelité*, tragi-comédie (Paris: A. de Sommaville, 1637).
— *Les Ménèchmes*, comédie (Paris: A. de Sommaville, 1636).
— *La Pèlerine amoureuse*, tragi-comédie (Paris: A de Sommaville, 1637).
— *Les Sosies*, comédie (Paris: A. de Sommaville, 1638).
Scarron, Paul *Jodelet, ou Le Maître Valet*, comédie (Paris T. Quinet, 1645).
Schelandre, Jean de *Tyr et Sidon*, tragi-comédie divisée en deux journées (Paris: R. Estienne, 1628); ed. J. W. Barker (Paris: Nizet, 1974).
Scudéry, Georges de *L'Apologie du théâtre* (Paris: A. Courbé, 1639).
— *La Comédie des comédiens*, poème de nouvelle invention (Paris: A. Courbé, 1635); ed. J. Crow, Textes Littéraires, 19 (University of Exeter, 1975).
— *Le Fils supposé*, comédie (Paris: A. Courbé, 1636).
— *Ligdamon et Lidias, ou La Ressemblance*, tragi-comédie (Paris: F. Targa, 1631).
— *Le Prince déguisé*, tragi-comédie (Paris: A. Courbé, 1636) (1635).
— *Le Trompeur puny, ou l'Histoire septentrionale*, tragi-comédie (Paris: A. de Sommaville, 1634).
D'Urfé, Honoré *L'Astrée*, ed. H. Vaganay, 5 vols (Lyon: Masson, 1925–8).
— *La Sylvanire, ou La Morte-vive*, fable bocagère (Paris: R. Fouet, 1627).

3 *Other works cited*

Alarcón y Mendoza, Juan Ruiz de *La Verdad sospechosa*, ed. E. Barry, fourth edition (Paris: Garnier, n.d.).
— *Théâtre*, trans. A. Royer (Paris: M. Lévy, 1865).
Vega Carpio, Lope de *Obras*, publicadas por la Real Academia Espanola, ninth edition, 13 vols (Madrid: Galo Saez, 1916–30).
— *Théâtre*, trans. D. Hinard (Paris: G. Charpentier, 1881).
The Complete Works of Voltaire Volumes 53–5, 'Commentaires sur Corneille', ed. D. Williams, 3 vols (Banbury: The Voltaire Foundation, 1974–5).

II Secondary sources

1 *Books and articles on Corneille*

Bourdat, Pierre 'Une Source cornélienne du *Misanthrope: La Veuve*', *Information Littéraire*, 20 (1968), 129–31.
Brasillach, Robert *Pierre Corneille* (Paris: Arthème Fayard, 1938).
Bürger, Peter *Die frühen Komödien Pierre Corneilles und das französische Theater um 1630; eine wirkungsästhetische Analyse* (Frankfurt: Athenäum, 1971).

Cherpack, Clifton 'The Captive Audience in *L'Illusion Comique*', *Modern Language Notes*, 81 (1966), 342–4.

Cosnier, Colette 'Un Étrange Monstre–*L'Illusion Comique*', *Europe*, 540–541 (April–May 1974), 103–13.

Couton, Georges *Réalisme de Corneille* (Paris: Les Belles Lettres, 1953).

— 'État présent des études cornéliennes', *Information Littéraire*, 8 (1956), 43–8.

— *Corneille*, Connaissance des Lettres, 52 (Paris: Hatier, 1969).

Cuche, François Xavier 'Les Trois Illusions de *L'Illusion Comique*', *Travaux de Linguistique et de Littérature*, IX 2 (1971), 65–84.

Dorchain, Auguste *Pierre Corneille* (Paris: Garnier, 1918).

Dort, Bernard *Pierre Corneille, dramaturge*, Les Grands Dramaturges, 16 (Paris: L'Arche, 1957).

Doubrovsky, Serge *Corneille et la dialectique du héros*, Bibliothèque des Idées (Paris: Gallimard, 1963).

Fournier, R. J. 'Corneille's Early Comedies: A Study in Dramatic Development' (unpublished Ph.D. dissertation, University of Western Ontario, 1973).

— 'A Prefigurement of *Le Cid*: Pierre Corneille's *La Suivante*', *Revue de l'Université d'Ottawa*, 46 (1976), 271–7.

Francq, H. 'Corneille: premières amours et première comédie', *Revue de l'Université d'Ottawa*, 38 (1968), 177–209.

Fumaroli, Marc 'Rhétorique et dramaturgie dans *L'Illusion Comique* de Corneille', *XVIIe Siècle*, 80–1 (1968), 107–32.

Gaubert, Serge 'De la Comédie des signes aux signes de la comédie', *Europe*, 540–1 (April–May 1974), 76–86.

Harvey, Lawrence E. 'The Dénouement of *Mélite* and the Role of the Nourrice', *Modern Language Notes*, 71 (1956), 200–3.

— 'The Noble and the Comic in Corneille's *La Veuve*', *Symposium*, 10 (1956), 291–5.

— 'Intellectualism in Corneille: the Symbolism of Proper Names in *La Suivante*', *Symposium*, 13 (1959), 290–3.

Hatzfeld, Adolphe *Les Commencements de P. Corneille* (Grenoble: Prudhomme, 1857).

Helmreich-Marsilien, Armand 'Un Inspirateur paradoxal du tragique racinien: Corneille comique', *Australian Journal of French Studies*, 2 (1965), 291–312.

Hubert, Judd D. 'Le Réel et L'Illusoire dans le théâtre de Corneille et dans celui de Rotrou', *Revue des Sciences Humaines*, 91 (1958), 333–50.

— 'Le Jeu de l'amour et de l'honnêteté', *Esprit Créateur*, 15 (1975), 49–58.

Huszar, Guillaume *Pierre Corneille et le théâtre espagnol* (Paris: Bouillon, 1903).

Kerr, Cynthia B. 'Violence et obstacle dans *La Place Royale*', *French Review*, 49 (1975–6), 496–504.

— *L'Amour, l'amitié et la fourberie: une étude des premières comédies de Corneille*, Stanford French and Italian Studies, 20 (Anna Libri, 1980).

Koch, Philip 'Cornelian Illusion', *Symposium*, 14 (1960), 85–99.

— 'The Hero in Corneille's Early Comedies', *PMLA*, 78 (1963), 196–200.

Küchler, Walther 'Pierre Corneille's *Mélite'*, *Germanisch–Romanische Monatsschrift*, 5 (1913), 677–89.

Lanson, Gustave *Corneille*, Les Grands Ecrivains Français (Paris: Hachette, 1946).

Larroutis, M. 'Corneille et Montaigne: l'égotisme dans *La Place Royale'*, *RHLF*, 62 (1962), 321–28.

Lebègue, Raymond 'Cet étrange monstre que Corneille a donné au théâtre', *Mélanges de littérature comparée et de philologie offerts à Mieczyslaw Brahmer* (Warszawa: PWN, 1967), pp. 281–94.

Lemonnier, Léon *Corneille* (Paris: Tallandier, 1945).

Litman, Théodore A. *Les Comédies de Corneille* (Paris: Nizet, 1981).

McFarlane, I. D. 'A Reading of *La Veuve'*, *The Equilibrium of Wit: Essays for Odette de Mourgues*, ed. P. J. Bayley and D. G. Coleman (Lexington: French Forum, 1982), pp. 135–49.

Mallinson, G. J. 'The Variants of Corneille's Early Plays'. *Modern Language Review*, 77 (1982), 547–57.

Maurens, Jacques *La Tragédie sans tragique: Le neo-stoïcisme dans l'oeuvre de Pierre Corneille* (Paris: A. Colin, 1966).

May, Georges 'Sept années d'études cornéliennes', *Romanic Review*, 43 (1952), 282–92.

Mertens, C. J. 'Alidor, bon ami, mauvais amant', *RHLF*, 72 (1972), 400–5.

Moisan-Morteyrol, Christine 'Les Premières Comédies de Corneille: prélude à *la Place Royale'*, *Europe*, 540–1, (April–May 1974), 91–9.

Morel, Jacques 'Le jeune Corneille et le théâtre de son temps', *Information Littéraire*, 12 (1960), 185–92.

Nadal, Octave *Le Sentiment de l'amour dans l'oeuvre de Pierre Corneille*, Bibliothèque des Idées (Paris: Gallimard, 1948).

Nelson, Robert J. 'Pierre Corneille's *L'Illusion Comique*: the Play as Magic', *PMLA*, 71 (1956), 1127–40.

— *Corneille: His Heroes and their Worlds* (Philadelphia: University of Pennsylvania Press, 1963).

Paquot-Pierret, Léon *Les Comédies de Corneille*, Collection Lebègue, 60 (Bruxelles: Lebègue & Cie., 1944).

Pedersen, John 'Le Joueur de rôles: Un personnage typique des comédies de Corneille', *Revue Romane*, 2 (1967), 136–48.

Poole, M. S. 'A Re-reading of Corneille's *Mélite'*, *The Classical Tradition in French Literature: Essays presented to R. C. Knight*, ed. H. T. Barnwell *et al.* (London: Grant and Cutler, 1977), pp. 49–60.

Reiss, T. J. 'The Dialectic of Language in the Theatre: Corneille from *Mélite* to *Le Cid'*, *Yale French Studies*, 45 (1970), 87–101.

— '*Le Menteur* de Corneille: langage, volonté, société', *Romance Notes*, 15 (1973–4), 284–96.

Rivaille, Louis *Les Débuts de P. Corneille* (Paris: Boivin, 1936).

Rizza, Cecilia 'La Condition de la femme et de la jeune fille dans les premières comédies de Corneille', *Onze Études sur l'image de la femme dans la littérature française du dix-septième siècle*, ed. W. Leiner (Paris: J.-M. Place, 1978), pp. 169–93.

Rubin, David Lee   'The Hierarchy of Illusions and the Structure of
   L'Illusion Comique', La Cohérence Intérieure: Études sur la littérature
   française du XVIIe siècle présentées en hommage à Judd D. Hubert (Paris: J.-M.
   Place, 1977), pp. 75–93.
— 'On Theatricality in Pierre Corneille's Later Comedies, Papers on French
   Seventeenth Century Literature, 7 (1977), 81–101.
Scherer, Jacques   'Activités cornéliennes 1939–49', Revue d'Histoire du
   Théâtre, 2 (1950), 59–70.
Schlumberger, Jean   Plaisir à Corneille, promenade anthologique (Paris:
   Gallimard, 1936).
Sellstrom, A. Donald   'L'Illusion Comique of Corneille: the Tragic Scenes
   of Act V', Modern Language Notes, 73 (1958), 421–7.
— 'Addenda to the Sources of Corneille's L'Illusion Comique', Modern
   Language Notes, 76 (1961), 533–6.
Sénart, Philippe   'La Place Royale au Théâtre de l'Est parisien', Nouvelle
   Revue des Deux Mondes (December 1973), pp. 691–3.
Smith, C. N.   'Towards coherence in comedy: Corneille's Le Menteur',
   Form and Meaning: Aesthetic Coherence in Seventeenth-Century French
   Drama (Studies presented to Harry Barnwell), ed. W. D. Howarth et al.
   (Avebury, 1982), pp. 63–74.
Starobinski, Jean   'Sur Corneille', Temps Modernes, 10 (1954–5), 713–29.
Staves, Susan   'Liars and Lying in Alarcón, Corneille and Steele', Revue
   de Littérature Comparée, 46 (1972), 514–27.
Stegmann, André   L'Héroïsme cornélien: Genèse et Signification, 2 vols.
   (Paris: A. Colin, 1968).
Sweetser, Marie-Odile   La Dramaturgie de Corneille (Genève: Droz, 1977).
Tancock, L. W. 'Work on Corneille since 1945', Modern Languages, 40
   (1959), 109–14.
Temkine, Raymonde   'A propos d'une représentation de la Place Royale',
   Europe, 540–1 (April–May 1974), 99–102.
Van Roosbroeck, Gustave L.   'A Commonplace in Corneille's Mélite: the
   Madness of Eraste', Modern Philology, 17 (1919–20), 141–9.
— 'Corneille's Early Friends and Surroundings', Modern Philology, 18
   (1920–21), 361–81.
— 'Preciosity in Corneille's Early Plays', Philological Quarterly, 6 (1927),
   19–31.
— The Genesis of Corneille's 'Mélite' (Vinton: Kruse Publishing Co., n.d.).
Verhoeff, Han   Les Comédies de Corneille: une psycholecture (Paris: Klinc-
   ksieck, 1979).
Walters, Gordon B. Jnr.   'Society and the Theatre in Corneille's L'Illusion
   Comique', Romance Notes, 10 (1968–9), 324–31.
Yarrow, P. J.   Corneille (London: Macmillan, 1963).

2   General background
Adam, Antoine   Histoire de la littérature française au XVIIe siècle, 5 vols.
   (Paris: Domat, 1948–56).
Brereton, Geoffrey   French Comic Drama from the Sixteenth to the Eighteenth
   Century (London: Methuen, 1977).

Brunetière, Ferdinand *Les Epoques du théâtre français, 1636–1850* (Paris: Hachette, 1896).

Buffum, Imbrie *Studies in the Baroque from Montaigne to Rotrou* (New Haven: Yale University Press, 1957).

Emelina, Jean *Les Valets et les servantes dans le théâtre comique en France de 1610 à 1700* (Grenoble: Presses Universitaires de Grenoble, 1975).

Gaiffe, Felix *Le Rire et la scène française* (Paris: Boivin, 1931).

Garapon, Robert *La Fantaisie verbale et le comique dans le théâtre français du moyen âge à la fin du XVIIe siècle* (Paris: A. Colin, 1957).

Guichemerre, Roger *La Comédie avant Molière, 1640–1660* (Paris: A. Colin, 1972).

Howarth, W. D. 'La Notion de la catharsis dans la comédie française classique', *Revue des Sciences Humaines*, 152 (1973), 521–39.

Lancaster, Henry Carrington *A History of French Dramatic Literature in the Seventeenth Century*, 9 vols. (Baltimore: Johns Hopkins Press, 1929–42).

Mallinson, G. J. 'L'Hospital des Fous of Charles Beys: the Madman and the Actor', *French Studies*, 36 (1982), 12–25.

— 'Mareschal's Le Railleur: Topicality and the Search for the Comic', *Newsletter of the Society for Seventeenth-Century French Studies*, 4 (1982), 40–7.

Marsan, Jules *La Pastorale dramatique en France à la fin du XVIe et au commencement du XVIIe siècle* (Paris: Hachette, 1905).

Martinenche, Ernest *La Comedia espagnole en France de Hardy à Racine* (Paris: Hachette, 1900).

Morçay, Raoul (and Pierre Sage) *Le Préclassicisme* (Paris: del Duca, 1962).

Reiss, T. J. *Toward Dramatic Illusion: Theatrical Technique and Meaning from Hardy to 'Horace'* (New Haven: Yale University Press, 1971).

Rousset, Jean *La Littérature de l'âge baroque en France: Circé et le Paon* (Paris: Corti, 1953).

Scherer, Jacques *La Dramaturgie classique en France* (Paris: Nizet (1950)).

Voltz, Pierre *La Comédie*, Collection U, Série 'Lettres Françaises' (Paris: A. Colin, 1964).

Winkler, Emil 'Zur Geschichte des Begriffs "comédie" in Frankreich', *Sitzungsberichte der Heidelberger Akademie der Wissenschaften: philosophisch–historische Klasse*, 28:1 (1937–8), 1–31.

Index of primary sources

Alarcón y Mendoza, J. R. de
  La Verdad Sospechosa, 190–209, 232, 233
Anon.
  Le Capitan, 144, 188, 230
  La Comédie de chansons, 21, 226
  La Folie de Silène, 41, 228
  Le Mercier Inventif, 75, 77, 229
Aubignac, F. H. abbé d'
  La Pratique du théâtre, 12, 26, 186–7, 225, 227
Auvray, J.
  Le Banquet des Muses, 45, 228
  Dorinde, 36, 53, 56, 66, 68, 137, 145, 181–2, 228, 232
  Madonte, 36, 37, 43, 227, 228

Baro, B.
  Célinde, 10, 11, 15, 58, 172, 181, 182, 224, 227, 228, 232
  Clorise, 10, 12, 17, 60, 62, 67, 224, 229, 230
Beys, C. de
  Céline, 33, 180, 227
  Le Jaloux sans sujet, 16, 26, 33, 98, 131, 138, 152, 225, 226
  L'Ospital des Fous, 232
Boisrobert, F. Le Métel de
  La Jalouse d'elle-mesme, 195, 233

Pyrandre et Lisimène, 65, 115, 225, 230
Brosse, de
  Les Innocens coupables, 188, 189, 232
  Les Songes des hommes esveillez, 188, 232

Chapelain, J., 15, 225
Chevreau, U.
  L'Advocat duppé, 24, 226, 227
Claveret, J.
  L'Esprit fort, 23, 49, 61, 64–5, 68, 75, 78, 80–1, 93, 95, 99, 102, 110, 135, 137–8, 157, 226
Corneille, P.
  Agésilas, 221
  Le Cid, 167, 220
  Clitandre, 14, 55, 220
  La Galerie du Palais, 6, 77–106, 114, 127, 132, 134, 136, 148, 171, 186, 204, 209, 217, 218, 220, 229
  L'Illusion Comique, 163–87, 216, 217, 219, 220, 231, 232, 234
  Mélite, 5, 34–54, 55, 56, 72, 82, 104, 105, 107, 109, 129, 137, 145, 157, 186, 200, 217, 218, 219, 227, 228

Le Menteur, 187, 188–209, 210, 213, 214, 215, 216, 217, 218, 219, 220, 232, 233

Nicomède, 220

La Place Royale, 7, 134–62, 178, 186, 204, 209, 217, 218, 220, 230, 231

La Suite du Menteur, 210–16, 220, 233

La Suivante, 7, 107–33, 134, 136, 171, 172, 185, 217, 218, 220, 229, 230

La Veuve, 4, 6, 55–76, 78, 105, 109, 111, 114, 125, 186, 204, 217, 218, 219, 220, 228, 229

Corneille, T.
L'Amour à la mode, 205, 233

Coste, G. de
Lizimène, 19, 55, 77, 84, 159, 225

Cyrano de Bergerac, S. de
Le Pédant joué, 205, 233

D'Alibray, C. de Vion
L'Aminte du Tasse, 11–12, 26, 29, 55, 56, 63, 141, 184, 224

Desmarets de Saint-Sorlin, J.
Aspasie, 10, 11, 224
Les Visionnaires, 24–5, 200, 226

Discret, L.-C.
Alizon, 20, 32, 226
Les Nopces de Vaugirard, 21, 226

Du Peschier, N.
La Comédie des comédies, 22, 226

Du Rocher, R.-M.
La Mélize, 32, 227

Du Ryer, P.
Alcimédon, 94, 98, 102, 229
Amarillis, 23, 78, 80, 87, 91, 128, 149, 159, 160, 226, 230, 231
Arétaphile, 230
Argenis et Poliarque, 10, 33, 49, 56, 72, 224, 230
Cléomédon, 28, 183, 227

Clitophon, 9, 60, 144, 149, 184, 224, 227, 232

Lisandre et Caliste, 13, 15, 77, 93, 102, 104, 225

Les Vendanges de Suresne, 24, 30, 33, 127, 129, 130, 135, 226, 230

Furetière, A., 85, 229

Gaillard, A.
La Carline, 27, 52, 227

Gaultier Garguille, 32, 131, 227

Gillet de la Tessonerie
La Comédie de Francion, 207–8, 233

Gombauld, J.-O. de
Amaranthe, 24, 73, 118–19, 225, 227

Gougenot
La Comédie des comédiens, 124, 128, 168, 182, 230

Guarini, G.
Il Pastor Fido, 19, 137

Guérin de Bouscal, G.
Dom Quixote de la Manche, 207, 233
Le Gouvernement de Sanche Pansa, 189, 232

Hardy, A.
Alcée, 232
Alcméon, 179
Alphée, 231
Corine, 28, 227, 228
Gésippe, 47, 67, 228
Le Triomphe d'Amour, 230

La Bruyère, J. de, 1, 222

La Croix, C.-S. de
La Climène, 40, 101, 227, 228, 229
L'Inconstance punie, 11, 35, 60, 225, 227, 228, 229

Le Vert

Le Docteur amoureux, 21, 226

Mairet, J. de
 Chryséide et Arimand, 18, 60, 225, 232
 Les Galanteries du duc d'Ossonne, 19–20, 93, 97, 120, 175, 226, 227
 La Silvanire, 10, 22, 25, 27, 28, 32, 50, 55, 56, 57, 59, 72, 83, 137, 170, 181, 224, 225, 226, 228, 229, 230
 La Sylvie, 10, 17, 28, 44, 48, 101, 112, 224, 227, 228, 230
Mareschal, A.
 La Généreuse Allemande, 33, 36, 46, 88, 178, 227, 228
 L'Inconstance d'Hylas, 22–3, 33, 61, 68, 95, 137, 139, 140, 157, 159, 226
 Le Railleur, 20, 23, 33, 164–5, 226, 230
 Le Véritable Capitan Matamore, 20, 160, 188, 207, 226
Monléon, de
 L'Amphytrite, 15, 225
Montluc, A. de
 La Comédie de proverbes, 22, 32, 226

Ogier, F., 9, 172–3, 177
D'Ouville, A. Le Métel
 L'Absent chez soy, 188, 232
 La Dame suivante, 189, 205, 232
 L'Esprit folet, 189, 232, 233
 Les Fausses Véritez, 188, 232

Pichou
 La Filis de Scire, 33, 40, 67, 113, 144, 227
 Les Folies de Cardenio, 19, 33, 39, 40, 41, 43, 51, 53, 137, 164, 168, 207, 226, 227, 229, 231

L'Infidèle Confidente, 43, 155, 156, 228

Racan, H. de Bueil
 Les Bergeries, 10, 27, 28–9, 39, 61, 75, 80, 153, 224, 225, 227, 228, 229
Rayssiguier, de
 L'Aminte du Tasse, 9, 17, 33, 130, 183, 224
 La Bourgeoise, 78, 88, 89, 91, 103, 122, 164, 229, 231
 La Célidée, 10, 141–2, 143, 153–4, 224
 Palinice, Circeine et Florice, 31, 33, 121–2, 128, 226, 233
 Les Thuilleries, 16, 137, 148, 155–6, 177, 225, 230
 Tragi-comédie pastorale, 10, 11, 63, 104, 137, 157, 158, 224, 229
Rotrou, J. de
 Agésilan de Colchos, 231
 Amélie, 83–4, 149, 169, 229
 La Bague de l'oubly, 19, 53, 133, 137, 175, 226, 228
 La Belle Alphrède, 33, 164, 165, 179, 225, 231, 232
 Les Captifs, 14, 225
 Céliane, 18, 78, 91–2, 97, 142, 154, 226, 229
 Célimène, 18, 226, 232
 Clarice, 20, 226
 Cléagenor et Doristée, 33, 110, 124, 178, 227
 Clorinde, 33, 154, 226, 230
 Les Deux Pucelles, 146, 230
 Diane, 16–17, 29–30, 78, 89, 90, 98, 120–1, 127, 225, 232
 Filandre, 18, 19, 31–2, 33, 88, 89, 105, 129, 226
 Florimonde, 17, 154, 225, 231
 L'Heureuse Constance, 15, 225
 L'Hypocondriaque, 39, 51, 53, 56,

207, 227
L'Innocente Infidelité, 177–8, 232
Les Ménèchmes, 20, 61, 70, 119,
    133, 139, 140, 226
Le Pèlerine amoureuse, 79, 120,
    121, 148, 149, 229, 231
Les Sosies, 20, 188, 226

Scarron, P.
    Jodelet, 189–90, 232
Schelandre, J. de
    Tyr et Sidon, 9, 53, 172–3, 180,
        224, 232
Scudéry, G. de
    L'Apologie du théâtre, 15, 225
    La Comédie des comédiens, 12, 84,
        99, 182, 183, 224
    Le Fils supposé, 10, 27, 33, 99, 149,
        224, 226, 232
    Ligdamon et Lidias, 17, 33, 36,

183, 225, 227, 229, 232
Le Prince déguisé, 174, 179, 232
Le Trompeur puny, 13, 59, 61, 66,
    72, 80, 97, 117, 146, 179, 225,
    229, 231

Tasso, T.
    Aminta, 19, 35, 137

D'Urfé, H.
    L'Astrée, 12, 28, 30–1, 45, 62, 63,
        67, 80, 97, 111, 137, 138, 149,
        154, 155, 172, 211, 227, 228,
        229, 231
    La Sylvanire, 227

Vega Carpio, L. de
    Amar sin saber a quién, 210–16,
        233
Voltaire, 233, 234